The New York Times
More 60-Minute Gourmet

The New York Times
More 60-Minute Gourmet

Pierre Franey

WITH AN INTRODUCTION BY
Craig Claiborne

Fawcett Columbine • New York

A Fawcett Columbine Book
Published by Ballantine Books
Copyright © 1981 by The New York Times Company

All rights reserved. No part of this book may be reproduced in any form or by any electronic or mechanical means, including information storage and retrieval systems, without permission in writing from the publisher, except by a reviewer who may quote brief passages in a review. Published in the United States by Ballantine Books, a division of Random House, Inc., New York, and in Canada by Random House of Canada Limited.

Library of Congress Catalog Card Number: 82-90837
ISBN 449-90194-7
This edition published by arrangement with Times Books

Manufactured in the United States of America
First Ballantine Books Trade Edition: May 1983

10 9

To Betty,
Claudia, Diane, and
Jacques

Contents

Introduction | Page 3

The Gourmet in the Kitchen | Page 5

Appetizers | Page 13

Poultry | Page 27

Eggs | Page 79

Fish | Page 93

Shellfish | Page 129

Lamb | Page 167

Veal & Calves' Liver | Page 183

Beef | Page 205

Pork & Ham | Page 223

Pasta | Page 245

Vegetables | Page 257

Desserts | Page 267

Index | Page 287

Introduction

WHEN IT WAS PROPOSED TO PIERRE FRANEY that he write a column called "The 60-Minute Gourmet" for *The New York Times,* we were, as collaborators, fascinated by the challenge and amused by the thought.

Pierre had worked in a professional kitchen as a professional chef for more than fifty years. I had worked as a professional food writer for more than twenty years, since I had been trained in international cookery at a Swiss hotel school.

Neither of us had ever given serious consideration to cooking by the clock; although I, too, have had to race against time when one catastrophe or another has befallen my kitchen. On one occasion—too well remembered—when I lived in a small apartment in Greenwich Village, I had invited a very important magazine editor and his wife to dinner. I had arrived home late and before they were to arrive I turned on the cold water spigot to rinse a batch of lettuce leaves only to discover a second later that I was out of butter. I dashed out the door to the nearest grocery only to return to discover the sink overflowing and the floor a miniature swimming pool. By the time that mess was mopped up, there was a knocking on the door and the guests walked in, not to find a cool, calm, and collected host, but me in a slightly mesmerized state. Still, we sat down to dine within the hour on a four-course meal including a hastily put together appetizer, roast duck with Cassis, salad with Brie, and a hot-from-the-oven apple tart. I simply gave them my first and wholly unintended lesson in hasty food preparation.

It is an evident fact that in the world we live in today, there are thousands of folks out there, good cooks and not-so-good, who take pleasure in entertaining on evenings when time is an essential element in food preparation. And that, of course, is the audience to whom that hasty cooking column was directed from the beginning. Our initial effort, and these are the recipes that were included in Volume I of Pierre's book, consisted primarily of main courses.

We were somewhat tardy in reckoning that there are a good many cooks out there who hanker for more ambitious menus to serve their guests. Numerous readers wrote to ask us to supply them with appetizers for meals to be cooked or put together in less than an hour. And even more asked for recommendations for desserts with which to end the meal. We had previously recommended a simple assortment of fresh fruits with cheeses or a mélange of fresh fruits or a scoop of the finest ice cream.

As time progressed, it occurred to us that there are many first courses which can be put together with little effort and be as impressive as all get-out as well: a quick smoked salmon mousse, various dips, such as Gorgonzola cheese and walnuts, cream cheese with fresh crabs, avocado with an easily put together crab salad.

Among the desserts, we developed hastily made soufflés, an assortment of mousses, and even crêpes, some filled with ice cream and using various easily made garnishes.

As Pierre points out, the very soul and saving grace of a first rate, but hastily made meal, is in its organization. If you plan to serve an appetizer or dessert, you should tailor your main course accordingly. It should be a preparation that requires little attention as it cooks—broiled chicken, fish, or steak, for example—so that the dessert or appetizer can be made during the cooking "lull."

You might also keep in mind that some foods are excellent when prepared in advance and frozen. I have such things as crêpes in mind, in particular. If you are going to make a batch of crêpes you might consider doubling the recipe (the basic batter can be made in seconds and the crêpes must, by their very nature, cook quickly). Crêpes freeze particularly well.

Some of the appetizers included are also excellent when served second time around. Take the chicken liver mousse, for instance. It is very good when served warm on the first evening or day it is made, but it *does* improve with standing overnight. And, thus, you may serve it as a preface to two meals running.

Craig Claiborne
East Hampton, New York
August 1981

The Gourmet in the Kitchen

IT ALMOST GOES WITHOUT SAYING THAT I came late to the world of newspaper "reporting." As a matter of fact, when I was born in that small town in Burgundy called Saint Vinnemer (population 398), I would suspect that the last occupation or profession on earth that my parents might have pondered or foreseen for me would be spreading the gospel of cooking to a fairly wide audience of people who hungered for and wanted to prepare good food in their own homes. And, more importantly, perhaps, within the space of sixty minutes, a fact which vastly amused my late mother in her later years.

I was born in a rural area where the clock simply didn't count when you were cooking or doing many other things in life. But one of the chief pleasures of life back in those days was dining well. Although my father's occupation was that of a plumber, he was, as mayor of his town, a favorite citizen. He held the position of mayor for more than thirty years.

My family lived in a small house and the center of it was a large iron stove that burned both coal and wood. It served a double purpose: to provide heat for cooking and, in winter, the principal source of warmth. Family dinners were often made with produce from the family garden and from the animals that ran in the *bassecour* or poultry yard where there was a year-round supply of chickens, geese, and eggs. In autumn, there were many game dishes on the family table, among them a ragoût of lapin or rabbit, a personal favorite.

I remember in particular the trips to Auxerre. No matter what time of day, my father, like most Frenchmen, would stop by the local bar for a glass or two of white wine. But first we'd stop at a nearby charcuterie and buy sausages or rillettes (a kind of pork spread) and fresh loaves of bread, hot from the oven. My wine, of course, was always diluted with a good deal of water.

Curiously, although my family lived about three hundred kilometers from the sea, fish and seafood figured largely in our weekly diet. On Fridays my father and I would bicycle to the local railroad station to meet the fish train that came overnight from Boulogne sur Mer on the Channel. There would be cartons and crates of fish on ice—oysters, mussels, raye or skate, herring, and so on.

My uncle was a wine merchant and I traveled a good deal with him, too, when he visited the caves in the area.

In those years almost all children in middle-class circumstances in rural regions were apprenticed at one occupation or another. I don't recall when the decision was made that I should train to become a chef. The decision was doubtless influenced by my uncle who, because of his wine trade, had many connections with Paris restaurants. I was placed in a small restaurant, the now defunct Restaurant Thenint on the Place de la Republique. My parents drove there for the first time in 1935, when I was fourteen years old.

After my apprenticeship, I worked many hours a day in several restaurants, first as a sauce cook, then as a fish cook, roast cook, and hors d'oeuvre and salad maker for many years both in Paris and New York. Never once did it occur to me that a "deadline" in the preparation of a meal might be an important factor in the lives of many Americans.

When I joined the staff of *The New York Times,* however, it was proposed that given the pace of life in this country, considering the number of women and other cooks who are gainfully employed outside the home on a nine-to-five basis, time in food preparation was, indeed, of the essence. Particularly for those who set not only a good but an impressive table. And all this came about during the course of this nation's food revolution coast to coast. People had developed an enthusiasm for home cookery that surpassed anything that ever happened in France or anywhere else in Europe for that matter. They were buying the finest olive oils and vinegars and mustards and exotic spices and the greatest, most varied and ingenious kitchen equipment known to any civilization.

From the very beginning I have tried to analyze and formulate in my own mind precisely the things that should be done to facilitate cookery so that great meals can be produced within the space of sixty minutes and my ideas now are approximately what they were when I compiled the first volume of my recipes for "The 60-Minute Gourmet."

In the first place you should outfit your kitchen with the finest and most efficient equipment—knives, blender or food processor, mixing bowls, and so on—that your purse can afford. Just as you would not run or jog in bedroom slippers, you should not try to cut with dull knives, or make sauces with a wooden or metal spoon rather than a wire whisk. That is not to say that you need an elaborate set of gadgets and utensils such as you would find in a professional kitchen. To choose one example of my thinking: If your budget is limited, you can very easily get by with two knives, provided they are of good quality—a sharp and sturdy chef's knife (sometimes called a butcher knife) and a sharp and sturdy paring knife. You can build on this basic set as time progresses, and add a swivel-bladed vegetable paring knife, a bread knife, and so on.

If you do have the most important "basics" for cooking (one large and one small mixing bowl, one medium-size skillet, one medium- and one small-size saucepan, a "spaghetti" pot, and so on), my next advice for "speedy" or hasty cooking would be organization.

At the risk of being repetitious, I would like to repeat some of the most salient points that I stressed in my first volume:

The second most important asset for hasty cooking with comfort and ease is that of organization. This "organization" should commence before you buy a single ingredient or take a saucepan down from the rack. You should take into thorough consideration, making a list as necessary, of the ingredients and utensils you will need to prepare the dishes you have in mind. Don't take anything for granted, be it a pound of butter you *thought* you had in the refrigerator or the carton of cream you were *sure* was sitting next to the milk.

Once you are ready to attack a dish, I strongly recommend that you assemble all the ingredients necessary for the preparation of the dish in one area. To choose one simple and obvious dish, consider the preparation of fish chowder. Bring to your work surface the following: onions, celery, potatoes, the fish, milk, butter, and whatever else the recipe requires. Gather these into a neat grouping. Get out the proper saucepan or pot and put it on the stove.

You will save yourself a good deal of time and bother if you lay out a length of waxed paper on the work surface and start peeling and trimming the onions, celery ends, and so on. When the peeling and trimming are done, simply gather the sheet of paper together and discard it.

Now proceed to the cubing of the potatoes (which must be dropped into cold water to prevent discoloring), the chopping of the onions and celery, adding them to glass measuring cups as they are prepared. Keep the ingredients neatly grouped and always keep your working surface wiped and clean between the cubing, chopping, and so on. Always keep in mind that clutter is distracting, a hindrance, and an enemy of time.

And incidentally, have a place for everything—the salt container, the pepper, the milk, and so on. Don't shift things about from day to day. Have a spot in the refrigerator for the butter, the milk, the cream, so that your hand projects automatically to the right place. It's a great time saver.

You can save yourself time and money if you will exercise forethought a day or an evening ahead. For example, if a dish you have planned for tomorrow's dinner calls for cooked shrimp, lobster, or chicken you will greatly simplify matters if you cook the shrimp, lobster, or whatever the night before. Remember that precooked seafood, to choose one example, costs more than the raw product.

And there are many vegetables and seasonings that can be chopped or minced or otherwise prepared the night before. Garlic can be finely minced and stored compactly in a small container and covered with plastic wrap so that air does not circulate around it. (It can also be covered with a little oil to keep air out.) Onions can be chopped, added to a bowl, and covered with plastic wrap and kept for many hours without damage to taste. So can shallots and fresh parsley.

Lettuce leaves can be rinsed clean in cold water and patted or spun dry before storing in plastic wrap or bags for use the next day. Potatoes can be peeled and cubed and kept in a basin of cold water in the refrigerator for a day or so. You can scrape carrots the day before, core green peppers or cabbage, and so on.

Think twice before throwing things out, half an onion, say. If you only use one-half for a meal, cover the other half closely in plastic wrap and refrigerate. It will be in good condition for at least one more day.

If circumstances permit (and there are rare exceptions in my mind when they would not) you might consider extending your night-before programming to the dinner table. If you know you will be pressed for time when you come home to prepare a meal, it would seem the most logical thing in the world if your preparations included setting the table as completely as possible to receive guests. Place mats or tablecloths could be installed on the table, the places set with silver, napery, wine glasses, and the like. If you're going to be all-out fancy with flowers, an arrangement of blooms will also keep very neatly in the refrigerator.

If you are a really conscientious host or hostess and are pressed for time, as this book presumes you to be, you will probably want to serve coffee at the end of the meal. Therefore, as long as you are organizing to the last degree, you might make all preparations the night before for coffee brewing and serving. Make ready the coffee cups and spoons, have the cream in a pitcher in the refrigerator (if the cream is fresh it won't spoil) and the sugar spooned into a proper server. If you plan to serve cordials or after-dinner liqueurs, bring those glasses out, too.

You will probably serve a beverage of some sort, probably wine or beer (if there is sauerkraut). You can deposit a bottle of white wine in the refrigerator the night before. As a matter of fact, you can uncork it the night before if you recork it immediately and refrigerate it. The red wine can be placed in a cool place, but don't refrigerate it the night before. I hasten to add that some red wines benefit from a little chilling, a Beaujolais or an Italian wine, say, half an hour before they are served.

If you have a fine hand at cooking, if you cook at all properly, you will need access to a decent number of herbs and spices. In season I use fresh herbs to the greatest extent possible. My herb garden is fairly modest, but throughout the summer I have a constant supply of such herbs as tarragon, rosemary, thyme, parsley, sorrel, and basil. I have a fresh bay bush for bayleaves, but that is a rarity. I buy other herbs in season at a greengrocer—fresh coriander, dill, and so on.

In winter, however, like everyone else, I am largely dependent on dried herbs and spices. These, with the exception of bay leaf and thyme, are kept in a cool, dark place in the pantry to preserve their color and flavor. I have my bay leaf and thyme in a cool place next to the stove, and the reason for this is that I use both in considerable quantity while testing recipes. Otherwise I would leave these too in a cool, dark place.

Remember that a bright color, even for dried herbs and spices, is an indication of freshness in season.

There follows an alphabetical list of dried herbs and spices that I would consider essential for a spice rack. The most important of these are italicized, with bay leaf and thyme the most important of them all.

Allspice, whole or ground
Basil
Bay leaves
Caraway seeds
Cayenne pepper or hot ground red pepper
Chili powder
Cinnamon, ground and/or in stick form
Cloves, whole and/or ground
Coriander, seeds or ground
Cumin, seeds or ground
Curry powder
Marjoram
Mustard powder
Nutmeg, whole and/or ground
Oregano
Paprika
Black peppercorns and ground black pepper
White peppercorns and ground white pepper
Hot red pepper flakes and/or whole dried hot red pepper pods
Rosemary
Saffron, in stem form or powdered
Tarragon
Thyme
Vanilla extract

I am one of those people—as many of my friends are—who believe that some foods are equally if not more delicious when used as leftovers rather than when freshly cooked. Like many another, I prefer cold turkey sandwiches with fresh mayonnaise to the original roast bird. Cold leftover poached fish makes one of the best cold salads. Cold leftover duck is delicious although it must not be kept too long. And turkey soup made with the carcass and other bits of leftovers is superb.

If you dine and/or entertain often at home, and time is a factor (which is almost assuredly the case if you are reading this), there are many delectables—standbys, if you will—that you might consider always keeping in stock either in the refrigerator or on the pantry shelf, such as the case may be. Some of the finest meals I can recall were those that required no more effort than slicing and arranging foods in an appetizing fashion on platters. You might keep on hand well-flavored salamis and smoked meats, head cheese and pâtés (the keeping time of these goods varies, of course, and some must be eaten within a reasonably short time after purchase). Have on hand for a platter of such charcuterie (or cold meats or cold cuts, as it is listed in America) a jar or two of fine imported mustards (kept in the refrigerator) and imported cornichons (small, sour French pickles) to use as garnish. Plus a crusty French or Italian loaf. Stocks of such breads, tightly wrapped, keep well in the freezer and can be reheated before serving.

I also almost always have in my home refrigerator a wheel or two of Brie or Camembert or other cheeses that could be served on the spur of the moment. When tightly wrapped in plastic wrap or foil and refrigerated, the shelf life of most cheese is far greater than most people suspect. And, for cooking purposes, I always have—closely wrapped—a supply of Swiss or Gruyère cheese for "grantinéed" dishes, plus Parmesan (whole chunks; Parmesan is always best if freshly grated the moment before it is used) for gratinéed dishes or to sprinkle on pasta.

In addition to this, on my pantry shelves I keep a constantly replenished supply of canned fish products—sardines, tuna, and salmon mostly—for hasty meals. For such meals—whether of sliced meats or sardines—I would generally serve a cold salad and there will almost always be in my refrigerator fresh cucumber, tomatoes, and eggs for hard-cooking and/or turning into fresh mayonnaise.

Which reminds me that many new cooks over the years have asked about how to best maintain salad oils such as olive oil if they are to be maintained over a long period of time. Refrigeration is the answer, although I must confess that in my own home, oils, whether olive or corn oil, are used in such quantities that rancidity through nonuse is almost out of the question.

A few words might be added here about expediting the cooking of certain foods. If you have a dish that is to be baked—let us say a chicken that is to be cut into serving pieces and baked with a liquid poured around it—it will hasten the cooking time a great deal if you use a metal baking dish, one that can be heated on top of the stove. Place the dish on the stove and get the liquid to the boil before placing the dish in the oven.

I am also often asked if I make everything from scratch, especially such staple and often called for ingredients as chicken stock or beef broth, and the answer is no. It is certainly true that I prefer to use fresh chicken or beef broth, but like everyone else, I am frequently caught in the web of needing either chicken or beef broth on the spur of the moment. Thus I keep in my larder for such emergencies an ample supply of canned broths. Plus bottles of clam broth, which can—in an emergency—be substituted for fish stock. I also almost always have a case or so of canned tomatoes on my shelves, and tomato paste. I would no more use a can of tomato sauce (the flavor is terrible) than dehydrated onion or garlic, or instant rice (an abomination and insult to a cook's intelligence) because a sauce made with canned tomatoes is infinitely preferable and easy to make. And when fresh tomatoes are out of season, canned tomatoes are far superior for other uses as well.

I would also point out that the freezer is a great boon for home cooks. The use of a TV dinner is, to my mind, unthinkable. But there are many foods that can be frozen to advantage—including tomato sauce, meat casseroles, and so on.

A word of caution about reheating foods that have been frozen. Freezing tends to dilute the strength of various spices in any dish. Therefore, it is best to always taste the defrosted product and add more seasonings according to taste. And speaking of seasonings, always use salt sparingly when cooking. Remember that it can always be added at the end of cooking time. It can't be taken away, no matter what people say about adding raw potatoes to the dish to extract the salt.

At times there have been two "quarrels" with the column known as "60-Minute Gourmet" and by way of expiation I would like to point out the following:

It has been said that there might seem to be an excessive number of recipes for rice, noodles, and potatoes. The answer is that these foods have been considered, in the finest kitchens in the world, the basic and ideal accompaniments for main courses. Certain stews and ragouts, for example, simply go with noodles in one form or another. Rice is the best and most logical accompaniment for many dishes, be they meat, poultry, or fish. The same is true of potatoes. For subtle, psychological reasons, these "starches" are not always interchangeable where taste is concerned. I have done my utmost in the menu planning here to choose the ideal accompaniment (noodles, rice, or potatoes) and to vary the preparation to the greatest degree possible.

In addition to the appliances and gadgets mentioned earlier, you can make your cooking more comfortable and pleasurable if you have the following:

A wire whisk of respectable weight and size; a large, plain metal spoon; a large, slotted or perforated metal spoon; a kitchen timer; a large two-pronged fork; a pancake turner; a swivel-bladed vegetable scraper; a colander or sieve of suitable size; a set of graduated glass measuring cups (from one to four cups); a standard set of metal measuring spoons; a nest of mixing bowls; a can opener; a beer can opener; a flour sifter; a grater with assorted grating surfaces; a heavy pair of kitchen scissors; a salad basket (preferably a spin-dry utensil); rubber or plastic spatulas.

Other utensils or gadgets that would be valuable if not essential include a pair of kitchen tongs; a large spatula; a lemon squeezer; a large wooden spoon for stirring; a rolling pin; a pastry blender; a dish-draining rack; a spice rack; an ice pick; a dispenser for paper towels, plastic wrap, waxed paper, and aluminum foil; an electric juice extractor; and a pastry brush. You may wish to add an electric toaster, although I prefer toast made in the oven.

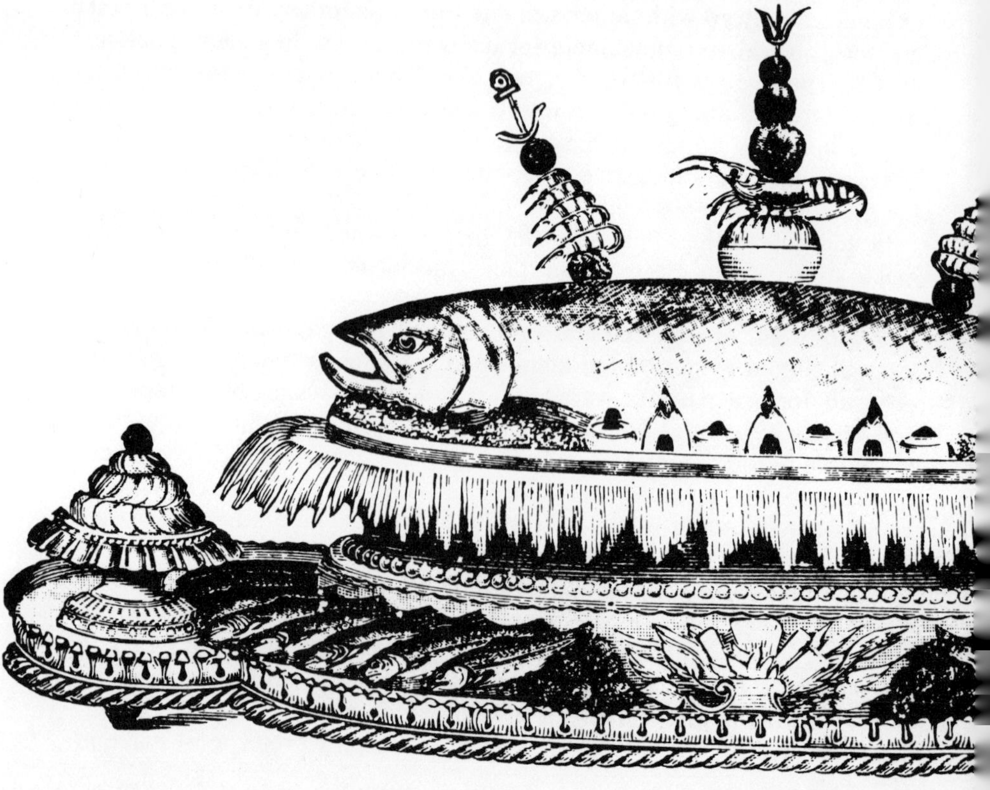

Appetizers

O**NE OF THE MOST FASCINATING ASPECTS OF MY** column is the comments from readers making special requests for various kinds of foods for menus. Some of them are wholly surprising.

For instance, it has rarely, if ever, occurred to me to suggest the preparation of appetizers or first courses to be served as part of a meal to be prepared, start to finish, in 60 minutes. Recently, however, I have twice been asked by readers if I could provide such appetizers. I have prepared two mousses, either of which might add that extra touch of special effort—without a great deal of it. The mousses that I prepared were one with smoked salmon, the other with chicken livers.

Both are almost embarrassingly easy to make; either can be made within 20 minutes. The salmon mousse, in fact, can be prepared in 5. I also prepared another easy, quickly made appetizer—smoked brook trout with horseradish sauce.

Making a first course does not necessarily demand an even more rapidly made main course. Consider a roast chicken as a main course: You could begin preparation of the chicken, put it in the oven, and it will be ready to serve in about 45 minutes.

After the chicken has begun to cook there would be ample time to go about the preparation of one of the appetizers. The salmon mousse, as a matter of fact, is excellent and ready to serve the moment it is blended and removed from the food processor. You will find, however, that the mousse improves on standing, overnight or even longer.

The chicken liver mousse is best if it is cooled to at least lukewarm, once it is removed from the food processor. It is good with buttered toast and can be served to advantage the second day.

Mousse de Saumon Fumé
(Smoked salmon mousse)

½ pound smoked salmon
½ pound cream cheese
⅓ cup chopped scallions
¼ cup finely chopped dill
Juice of half a lemon
Freshly ground pepper to taste

Tabasco sauce to taste
2 tablespoons aquavit, optional
Buttered toast
Chopped raw onion
Drained capers

1. Combine all the ingredients, except the toast, chopped onion, and capers, in the container of a food processor or blender. Blend to a fine purée. Pour the mixture into a serving dish. Smooth the top and chill.

2. Serve with buttered toast, chopped onion, and drained capers on the side.

Yield: About 4 cups.

Mousse de Foie de Volaille
(Chicken liver mousse)

¾	pound chicken livers	¼	pound butter or melted chicken fat
	Salt and freshly ground pepper	½	cup thinly sliced shallots
¼	bay leaf, broken into small pieces	¼	pound mushrooms, thinly sliced, about 2 cups
⅛	teaspoon dried thyme	1	tablespoon cognac
⅛	teaspoon ground allspice		Thinly sliced rye bread
⅛	teaspoon ground cinnamon		Chopped raw onions, optional
	Pinch of cayenne pepper		

1. Pick over the livers. Cut away and discard any tough connecting tissues or blemished portions. Put in a bowl and add salt and pepper to taste, the bay leaf, thyme, allspice, cinnamon, and cayenne.
2. Melt the butter in a heavy skillet and add the shallots and mushrooms. Cook, stirring often, until the mushrooms give up their liquid. Cook until most of this liquid evaporates. Add the livers and seasonings and stir. Cook, stirring occasionally, about 10 minutes.
3. Pour and scrape this mixture into the container of a food processor or blender. Add the cognac and blend to a fine purée.
4. Spoon and scrape the mousse into a small serving dish. Smooth over the top. Let cool. Chill. Serve with thinly sliced rye bread and chopped onion on the side.

Yield: About 2 cups.

Smoked Brook Trout with Horseradish Sauce

2	whole smoked brook trout, available at specialty shops		Salt
			Parsley or dill sprigs for garnish
½	cup heavy cream		
2	tablespoons or more horseradish	4	seeded lemon halves

1. Carefully remove the skin from each trout. Using a knife, carefully fillet the trout, removing all bones, large and small. Carefully arrange 1 trout fillet on each of four plates.
2. Whip the cream until stiff. Fold in the horseradish and add salt to taste. Garnish each serving with parsley sprigs and half a lemon. Serve the horseradish sauce on the side.

Yield: Four servings.

ONE OF THE FIRST THINGS I LEARNED ABOUT great French cooking when I became an apprentice many years ago in Paris is that there are many categories of appetizers on French menus. They may be as basic and bourgeois as steamed potatoes served with anchovies, or they may fall into the category of pâtés and terrines. The ultimate hors d'oeuvres bear a special name: They are called hors d'oeuvre riches, pronounced "reesh." The three foods in France that fall into this category are caviar, foie gras, and the very finest smoked salmon.

I sometimes think that if we had in France the great crabmeat that is available in America that, too, might be included among the hors d'oeuvre riches. To my thinking, there are few things better, with finer texture or a "sweeter" taste, than the highest quality lump crabmeat.

It almost goes without saying that crabmeat in almost any of its preparations is ideal for a "hasty" dish, whether as an appetizer or in a main course.

A friend of mine recently returned from Maryland, which has some of this country's finest crabmeat. He brought with him enough crabmeat to be used for several meals. We had plain lump crab with a fine homemade mayonnaise, a crab casserole, a crab salad, and crab soup. One of the dishes we made was a cold Mexican-style salad with a mayonnaise and chopped jalapeño chilies, which are widely available in cans in this country. The chilies added a special spice that was both interesting and worthwhile. The basic salad is quick to prepare and is good simply served on a bed of lettuce. Because we were in possession of excellent avocados at the time, we served the crab salad with avocado and tomatoes wedges.

This dish takes less than 60 minutes to prepare and is good served as a luncheon course or as an appetizer.

Avocado and Crabmeat Salad

2 ripe, firm, unblemished avocados
Juice of one lime
Salt
2 red, ripe, medium-size tomatoes

Crab mayonnaise Mexicaine (see recipe)
Finely chopped parsley for garnish

1. Peel the avocados, cut them in half, and discard the pits. Cut each half into 6 wedges. Squeeze the lime juice over the wedges to prevent discoloration. Sprinkle the wedges lightly with salt.

2. Core the tomatoes and cut each tomato into 8 wedges. Sprinkle each wedge lightly with salt.

3. Spoon equal portions of the crab mixture on each of four luncheon

plates. Garnish each serving with 6 avocado slices and 4 tomato wedges. Sprinkle with chopped parsley and serve.

Yield: Four servings.

Crab Mayonnaise Mexicaine
(Crab salad with jalapeño chilies)

- 1 pound fresh crabmeat, preferably lump
- 1 cup fresh mayonnaise (see recipe)
- Juice of one lime
- 2 jalapeño chilies, chopped, about 1 tablespoon
- ¼ cup finely chopped, loosely packed fresh coriander
- 3 tablespoons finely chopped chives, or 2 tablespoons finely chopped white onion
- Salt and freshly ground pepper

1. Pick over the crab to remove any bits of shell or cartilage.
2. Put the mayonnaise, lime juice, chilies, coriander, chives, and salt and pepper to taste into a bowl. Add the crabmeat and toss lightly to blend without breaking up the crab lumps.

Yield: Four to six servings.

Mayonnaise

- 1 egg yolk
- Salt and freshly ground pepper
- 1 teaspoon imported mustard such as Dijon or Düsseldorf
- 1 teaspoon vinegar or lemon juice
- 1 cup peanut, vegetable, or olive oil

1. Place the yolk in a mixing bowl and add salt and pepper to taste, mustard, and vinegar. Beat vigorously for a second or two with a wire whisk or electric beater.
2. Start adding the oil gradually, beating continuously with the whisk or electric beater. Continue beating and adding oil until all of it is used. If the mayonnaise is not to be used immediately, beat in a tablespoon of water. This will help stabilize the mayonnaise and retard its turning when stored in the refrigerator.

Yield: About 1 cup.

ALTHOUGH I WAS BORN AND SPENT MY FORMative years in France, I learned a good deal about European food after I came to America. I have stated before that I was largely unfamiliar with the many varieties of pasta known for generations in Italy until I came here. I have come to appreciate Greek and Spanish and Turkish foods that were not known in my home region of Burgundy and which I did not find in Paris during my apprenticeship there.

It has, in fact, been within the past decade that I have learned to appreciate the fine merits of that most curious seafood known in English as squid and in Italian as calamari. I must confess that I had to refer to a bilingual dictionary to discover the French name for the mollusk—it is calmar.

Although many recipes call for long cooking of squid, I found that it cooks rather quickly and is much better in texture if it is not overcooked. I have cooked it in many fashions but there are two preparations that seem ideally suited to the preparation of a meal in 60 minutes or less.

It is true that the cleaning of squid is a little time consuming but it is easily done once mastered. You simply rinse the squid in cold water and pinch off the head where the eyes are and pull. This should remove most of the interior material or viscera to be discarded. You can scrape out any remaining viscera. You then pull off the skin. Coarse salt rubbed with the fingers all over the squid can help this skin removal. Rinse the squid once more and it is ready to prepare.

A squid salad and a sort of soup with squid and anchovies are two dishes I recommend for a hasty summer meal. Either the salad, a fancy blend of flavors and textures, or the soup, a tangy pungent, sharp-flavored liquid, makes an ideal luncheon course or first course of a meal. The salad requires about half an hour to cook and blend, the squid in anchovy sauce about ten minutes less. Either of them is best served with a crusty loaf of French or Italian bread—or garlic bread. A well-seasoned green salad would go neatly with the soup.

Italian-style Shrimp and Squid Salad

¾ pound shrimp
1 pound squid
2 tablespoons red wine vinegar
½ cup water
1 bay leaf
¼ teaspoon dried hot red pepper flakes
  Salt
10 peppercorns

⅓ cup olive oil
½ teaspoon dried oregano
3 tablespoons red wine vinegar
1 tablespoon finely chopped garlic
  Juice of one lemon or to taste
¼ cup finely chopped parsley
½ cup chopped celery
1 sweet red pepper, chopped, optional

1. Peel and devein the shrimp. There should be about 1½ cups. Put them in a saucepan.

2. Cut off the tentacles and eyes of the squid. Pull and squeeze out the beak of the squid. Remove the skin of the bodies and tentacles of the squid by holding them under cold running water and rubbing with coarse salt or simply by pulling and rubbing with the fingers. Rinse the squid and drain thoroughly.

3. Cut the squid bodies crosswise into 1-inch rings. Cut the tentacles apart. Add the squid to the shrimp. Add the 2 tablespoons of vinegar, water, bay leaf, hot pepper flakes, salt to taste, and peppercorns. Cover, bring to the boil, and boil about 2 minutes.

4. Remove the shrimp and squid rings and put them in a mixing bowl. Add the remaining ingredients and toss well to blend. Serve at room temperature.

Yield: Six servings.

Squid in Anchovy Sauce

3 pounds baby squid, cleaned and cut into 2-inch squares	1 cup fresh or bottled clam juice
½ cup olive oil	¼ cup finely chopped parsley
1 cup chopped onion	Juice of one and one-half lemons or juice to taste
Freshly ground pepper	
2 2-ounce cans flat anchovies, drained	

1. The squid must have the ink sac removed and they should be rubbed under cold running water to remove the brownish-purple outer skin. They should be rinsed and drained well.

2. Heat the oil in a saucepan and add the onion. Cook until the onion is translucent. Sprinkle with pepper and add the squid and anchovies. Do not add salt until the very end, if ever. The anchovies are already salty.

3. Add the clam juice and parsley and simmer 30 minutes. Add the lemon juice and serve hot in small soup bowls with parsley sprinkled over. Serve with a pepper mill, if desired.

Yield: Four to six servings.

Les Huîtres au Beurre Blanc
(Oysters with white butter sauce)

3   dozen oysters on the half shell
1¼ cups beurre blanc (see recipe)
1¼ cups finely chopped scallions

1. Preheat the broiler.
2. Arrange the oysters on flameproof baking dishes and place under the broiler for 3 minutes or just until heated without cooking.
3. Remove from the broiler
4. Blend the butter sauce and scallions and spoon this over the oysters. Serve with a pepper mill on the side.

Yield: Six servings.

Beurre Blanc
(White butter sauce)

6   tablespoons finely chopped shallots
1½ cups dry white wine
12 tablespoons butter
Salt and freshly ground pepper

1. Combine the shallots and wine in a saucepan and bring to a vigorous boil.
2. Let the wine cook down to about ⅓ cup. Continue cooking over high heat, stirring rapidly with a wire whisk, and add the butter about 2 tablespoons at a time.
3. Add salt and pepper to taste.

Yield: About 1¼ cups.

Clams Posillipo

48 littleneck or cherrystone clams	Freshly ground pepper
½ cup olive oil	1 tablespoon dried oregano
1 tablespoon finely minced garlic	¼ cup finely chopped parsley
2 dried hot red peppers	
½ cup dry white wine	
3 cups canned tomatoes with tomato paste	

1. Wash the clams well and drain.

2. Heat the oil in a large, heavy skillet and add the garlic and hot peppers. Cook briefly and add the wine. Cook to reduce the liquid by half, then add the tomatoes with tomato paste. Add pepper to taste and the oregano. Cover and bring to the boil. Cook about 15 minutes.

3. Add the clams and cover closely. Cook until the clams open, 5 to 10 minutes. Sprinkle with chopped parsley and serve.

Yield: Four servings.

IT IS THE PREMISE OF MY COLUMN, OF COURSE, that the preparation of a first-rate meal within the span of 60 minutes requires neither hocus-pocus nor a great deal of prestidigitation. Generally speaking, when working within that time I have limited myself largely to main courses with accompanying side dishes such as rice or noodles plus a salad with cheese.

There is no reason why, with a touch more effort, a menu prepared in less than an hour could not easily embrace an appetizer or first course as well. Part of my thinking in this area is that if you serve a vegetable such as leeks as a first course, there is no need, with good menu-planning, to offer a vegetable as a side dish.

After that column, a reader wrote to ask if artichokes vinaigrette could also be used as a first course, considering a one-hour preparation time for a meal, and the answer is yes. She added that although she had dined on artichokes many times, she had never prepared the vegetable herself and asked for advice on how to go about it.

Artichokes demand more time than most vegetables, but they are, nonetheless, easily prepared if you have a sharp and sturdy chef's knife (and no well-equipped kitchen should be without one) and a pair of kitchen scissors.

Cut off the very top of the artichoke, slice off the stem, trim the tip of the outer leaves with the scissors and the artichoke is then ready for the pot. The average artichoke requires a longer cooking time than most vegetables, about 45 minutes. It may be served hot or cold with a vinaigrette sauce. (Artichokes are also excellent served directly from the kettle with hot melted butter.)

Leeks vinaigrette seem to be an almost ideal first course, for their preparation is simplicity itself. You trim and rinse the vegetable and put it on to cook in water. After draining, the leeks are left to cool (the dish may be served at room temperature or lukewarm) and served with a vinaigrette sauce, one that can be made, literally, in less than a minute.

While the leeks simmer you have a good deal of time on your hands to turn to the main course.

Artichauts Vinaigrette
(Artichokes vinaigrette)

4 artichokes, about ¾ pound each
Salt
1 tablespoon imported mustard, preferably Dijon
2 tablespoons red wine vinegar
Freshly ground pepper
¾ cup peanut, vegetable, or corn oil
Finely chopped parsley

1. Place the artichokes, one at a time, on their sides and, using a sharp knife, cut off the upper leaves about 1 inch from the top. Slice off the

bottom stem, leaving a neat, flat base. Using a pair of kitchen scissors, cut off the top of the artichoke leaves, about 1 inch from the tip of each.

2. Put the artichokes in a large pot with cold water to cover. Add salt to taste. Closely cover the artichokes with a clean cloth only, and bring to a boil. Let simmer 45 minutes, or until tender. Do not overcook. Drain well and let stand until ready to serve.

3. Put the mustard, salt to taste, vinegar, and pepper to taste in a small mixing bowl. Beat vigorously with a wire whisk. Gradually add the oil, beating constantly. Add the parsley.

4. Serve the artichokes with small bowls of the sauce on the side.

Yield: Four servings.

Poireaux Vinaigrette
(Leeks vinaigrette)

4	large unblemished leeks, about 2 pounds		Freshly ground pepper
	Salt	¾	cup peanut, vegetable, or corn oil
1	tablespoon imported mustard, preferably Dijon	1	tablespoon finely chopped parsley
2	tablespoons red wine vinegar		

1. Trim off the root ends of the leeks, but leave the bases solid and intact. Trim off the green tops crosswise, leaving a base about 5 or 7 inches long. Use the green parts of the leeks for soups and seasoning in other dishes. The trimmed weight is about 1¼ pounds.

2. Using a sharp knife, split the leeks in half lengthwise, starting about 2 inches from the stem end and cutting through the leaves. Rinse the leeks well under cold running water to remove the dirt between the leaves. You may tie the leeks back into their original shape with string. Put the leeks in a saucepan and add cold water to cover with salt to taste. Bring to the boil and simmer 10 to 15 minutes or until tender. The cooking time of the leeks will vary, depending on the size and age of the leeks. Take care never to overcook the leeks or they will be mushy.

3. Drain the leeks thoroughly and let them stand until cool enough to handle, then press them between the hands to extract any excess liquid.

4. Split the leeks in half crosswise. Arrange them nealty on a serving dish.

5. Put the mustard, vinegar, with salt and pepper to taste in a small bowl. Beat vigorously with a wire whisk. Gradually add the oil, beating constantly.

6. Spoon the sauce over the leeks and sprinkle with finely chopped parsley.

Yield: Four servings.

MANY TIMES, OVER THE YEARS, I HAVE BEEN asked, to offer recipes for crudités, those crisp, raw vegetables—celery, carrots, scallions, and such—that are encountered on the menus of southern France where they are, more often than not, served with a vinaigrette sauce.

Some time ago I decided to make four hasty and excellent dips to be served with crudités, and for a very good reason. I have attended many cocktail parties over a period of years in this country, and most of the dips that are served are of the cream-cheese-and-dry-onion-soup-mix variety. The dip is usually served with spears of cucumber and zucchini and bits of cauliflower and other seasonal crisp vegetables that are good in themselves.

All the dips outlined here are very much on the order of hasty food preparation and they are fashioned to offer contrasts in flavor—a combination of Gorgonzola cheese and walnuts, for example, or a blend of cream cheese with three interesting flavors—anchovy, roasted peppers, and clams.

These recipes are tailored for people who have to rush home from the office to prepare a quick snack for guests who will arrive shortly. But they are also excellent for those with time on their hands. As a matter of fact, while the dips are quite tasty when first made, they also keep well in the refrigerator and will develop flavor as they stand.

Cream Cheese and Anchovy Dip

- ¼ pound cream cheese
- 4 flat anchovy fillets
- 2 tablespoons drained capers
- ½ cup thinly sliced or chopped onion
- 1 clove garlic, finely minced
- ¼ to 1 cup sour cream
- 1 tablespoon finely chopped chives

1. Combine the cream cheese, anchovies, capers, onion, and garlic in the container of a food processor. Process until almost fine.

2. Add the sour cream according to the consistency desired. Scrape into a bowl and stir in the chives and chill. Serve as a spread or dip with raw vegetables, potato chips, or crackers.

Yield: About ¾ to 1¼ cups.

Gorgonzola Dip with Walnuts

- ¼ pound Gorgonzola cheese
- ¼ pound cream cheese
- ¼ cup heavy cream
- 3 tablespoons coarsely chopped walnuts
- 1 teaspoon cognac

1. Combine the Gorgonzola cheese, cream cheese, and heavy cream in the container of a food processor. Process well.

2. Scrape the mixture into a mixing bowl and fold in the walnuts and cognac and chill. Serve as a dip for raw vegetables, such as zucchini or celery sticks, or as a spread for toast and or crackers.

Yield: About 1¼ cups.

Cream Cheese and Roasted Pepper Dip

1	small green pepper	4	drops Tabasco sauce
¼	pound cream cheese	¼	teaspoon Worcestershire sauce
½	cup sour cream		Salt
¼	cup thinly sliced onion	1	tablespoon finely chopped chives
1	clove garlic, thinly sliced		

1. Put the pepper under a broiler and cook, turning often, until the skin is burned all over. Put the pepper in a brown paper bag and close tightly to seal.

2. When cool, remove the pepper from the bag. Peel it and cut it in half. Discard the stem, inner membranes, and seeds. Cut the pepper into fine dice and set aside.

3. Put the cream cheese, sour cream, onion, garlic, Tabasco, Worcestershire sauce, and salt to taste into the container of a food processor. Process thoroughly.

4. Scrape the mixture into a mixing bowl and add the roasted pepper and chives and chill. Serve as a dip for raw vegetables.

Yield: About 1¼ cups.

Cream Cheese and Fresh Clam Dip

12	cherrystone clams	½	cup sour cream
1	cup water	1	teaspoon celery salt or celery seed
¼	pound cream cheese		

1. Scrub and rinse the clams well and put them in a small kettle or a large saucepan. Add the water and cover tightly.

2. Bring to the boil and cook about 5 minutes or until the clams open. Drain the clams. Reserve the clam juice for another use if desired.

3. Remove the clams from the shell and put them into the container of a food processor. Process until fine but not to a purée.

4. Add the cream cheese, sour cream, and celery salt or celery seed. Blend to the desired texture. Scrape into a bowl and chill.

Yield: About 1 cup.

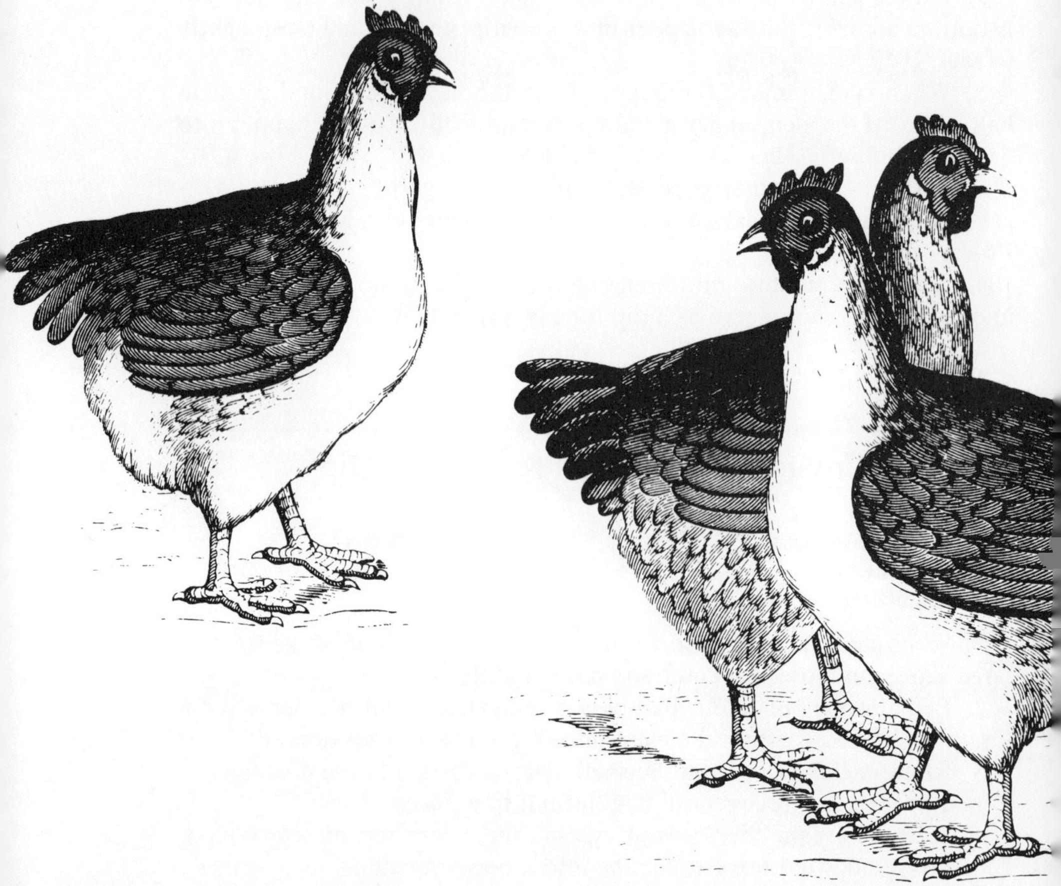

Poultry

ONE OF THE QUIET BUT IMPORTANT ADVANCES of the present-day kitchen in the United States is the availability of ready-boned chicken breasts in the nation's supermarkets. Twenty years ago it was necessary to ask your butcher to perform this task and some butchers would respond with a bit of irritability and hesitation. Boneless chicken breasts are, of course, a great boon to any cook with two hands on a saucepan and one eye on the clock. The cooking must be done quickly to avoid a dry, unpalatable taste.

Although chicken has its own admirable and delicate flavor, it is the perfect foil for foods that are more pronounced in flavor. And because it takes so well to such a multitude of other ingredients, chicken is one of the most versatile of meats. It is complemented by foods as subtle as mushrooms or herbs as assertive as rosemary or oregano. Sweet peppers offer an excellent contrast, and that is the combination in the recipe here. The dish's other principal ingredients are garlic, a bit of dry white wine, and parsley. The total cooking time is less than half an hour.

To hasten this meal, which includes sautéed potatoes with mushrooms, it is best if you get all the ingredients ready for the skillet before you start cooking. As the chicken cooks, proceed to the final preparation of the potatoes and mushrooms.

Incidentally, if you can't find boned chicken breasts in your supermarket, or if your butcher is uncooperative, boning a breast is probably the easiest form of "butchering" in the world. It is something that a novice cook can do with a little practice and a paring knife.

Suprême de Volaille aux Poivrons
(Chicken breasts with peppers)

- 2 whole chicken breasts, about 2 pounds
- Salt and freshly ground pepper
- 3 tablespoons butter
- ½ teaspoon finely minced garlic
- ½ pound sweet red or green peppers, cored, seeded, and cut into thin strips, about 2 cups
- ½ cup dry white wine
- 1 tablespoon finely chopped parsley

1. You may purchase the chicken pieces already boned but with skin left on or you may do it yourself. If you choose to bone the chicken breasts yourself, split the breasts in half to produce four pieces. Leave the skin intact but, using the fingers and a paring or boning knife, cut between the flesh and bones to separate the flesh from the bones. The bones may be used for stock or discarded.

2. Sprinkle the chicken with salt and pepper to taste.

3. Melt 2 tablespoons of butter in a skillet and add the chicken pieces,

skin side down. Cook about 4 minutes or until golden brown on one side. Turn the pieces and continue cooking about 4 minutes.

4. Add the garlic and pepper strips. Cook about 4 minutes. Add the wine. Cover and cook about 4 minutes longer.

5. Remove the chicken pieces to a warm serving dish.

6. Add the remaining tablespoon of butter to the peppers in the skillet and stir until hot. Pour the peppers and sauce over the chicken. Sprinkle with parsley and serve.

Yield: Four servings.

Pommes Juliennes aux Champignons
(Sautéed potatoes with mushrooms)

3	medium-size potatoes, about 1½ pounds	2	tablespoons finely chopped shallots
½	cup peanut, vegetable, or corn oil	½	teaspoon finely minced garlic
¼	pound mushrooms, thinly sliced, about 1 cup		Salt and freshly ground pepper to taste
2	tablespoons butter	1	tablespoon finely chopped parsley

1. Peel the potatoes and cut them into quarter-inch-thick slices. Stack the slices and cut them into quarter-inch-thick strips as for french fries. There should be about 5 cups.

2. Put the potatoes in a colander and run piping hot water out of the tap over them. Drain well.

3. Heat the oil in a skillet and add the potatoes. Cook over high heat, stirring and shaking the skillet to cook the strips evenly. Cook about 10 to 12 minutes, until strips are golden brown. Add mushrooms and cook, shaking and stirring, about 4 minutes.

4. Drain the potatoes and mushrooms. Wipe out the skillet.

5. Add the butter to the skillet and, when it is hot, add the potatoes and mushrooms. Sprinkle with shallots and garlic and salt and pepper to taste. Sprinkle with parsley and serve.

Yield: Four servings.

I FIND WHEN I TRAVEL IN EUROPE THERE IS, generally speaking, one dish that sticks in the memory for each village and town in which I dine. It may be a simple omelet consumed in a small out-of-the-way inn in Burgundy; a wonderfully perfumed andouillette sausage hot from the fire in Sens, or spit-turned chicken cooked to a turn a kilometer or so from Bresse.

During a visit to Italy some years ago, we dined on a fine dish for which the city is known, a veal chop Modenese. It was an exceptionally tender, white-fleshed cut of veal, bone in, breaded and topped with a slice of prosciutto and Fontina cheese. The chop had been baked in a hot oven until the cheese took on a glossy, melted luster and still dribbled down the sides of the chop when it was served.

I have quite successfully duplicated this dish at home. On a recent occasion, however, I tried to reproduce it using a simple, inexpensive pound or so of skinless, boneless chicken breasts. It works admirably.

When I made this preparation a few days ago, I was able to buy imported Fontina, which is delectable both as a "melting" cheese as well as for a cheese tray. It is not easy to slice, however. I found that I could best "shape" the cheese, after cutting off a thin slab, by putting it on a flat surface, covering it with plastic wrap and pounding it lightly with a flat mallet. In Modena the dish was served with mashed potatoes. I have included a recipe for that as well as one for making fine fresh bread crumbs.

Suprême de Volaille Modenese
(Chicken breasts with cheese and ham)

2 whole skinless, boneless chicken breasts, about 1¼ pounds	¼ cup flour
1 egg	3 tablespoons butter, preferably clarified
Salt and freshly ground pepper	4 thin slices ham, preferably prosciutto, or boiled ham
1 teaspoon peanut, vegetable, or corn oil	4 thin slices cheese, preferably Fontina, although Swiss or Gruyère may be used
1 cup fine fresh bread crumbs (see technique)	

1. Preheat the oven to 400 degrees.

2. Using a sharp knife, split the chicken breasts lengthwise down the center. This will produce four pieces. Cut away the peripheral bits of fat from each piece. Place each piece between sheets of plastic wrap and pound lightly with a flat mallet.

3. Combine the egg, salt and pepper to taste, and oil in a flat dish. Beat well to blend.

4. Put the bread crumbs in another flat dish. Put the flour in another flat dish.

5. Dip each chicken piece first in flour, then in egg, and finally in bread crumbs. Pat lightly with the flat side of a heavy kitchen knife to make the crumbs adhere.

6. Melt the butter in a heavy skillet and just as it starts to turn brown add the chicken pieces. Cook about 4 minutes or until the pieces are nicely browned on one side. Turn and cook about 4 to 5 minutes until golden brown on the other side.

7. Arrange the chicken pieces in a baking dish. Cover each piece with a slice of ham. Top the ham with a slice of cheese.

8. Place the dish in the oven and bake 10 minutes.

Yield: Four servings.

How to make fine fresh bread crumbs

Put enough coarse-textured French or Italian bread cubes into the container of a food processor to make one cup. Process until fine. Put a sieve into a bowl and add the crumbs. Press and shake the crumbs through the sieve. Discard the crumbs that do not pass through the sieve.

Purée de Pommes de Terre
(Mashed potatoes)

4 Maine or Long Island potatoes, about 1¾ pounds	1¼ cups milk, approximately
Salt	2 tablespoons butter
	Freshly ground pepper

1. Peel the potatoes. Cut them into quarters. Put them in a large saucepan and add cold water to cover.

2. Add salt to taste. Bring to the boil and simmer until tender, about 20 minutes.

3. Meanwhile, bring the milk barely to the boil.

4. Drain the potatoes. Put them into a food mill or food ricer. Work the potatoes through to a fine purée and into a saucepan.

5. Add the butter and pepper to taste and beat with a wooden spoon until the butter is melted and blended. Gradually beat in the milk and test. Add more milk if a thinner purée is desired. Reheat briefly before serving.

Yield: Four servings.

WHEN I AM ASKED TO NAME THE ONE MAIN course that can be made in less than an hour, tastes best, and makes the greatest impression on guests, there are hundreds of foods that come to mind. But on consideration, it might just well be a platter of curried chicken.

There are several reasons for this. The flavor of curry appeals to almost all palates, East or West. Although I oftentimes add many other flavors to curried dishes—cumin, coriander, even fruits such as bananas and apples—the simple flavor of a fine curry powder can be sufficient unto itself.

And the simplest of all good curried dishes is outlined here. It is a breast of chicken in a curry sauce, the sort of dish that can be made within the space of one hour or less, even though you may start from "scratch" by cooking the chicken breast itself. It is also the kind of dish that can utilize leftover cooked chicken (or even veal or shrimp for that matter). The preparation of the meal entails the cooking of chicken breasts (ten minutes simmering time). As the chicken cooks you can start the sauce, the basis for which is butter, flour, and a good brand of curry powder.

Once the chicken is cooked and left to cool slightly (just until it can be handled without discomfort to the fingers), you add the broth from the chicken to the butter-flour mixture, stirring constantly and rapidly with a wire whisk. The completion of the dish is merely a matter of adding a touch of heavy cream. At times, I serve this dish as a "meal in one," and I have taken the liberty of including some chopped chutney in the sauce rather than serving it on the side.

The ideal accompaniment for almost any curried dish is rice and this can be prepared simultaneously—all things being equal—with the chicken in curry sauce. Here, too, for convenience sake and in the interest of saving time, I blend a couple of traditional, perhaps Western, curry accompaniments—shredded coconut and raisins or currants. The rice can be put on to cook the moment you put your saucepan with the chicken breasts on to simmer. The cooking time for the rice, as I have mentioned often, is only 17 minutes. Serve a well-seasoned green salad and a not-too-dry, well-chilled white wine to complement the meal.

Suprême de Volaille au Kari
(Breast of chicken with curry sauce)

- 2 tablespoons butter
- 3 tablespoons flour
- 1 tablespoon curry powder
- 1½ cups rich chicken broth, see recipe for poached chicken breast
- ½ cup heavy cream
- ¼ cup chopped chutney
- 2 whole poached chicken breasts (see recipe)

1. Melt the butter in a saucepan and add the flour and curry powder, stirring with a wire whisk. When blended and smooth add the broth, stirring constantly. Add the cream and the chutney and bring to the simmer.

2. Remove the skin and bones from the chicken. Carefully remove the breast halves, each in one piece. Arrange one breast half on each of four hot plates. Spoon equal portions of the sauce over each breast half. Serve with plain rice or rice with raisins and coconut.

Yield: Four servings.

Suprême de Volaille Poché
(Poached breast of chicken)

2	large, whole chicken breasts, about 2 pounds total weight	½	teaspoon dried thyme
1	cup fresh or canned chicken broth	1	bay leaf
	Water to cover		Salt to taste
½	cup coarsely chopped celery	12	peppercorns
½	cup coarsely chopped onion	1	sprig fresh parsley
		½	cup coarsely chopped carrot

1. Put the chicken breasts in one layer in a saucepan. Add the broth and water to barely cover.

2. Add the remaining ingredients and cover. Bring to the boil and let simmer about 10 minutes. Cover and let stand until ready to use.

Yield: Two cooked breasts of chicken.

Riz à l'Indienne
(Rice with raisins and coconut)

1	cup long grain rice	¼	cup dried, shredded coconut
1½	cups chicken broth	2	tablespoons butter, optional
¼	cup black raisins		

1. Combine the rice and broth in a saucepan. Bring to the boil and add the raisins and coconut.

2. Cover closely. Let simmer exactly 17 minutes. Uncover the rice and fluff in the butter.

Yield: Four servings.

ONE OF THE FIRST THINGS I LEARNED AS A young apprentice chef in Paris many decades ago is that "classic" French dishes go by a specific name that acts more or less as a code. One of these is Florentine to describe dishes made with spinach. Du Barry means dishes containing cauliflower and Argenteuil denotes the presence of asparagus. This greatly simplifies things for menu writers.

There are, of course, several thousand dishes that bear these code names, some of the most familiar of which are boeuf Bourguignonne (a beef stew made with Burgundy wine), fillet of sole Grenobloise (with capers and lemon) and lobster Américaine (with a light tomato-tarragon sauce plus a touch of cognac).

I was fascinated when I first worked in American kitchens to hear of a dish called chicken breasts Eugénie, because it *sounded* so French and yet I had never heard of it in my home country. It is a very good, very easily made dish (I once had to assist in preparing 2,000 servings of it for one banquet at the Waldorf Astoria Hotel, where I worked briefly before Le Pavillon opened), and I am resolutely convinced that it is wholly American in origin.

One French chef I know once told me that it is also called chicken breasts Virginie, which may well be true because it is made with not only breast of chicken but ham as well. And classically, my informant said, the ham should be Smithfield.

This is an excellent dish for entertaining. It consists of cooking skinless, boneless chicken breasts until cooked without browning. The breasts are placed on heated slices of ham, topped with mushrooms and served with a cream sauce lightly flavored with sherry. A dinner or supper for four can easily be made in less than an hour.

I have served this dish quite successfully with buttered green noodles sprinkled with Parmesan cheese plus a green salad.

Suprême de Volaille Eugénie
(Chicken breasts with mushrooms and ham)

- 2 large, whole skinless, boneless chicken breasts, about 1½ pounds total weight
- Salt and freshly ground pepper
- 2 tablespoons butter
- 12 large mushrooms, about ¼ pound
- 4 thin slices cooked Smithfield ham, prosciutto, or boiled ham
- 1 tablespoon finely chopped shallots
- ¼ cup dry sherry
- 1 cup heavy cream

1. Cut the chicken breasts in half. Trim away all fat and membranes.

2. Sprinkle the pieces with salt and pepper to taste. Melt the butter in a heavy skillet large enough to hold the chicken pieces and the mushrooms.

3. When the butter is hot, add the breasts and mushrooms. Cook the breasts on one side about 3 minutes and turn the pieces. In this recipe you are not supposed to brown the pieces. They should be cooked over low heat so that they cook gently. Cook on the other side about 5 minutes or until the pieces are barely cooked. As the breasts are turned, turn the mushrooms.

4. Transfer the chicken and mushrooms to a warm platter. Add the ham and cook just to heat through, turning once, about 30 seconds. Remove the ham and arrange one slice under each chicken breast.

5. Add the shallots to the skillet and cook briefly, stirring. Add the wine and cook until it is almost totally reduced.

6. Add the cream and cook down to about ¾ cup. Strain the sauce, pressing with a spatula to extract as much juice as possible from the solids. Reheat the sauce. Arrange the mushrooms over the chicken breasts and spoon the sauce over.

Yield: Four servings.

Nouilles Vertes au Parmesan
(Green noodles with Parmesan cheese)

½	pound fresh or packaged green noodles	2	tablespoons butter
	Salt	¼	cup freshly grated Parmesan cheese

1. Cook the noodles in boiling salted water to cover until tender. Fresh noodles will require 3 to 5 minutes; packaged noodles will take longer.

2. Drain the noodles and toss with butter. Sprinkle with cheese and serve.

Yield: Four servings.

I HAVE REMARKED MANY TIMES ON THE TRAditionally inexpensive role of chicken in cookery and the fact that, when economy in cooking is a factor, both chicken and turkey, properly treated, can be used as a substitute for veal, which is not only one of the finest and most delicate of meats but also a luxury. I can think of very few dishes in which chicken cannot be substituted for veal.

If you can make a fricassée of veal, you can prepare a fricassée of chicken by almost the exact same cooking procedure. In the home of an Italian friend, I have dined well on a platter of "vitello" tonnato, the well-known cold veal dish with tuna mayonnaise in which chicken breast was substituted for veal. As a matter of fact, most of the guests were unaware of the fact that they were not eating veal.

There is another Italian "invention" of which I am fond and another in which chicken serves very well for the traditional veal base. This is veal "milanese," in which scaloppine of veal is breaded, sautéed, and served with its customary side dish of macaroni or other pasta with a light tomato sauce.

The preparation of the dish is as simple as the results are tasty. And it is a dish that is easily prepared within the scope of one hour. You take skinless, boneless breasts of chicken and cut away all membranes and peripheral fat.

You dip the pieces (there are two pieces, of course, to each breast) first in flour, then in beaten egg, and finally in fine fresh bread crumbs.

Incidentally, when making bread crumbs using the blender or food processor, you might consider making them in a large batch. Leftover crumbs keep well tightly sealed for about a week in the refrigerator; indefinitely in the freezer.

You pat the crumbs with the flat side of a knife to help them adhere and then sauté the breaded meat in a blend of oil and butter. The reason for blending the oil and butter has to do with the burning point of butter. It is lower than that of oil. The butter is added for flavor.

The logical way to proceed with this meal is to prepare the chicken pieces first. You can bread them without cooking well in advance. As a matter of fact if, after you bread the pieces, you let them rest on a wire rack, the crumbs will adhere better.

Prepare the tomato sauce for the macaroni and, as it cooks, start sautéeing the chicken while simultaneously cooking the macaroni in boiling water.

Suprême de Volaille Milanaise
(Breaded chicken breasts)

2 whole skinless, boneless chicken breasts, about ¾ pound each	1 cup fine fresh bread crumbs
2 tablespoons flour	¼ cup freshly grated Parmesan cheese
1 large egg	1 tablespoon butter
2 tablespoons water	Macaroni with tomato sauce (see recipe)
4 tablespoons plus 1 teaspoon peanut, vegetable, or corn oil	
Salt and freshly ground pepper	

1. Split the chicken breasts in half down the center. Trim them neatly to remove peripheral membranes and bits of fat.
2. Put the flour in a plate.
3. Put the egg, water, one teaspoon of the oil, and salt and pepper to taste in another plate and beat well to blend.
4. Put the bread crumbs and cheese in another plate and blend well.
5. Dip the chicken, one piece at a time, first in the flour, then in the egg mixture, and finally the bread crumbs, making sure that the pieces are well coated. Pat lightly with the flat side of a knife to make the crumbs adhere well.
6. Heat the remaining 4 tablespoons of oil and the butter in a skillet large enough to hold the chicken pieces in one layer. Add the chicken pieces and cook over gentle heat until golden brown on one side, about 7 minutes. Turn the pieces and cook until golden brown on the other side, 5 to 7 minutes.

Yield: Four servings.

Macaroni Sauce Tomate
(Macaroni with tomato sauce)

2 cups canned tomatoes, crushed	1 bay leaf
2 tablespoons tomato paste	Salt and freshly ground pepper
2 tablespoons butter or olive oil	½ pound macaroni

1. Combine the tomatoes, tomato paste, butter, bay leaf, and salt and pepper to taste in a saucepan. Bring to the boil and simmer over moderate heat, stirring often, about 10 minutes.
2. Cook the macaroni according to your desired degree of doneness. Drain and serve with the tomato sauce.

Yield: Four servings.

IT SEEMS TO ME THAT THERE ARE TWO basic reactions to outdoor cooking in this country. There are those who admire it intensely and those who deplore it emphatically. I belong in the former category.

As a child I cooked chickens on a spit before an open fire. And one of the happiest vacations I've had involved preparing our own meals over a charcoal fire at a camp in Colorado.

I suspect that the reason some cooks don't admire charcoal-grilled foods is that they are not attuned to the pitfalls. A great deal depends on the heat from the coals, the distance the food is elevated above the coals, the direction of the wind, etc. And, unfortunately, the "rules" for such cookery are as unscientific as they are variable. You simply have to rely on your own good judgment to avoid burned, overcooked spareribs, hamburgers, leg of lamb, and so on.

One meal I prepared over the coals recently is my family's favorite—deviled chicken with a fresh tomato sauce. I used whole chicken breasts that had been coated lightly with mustard and oil before cooking. First, however, I had pounded them with a mallet. This makes them lie flatter and also expedites their cooking to some degree.

You must turn the breasts often but, if you know what you're about at the grill, you needn't stand and watch constantly to get the job done. There is ample time to prepare a simple fresh tomato sauce and seasonal salad. On this occasion I added to the chicken mushroom caps, brushed lightly with oil. The chicken, by the way, was sprinkled lightly with bread crumbs toward the end of the cooking period.

Poitrines de Volaille Diablées
(Breaded deviled chicken breasts)

4 whole chicken breasts with skin and bones, about 3½ pounds total weight	¼ cup peanut, vegetable, or corn oil
Salt and freshly ground pepper	8 tablespoons fine fresh bread crumbs
2 tablespoons mustard such as Dijon or Düsseldorf	Fresh tomato sauce (see recipe)

1. Preheat a charcoal broiler.

2. Put the chicken breasts skin side up on a flat surface. Flatten them one at a time, using a flat mallet or the bottom of a heavy skillet.

3. Sprinkle the breasts on both sides with salt and pepper to taste. Brush them all over with mustard and then with oil.

4. Place the breasts on the grill skin side down. Cook about 4 minutes, shifting them as necessary to prevent burning by flames that may appear on the coals. Ideally, you can create a grill pattern on the breasts by giving

them a 90-degree turn on the grill after they have cooked about 2 minutes longer skin side down or a total of about 4 to 5 minutes.

5. Turn the breasts skin side up and continue cooking, turning occasionally, about 15 minutes.

6. Turn the breasts skin side down and sprinkle the top of each with 1 tablespoon of bread crumbs.

7. Turn the pieces skin side up and sprinkle each with 1 tablespoon of crumbs. Continue cooking, turning as necessary, until the pieces are done, about 10 minutes longer. The total cooking time should be about 30 minutes. Serve with fresh tomato sauce.

Yield: Four servings.

Sauce Tomate
(Fresh tomato sauce)

- 2 tablespoons olive oil
- ½ cup finely chopped onion
- 1 teaspoon finely minced garlic
- 2 cups chopped skinned fresh tomatoes
- 1 bay leaf
- ½ teaspoon dried thyme
- Salt and freshly ground pepper to taste
- 1 tablespoon butter
- 1 tablespoon chopped fresh basil

1. Heat the oil in a saucepan and add the onion and garlic. Cook briefly until wilted.

2. Add the tomatoes, bay leaf, thyme, and salt and pepper to taste and bring to the boil. Cover and cook about 10 minutes. Stir in the butter and basil.

Yield: About 1½ cups.

Champignons Grillés
(Grilled mushrooms)

- 16 large mushrooms, about ¾ pound
- Salt and freshly ground pepper
- 2 tablespoons peanut, vegetable, or corn oil

1. Preheat a charcoal grill.

2. Sprinkle the mushrooms all over with salt and pepper to taste and brush with the oil.

3. Put the mushrooms stem side up on the grill and cook about 2 minutes. Turn the mushrooms and continue cooking about 3 minutes.

Yield: Four servings.

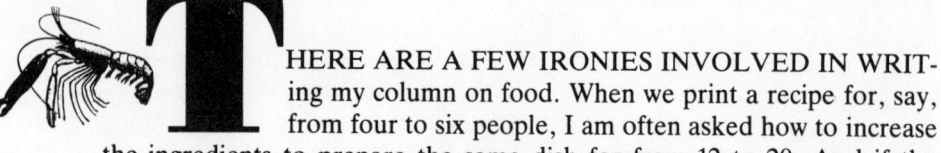

THERE ARE A FEW IRONIES INVOLVED IN WRITing my column on food. When we print a recipe for, say, from four to six people, I am often asked how to increase the ingredients to prepare the same dish for from 12 to 20. And if the recipe is for what might be called "crowd cookery," I am asked how to reduce the recipe for a small group, say four to six.

Within the last few weeks, we offered recipes for food that was destined to be served to a party of 30 or more, and among them was a recipe for food in an américaine sauce.

Américaine sauce is a light tomato sauce flavored with tarragon, shallots, and cognac and generally destined for lobster américaine, a difficult and time-consuming dish to prepare. For this book, I will set aside thoughts of the origin of the name of the dish and simply say that I am personally persuaded that it is not of American origin but was created in France and dubbed américaine for one reason or another.

In any event, I have twice been asked recently if that recipe for the américaine sauce could be reduced to a manageable amount to serve four, and the answer is an easy yes.

On a recent evening I made a combination of shrimp and chicken in an américaine sauce (I know that some purists are going to insist that you must use lobster, but I find it irrelevant). There were two reasons for blending the shrimp and chicken. One, the combination goes curiously well together. Two, I happened to have a limited amount of shrimp and a limited amount of chicken breasts on hand when I started to cook. Besides, with the cost of shrimp in today's market, it isn't a bad idea to stretch a cooking concept.

To my mind, this is a very fancy dish and perhaps not the sort you want to toss off for any commonplace occasion. It is easily and quickly made, however, and would be very good for a special occasion with a fine white Burgundy. The ideal accompaniment for the dish is rice followed by a salad and cheese and perhaps fresh fruit for dessert.

Crevettes et Filet de Volaille Américaine
(Shrimp and chicken breast in tomato sauce)

1 tablespoon olive oil	Salt and freshly ground pepper
½ cup finely chopped onion	1 pound uncooked shrimp
⅓ cup finely chopped celery	1 skinless, boneless chicken breast, about ¾ pound
⅓ cup finely chopped carrots	
4 teaspoons finely minced shallots	2 tablespoons butter
½ teaspoon finely minced garlic	2 tablespoons cognac
2 cups crushed tomatoes	½ teaspoon chopped fresh or dried tarragon
2 tablespoons tomato paste	
½ cup dry white wine	½ teaspoon finely chopped fresh parsley
¼ teaspoon dried tarragon	

1. Heat the oil in a saucepan and add the onion, celery, carrots, 1 teaspoon minced shallots, and garlic. Cook, stirring, briefly until the onion is wilted.

2. Add the tomatoes, tomato paste, wine, and ¼ teaspoon dried tarragon. Add salt and pepper to taste. Bring to the boil and let simmer about 15 minutes.

3. As the sauce cooks, peel and devein the shrimp. Set aside.

4. Cut away all membranes and fat attached to the chicken breast. Cut the chicken breast into half-inch shreds. Set aside.

5. Melt the butter in a skillet and, when it is quite hot but not brown, add the chicken. Sprinkle it with salt and pepper to taste. Cook, stirring to separate the pieces, about 45 seconds. Add the shrimp and stir. Cook, stirring occasionally, about 1 minute. Add the remaining 3 teaspoons of shallots and sprinkle with cognac. Add the fresh tarragon and the chopped parsley. Add the tomato sauce and bring to the boil. Serve with rice.

Yield: Four to six servings.

Riz Persillé
(Parsleyed rice)

3	tablespoons butter		Salt and freshly ground pepper
⅓	cup minced onion		Tabasco sauce to taste
1½	cups raw rice	3	tablespoons finely chopped parsley
2¼	cups water		
1	bay leaf		

1. Melt 2 tablespoons of butter in a saucepan and add the onion. Cook, stirring, until wilted. Add the rice and stir to make certain there are no lumps in the rice.

2. Add the water, bay leaf, salt and pepper to taste, and Tabasco.

3. Bring to the boil. Cover and simmer 20 minutes.

4. Discard the bay leaf. Using a two-pronged fork, stir in the remaining butter and chopped parsley.

Yield: Four to six servings.

A GOOD MANY YEARS AGO, THE FIRST TIME I saw the words "surf and turf" on a menu, I was puzzled. When it was explained to me that it meant lobster and steak served together, I was amused because it seemed such a bizarre and unlikely combination.

When I got around to sampling the dish, it turned out to be not such a bad combination at all. Since my initiation into the marriage of shellfish with meat or poultry, I have encountered many similar liaisons in the world of cuisine.

Veal Oskar links a broiled veal chop with (in this country, at least) crabmeat or shrimp plus asparagus spears and hollandaise sauce. The Chinese kitchen often combines poultry and other meats with various kinds of seafood: stir-fried chicken shreds with jellyfish; ham and chicken and shrimp in paper packages, and so on.

I realized that the surf and turf concept was actually very old. One of the most often-quoted anecdotes about French cookery has to do with chicken Marengo.

It seems that Napoleon's chef, after the battle of Marengo in Italy, scoured the countryside and came up with a dish composed of all the ingredients he could find in one afternoon: a chicken, crawfish, garlic, tomatoes, and eggs. All of these he combined, and the result was the Marengo creation. Few chefs today add the crawfish and fried egg garnish, but traditionally they should be included.

I was recently in an experimental mood and I brought together an assortment of foods I found in the refrigerator, including breast of chicken, mushrooms, and shrimp, plus about a pint of fresh tomato sauce left over from the evening before.

I cut the chicken into shreds, sautéed them along with the sliced mushrooms and shrimp and stirred in the tomato sauce. The end result was tasty enough. An acquaintance had stopped by and asked for a glass of Pernod and since the bottle was at my elbow, I added a splash of that. The dish, as it turned out, was neither East nor West, but it was different, good and easy to prepare in less than half an hour's time.

Blanc de Volaille aux Crevettes Roses
(Sautéed chicken breast with shrimp)

2 small skinless, boneless chicken breasts, about ¾ pound total weight	2 tablespoons finely chopped shallots
1 pound raw shrimp	½ cup dry white wine
½ pound mushrooms	2 cups fresh tomato sauce (see recipe)
3 tablespoons butter	1 tablespoon Pernod or Ricard liqueur
Salt and freshly ground pepper	

1. Split the chicken breasts in half lengthwise. Cut away all fibers, membranes, and bits of extraneous fat.

2. Place each breast half on a flat surface and cut the meat into half-inch strips. Set aside.

3. Peel the shrimp and run under cold water to remove the black vein. Drain well.

4. Rinse the mushrooms, pat dry and slice thinly.

5. Melt 2 tablespoons of the butter in a large, wide, heavy skillet and add the chicken. Cook over high heat, stirring, about 1 minute. Add the mushrooms and salt and pepper to taste. Cook, stirring, about 1 minute.

6. Add the shrimp and cook, stirring, about 1 minute or just until the shrimp turn red.

7. Using a slotted spoon, transfer the ingredients to a casserole. Leave any liquid or fat in the skillet.

8. To the liquid or fat add the shallots and cook briefly. Add the wine and cook until it is reduced to about half a cup.

9. Add the tomato sauce and bring to the boil.

10. Add the shrimp-mushroom-chicken mixture. Return to the boil, stirring, and swirl in the remaining tablespoon of butter. Stir in the Pernod or Ricard and serve.

Yield: Four servings.

Sauce Tomate
(Fresh tomato sauce)

¾ pound fresh tomatoes	1 teaspoon finely chopped garlic
1 tablespoon butter	1 bay leaf
½ cup finely chopped onion	Salt and freshly ground pepper

1. Cut out the cores of the tomatoes. Cut the tomatoes into cubes. There should be about 2 cups.

2. Melt the butter in a saucepan and add the onion and garlic. Cook, stirring, until wilted and add the tomatoes, bay leaf, and salt and pepper to taste. Cover and cook about 10 minutes.

3. Scrape the sauce into the container of a food processor. Process well.

4. Place a sieve in a large measuring cup and scrape the sauce into the sieve. Press the sauce through the sieve. Discard the solids.

Yield: About 2 cups.

THE FRENCH LANGUAGE HAS MANY SPELLINGS for the word curry. It is spelled kari, cari, curry, carri, and cary.

I had always presumed that the word had originated with the British, when India was a part of the British Empire. The Bloch and von Wartburg *Etymological Dictionary of the French Language,* however, points out that the word cari entered into the French language in 1602 and derives from kari, which is found in the Hindi language. According to this work, it was the English who "borrowed" from the French and called the dish curry.

There are, of course, many ways to make French curries. (My Indian friends, by the way, scoff at most dishes that Western cooks label curries.) They range from a simple addition of curry powder to a sauce to a more elaborate concoction that calls for finely diced apple and bananas, both of which give a pleasant, smooth softness to the flavor of the dish.

One of the simplest and most quickly made curries calls for skinless, boneless chicken breasts that are cut into bite-size strips and sautéed quickly in butter. The chicken must cook briefly—just until the meat loses its raw look—or it will tend to be dry. The strips are removed, and shallots, curry powder, and wine are added. This mixture is reduced over high heat, and heavy cream is added. When it cooks down to a saucelike consistency, the chicken pieces are returned to the skillet and heated. The dish is at that moment ready to be served.

Rice is an almost invariable accompaniment to a curry, and one that I especially like contains pine nuts and raisins. The rice, in fact, takes longer to cook (exactly 17 minutes) than does the main dish. Thus, in preparing the menu proposed here, it is best to begin the rice and then turn your attention to the curry.

Poulet au Kari à la Crème
(Chicken breasts in curried cream sauce)

1¾ pounds skinless, boneless chicken breasts	1 tablespoon or more curry powder
2 tablespoons butter	½ cup dry white wine
Salt and freshly ground pepper	1¼ cups heavy cream
¼ cup finely chopped shallots	

1. Trim around the chicken breasts to cut away and discard the fat and membranes. Cut the chicken into strips about ½ inch wide.

2. Melt the butter in a skillet and, when it is quite hot but not brown, add the chicken pieces. Sprinkle with salt and pepper to taste. Stir often until the chicken strips lose their raw look—about 2 minutes.

3. Sprinkle the chicken pieces with the shallots and curry powder. Stir well to blend and cook about 1 minute.

4. Transfer the chicken pieces to a bowl.

5. Add the wine to the skillet and cook over high heat about 3 minutes or until it is reduced to ¼ cup. Add any juices that have accumulated in the bowl containing the chicken.

6. Add the cream to the skillet and cook over high heat about 4 minutes. Add the chicken and stir to blend well. The chicken must be piping hot throughout. Serve hot with rice and cucumber and chili raita.

Yield: Four servings.

Riz au Sultan
(Rice with raisins and pine nuts)

2 tablespoons butter	1 cup rice
3 tablespoons finely chopped onion	¼ cup raisins
	1½ cups chicken broth
½ teaspoon finely minced garlic	¼ cup pine nuts

1. Melt 1 tablespoon of the butter in a saucepan and add the onion and garlic. Cook, stirring, until wilted. Add the rice and stir. Add the raisins.

2. Add the chicken broth and bring to the boil. Cover and let simmer exactly 17 minutes.

3. Add the pine nuts and remaining butter. Stir to fluff the rice while blending in the nuts.

Yield: Four servings.

Cucumber and Chili Raita

1 cucumber	¼ teaspoon ground cumin
1 cup plain yogurt	White pepper to taste
Salt to taste	
1 teaspoon or more finely chopped fresh hot green chilies	

1. Peel the cucumber and cut it in half lengthwise. Scrape out the seeds.

2. Cut the cucumber into quarter-inch-thick slices. Stack the slices and cut them into quarter-inch-thick strips. Cut the strips into quarter-inch cubes.

3. Combine the cucumber cubes with the remaining ingredients. Blend well. Serve with curries.

Yield: About 2½ cups.

IT IS CURIOUS THAT I HAVE SUCH A SERIOUS fancy for the uses of an outdoor grill. I don't ever recall having seen my family or any of our neighbors cooking on such an instrument when I was a child. (It is true that it was commonplace for us to do a great deal of cooking in the fireplace, which not only heated my childhood home, but served as a source for heat for good preparation.) In restaurants I have prepared many roasted chickens and other foods on a spit, or en brochette, but these were also done, more often than not, on professional rotisseries or on special grills constructed for fireplace use.

There are few things that please me more than the arrival of the warm weather, when I can dust off the barbecue grill, scrape it well on the surface, and fire up the charcoal. And one of my favorite entertainments is to prepare various foods en brochette for the delectation and delight of my guests.

One thing that pleases me is the great variety of marinades and basting sauces that can be used. I like to experiment with flavors. For the fun of it you might try shifting around and making up your own spice mixtures according to taste.

Poulet Grillé au Gingembre
(Grilled chicken with ginger)

- 1 2½- to 3-pound chicken, split in half for broiling
- 1 tablespoon finely chopped fresh ginger
- 1 teaspoon finely minced garlic
- ¼ cup lemon juice
- 2 tablespoons olive oil
- 1 bay leaf, broken into small pieces
- ½ teaspoon dried thyme
- Salt and freshly ground pepper
- Melted butter

1. Preheat a charcoal grill.
2. Put the chicken in a dish.
3. Blend the ginger, garlic, lemon juice, olive oil, bay leaf, thyme, and salt and pepper to taste in a small mixing bowl.
4. Pour the marinade over the chicken. Set aside for 15 minutes.
5. Drain the chicken and place it skin side down on the grill. Cook until nicely browned on the skin and turn. Baste the chicken with the marinade. Continue cooking and basting, turning the chicken every 5 minutes, for about 25 minutes or until the chicken is cooked. Serve with a little melted butter poured over.

Yield: Two servings.

Tomates Grillées
(Grilled tomatoes)

2	large red, ripe tomatoes
1	tablespoon plus 4 teaspoons peanut, vegetable, or corn oil
1	large clove garlic, cut into slivers
	Salt and freshly ground pepper

1. Preheat the broiler.
2. Core the tomatoes and slice them in half.
3. Grease a baking dish large enough to hold the tomato halves with 1 tablespoon oil. Arrange the halves in it, cut side up. Insert slivers of garlic inside the cut side of the tomatoes.
4. Sprinkle each half with salt and pepper to taste. Sprinkle about 1 teaspoon oil over each half and place them under the broiler. Broil about 5 minutes. Quickly remove the garlic slivers and serve.

Yield: Two servings.

ONE OF THE MOST INTERESTING FOODS IN THE luxury category of French cooking—a dish you will usually find served only on very festive and fancy occasions—is called demi-deuil. You can find various kinds of poultry that have been given this treatment, large chickens, capons, turkeys and so on.

To prepare a capon demi-deuil, for example, you start with a large, fine, fat capon and run your fingers gently through the neck opening to separate the skin from the flesh. You then insert the whole hand between the skin and flesh to separate them, not only over the breast but over the thighs and legs as well. At this point you insert slices of black truffles over the chicken flesh, so that when the chicken is steamed the truffle slices are seen as through a translucent covering over all the chicken. The capon is served carved with an ivory sauce, a rich concoction made with chicken broth and cream.

That preparation might seem a little ambitious for most home cooks. And it would never fit into the category of a 60-minute recipe. But mulling over the preparation, I thought of another dish. I decided to stuff various parts of chicken with a savory mushroom and herb mixture. I then decided that, instead of steaming the chicken, I would sauté it a bit and then bake it.

This is not at all a difficult recipe to prepare, and it is a bit more "dramatic" than a simple sauté of chicken.

Rice makes an ideal accompaniment for this dish, and, in that it takes something less than 20 minutes to cook, it may be best to ready your rice before starting the chicken preparation.

Poulet Poêlée aux Aromates
(Chicken stuffed with herbs and mushrooms)

2 chicken legs with thighs attached
2 boneless, unskinned chicken breasts with main wing bone attached
Salt and freshly ground pepper
6 small or 3 large mushrooms, about ⅛ pound
2 tablespoons finely chopped shallots
2 tablespoons finely chopped parsley
1 tablespoon finely chopped tarragon
1 teaspoon finely chopped fresh thyme or ½ teaspoon dried
3 tablespoons butter
Juice of half a lemon
¼ cup dry white wine
½ cup heavy cream
2 tablespoons finely chopped parsley

1. Preheat the oven to 375 degrees.
2. Sprinkle the chicken pieces with salt and pepper to taste.
3. Chop the mushrooms finely. There should be about ½ cup. Put the mushrooms in a clean towel and squeeze to extract the natural liquid.

4. Put the mushrooms in a mixing bowl and add the shallots, parsley, tarragon, thyme, 1 tablespoon of butter, and the lemon juice. Blend the ingredients well with the fingers.

5. Partly skin each of the chicken pieces, making a pocket large enough to hold about 2 tablespoons of the mushroom mixture. Fill each pocket with 2 tablespoons of the mushroom mixture. Replace the skin and press to distribute the filling more or less evenly under the skin. Partly cut through the joint where the leg and thigh meet. This will facilitate cooking.

6. Melt the remaining 2 tablespoons of butter in a large, heavy skillet and add the chicken pieces skin side down. Cook over low heat about 5 minutes or until lightly browned. Carefully turn the pieces to prevent the filling from falling out.

7. Place the skillet in the oven and bake 10 minutes.

8. Transfer the chicken pieces to a warm platter. Pour off most of the fat from the skillet. Add the wine and cook down until almost completely evaporated. Add the cream and cook over high heat about 1 minute, stirring.

9. Spoon the sauce over the chicken and serve sprinkled with finely chopped parsley.

Yield: Four servings.

Riz aux Poivrons
(Rice with peppers)

1 tablespoon butter	1 cup rice
½ cup finely chopped onion	1½ cups water
1 sweet red or green pepper, cored and chopped	Salt

1. Melt the butter in a saucepan and add the onion. Cook until wilted and add the chopped pepper, rice, water, and salt to taste.

2. Bring to the boil and cover closely. Cook exactly 17 minutes. Remove from heat and keep warm until ready to serve.

Yield: Four servings.

NEXT TO FRENCH COOKING, I SEEM TO HAVE had more exposure to the Italian kitchen than any other. And it is also true that my own children, when they were growing up, seemed to have a particular fondness for anything Italian that I would prepare for them—from pizza pie to various kinds of macaroni and spaghetti dishes.

We have had some fairly lengthy discussions of Italian cooking with our Italian friends, mostly chefs, including Luigi Nanni who has two very fine Italian restaurants in Manhattan, Nanni's and Il Valetto.

One of the curious things about many Italian menus is that they list various foods that are not to be found in the most reliable encyclopedias or authoritative books on regional Italian cooking. These are foods that may have been first created in America, vaguely reminiscent of something that does exist in Italy. One of these is Scarpariello, which means, literally, shoemaker-style.

This version of the dish, contributed by my friend Nanni, has a special excellence and is relatively easy to prepare in less than an hour.

Chicken Scarpariello alla Nanni

1	3½-pound chicken, cut into serving pieces	2	tablespoons butter
	Salt and freshly ground pepper	1	tablespoon finely minced garlic
3	tablespoons peanut, vegetable, or corn oil		Juice of half a lemon
		¾	cup dry white wine
		¼	cup finely chopped parsley

1. Sprinkle the chicken with salt and pepper to taste.
2. Heat the oil in a skillet and add the chicken pieces skin side down. Cook over moderately high heat about 5 minutes. Turn the pieces and cook about 3 to 5 minutes.
3. Pour off the fat. Add the butter and garlic and stir to coat the chicken pieces. Sprinkle with lemon juice.
4. Add the wine and cover. Cook about 5 minutes or until the chicken is done. Uncover and cook until the liquid almost evaporates.
5. Sprinkle with parsley and serve.

Yield: Four servings.

Nouilles Fines au Beurre
(Buttered fine noodles)

½ pound thin noodles
Salt

2 tablespoons butter at room temperature
Freshly ground pepper

1. Drop the noodles into a large quantity of boiling salted water. Cook about 2 or 3 minutes or until tender. Do not overcook.
2. Drain the noodles and return them to the pot. Toss them with the butter and add salt and pepper to taste. Serve hot.

Yield: Four servings.

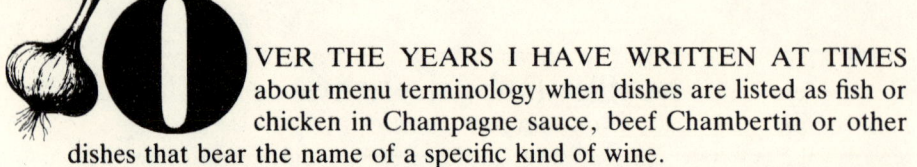

OVER THE YEARS I HAVE WRITTEN AT TIMES about menu terminology when dishes are listed as fish or chicken in Champagne sauce, beef Chambertin or other dishes that bear the name of a specific kind of wine.

I feel that chefs often take a permissible latitude in naming these dishes. My contention is that as long as the chef uses an excellent wine, even one that might be obscure to the average restaurant-going public, no great damage is done if he replaces one good Burgundy with another, or a first-rate Alsatian wine with another. But a case could be made for the fact that if a menu lists a Champagne sauce in the dining room, you should indeed use a Champagne in the kitchen.

When preparing a dish that calls for a wine, you should make certain that the wine is notably drinkable. If it is not good for the palate when taken from the glass, it will certainly not be good for the food that you will serve to your guests.

In specifying wines for cooking, we suggest more often than not a dry white wine or a dry red wine. There is a certain license in this. What you must guard against is the use of a wine that might be too dry, which is to say tart or acid, for good taste. If your wine is naturally "sour," then this quality will be reflected in the dish.

An excellent example of a dish made with wine is a poulet au riesling, in which a chicken is first sautéed and then cooked in a sauce of wine plus chicken broth with mushrooms and onions. To prepare this dish, you should, to be wholly authentic, use a true riesling, which is a white table wine with a fine bouquet and not too dry. The riesling grape is successfully cultivated in parts of the United States as well as in Alsace and in the Rhine and Mosel regions of Germany.

I have on occasion prepared the same dish using a good California chenin blanc, as well as a true Burgundy. I don't think it was deceptive when, if asked the name of the dish, I told them chicken with riesling. If pressed for details, I would have named the specific wine. In any event, it is an excellent dish and one that is easily prepared in less than an hour. Asparagus with a chopped-egg sauce goes well with the chicken.

Poulet au Riesling

- 1 chicken, 3 pounds, cut into serving pieces
- Salt and freshly ground pepper
- 2 tablespoons butter
- 12 small white onions, about ½ pound, peeled
- 1 bay leaf
- ½ pound mushrooms, thinly sliced, about 2 cups
- ¾ cup dry white wine, preferably riesling
- 1½ cups heavy cream

1. Sprinkle the chicken with salt and pepper to taste.
2. Melt the butter in a heavy skillet and add the chicken pieces skin side

down. Scatter the onions around the chicken. Add the bay leaf. Cook over moderate heat until the chicken skin is browned, about 5 minutes. Turn the pieces and add the mushrooms.

3. Cook, stirring gently so that the onions and mushrooms are redistributed around the chicken pieces. Add the wine and bring to the boil. Cover closely and continue cooking 20 minutes.

4. Transfer the chicken pieces to a warm serving dish. Using a slotted spoon, scoop out the onions, mushrooms, and bay leaf and scatter over the chicken.

5. Skim off and discard most of the fat from the juices in the skillet. Add the cream to the skillet and cook down over high heat about 2 minutes or until reduced to 2 cups. If desired, strain the sauce through a fine sieve. Pour the sauce over the chicken.

Yield: Four servings.

Les Asperges aux Oeufs Durs
(Asparagus with sieved egg)

1¼ pounds asparagus spears	Salt and freshly ground pepper
1 hard-cooked egg	⅛ teaspoon freshly grated nutmeg
3 tablespoons butter	
1 tablespoon finely chopped parsley	

1. Scrape the asparagus spears, starting about 2 inches from the top of each spear. Trim off the tough ends of each asparagus spear.

2. In a skillet bring enough water to the boil to cover the asparagus when they are added. Add the asparagus and let simmer from 2 to 4 minutes, depending on the size of the asparagus. Drain immediately.

3. Arrange the asparagus on a warm serving dish.

4. Put the egg through a fine sieve.

5. Melt the butter in a small skillet until it is hot and almost brown. Combine the egg and parsley and add it to the skillet. Sprinkle with salt and pepper to taste and nutmeg. Cook, stirring gently, about 30 seconds. Pour this over the asparagus and serve.

Yield: Four servings.

THERE IS ONE FACET OF AMERICAN MENU TERminology that has always fascinated French cooks—and Americans, too, or at least those who are aware of the subtleties in naming dishes. It has to do with one of the most celebrated of American creations, namely chicken à la king. No one knows the origin of the dish nor the origin of the name, but the ingredients are well known. It consists of cooked, cubed or shredded chicken, combined with mushrooms and pimientos, then blended in a cream sauce flavored with sherry and served, generally, on toast.

There are many variations of the theme of chicken in a cream sauce. One of these was much admired by Thomas Jefferson. It is said that one of his favorite dishes, when he was minister plenipotentiary to France, was something called capilotade, which is simply chicken in a cream sauce, generally baked in the oven.

When I was chef at Le Pavillon, one of the most popular items on the menu was a version of this very dish. It was called chicken hash Pavillon and was served on a bed of buttered noodles. This is an incredibly simple dish that can easily be made within the space of one hour and is excellent when made with leftover cooked chicken.

You will probably want to start from the beginning, however, and I offer here a basic recipe for poached chicken breasts (they cook in much less time than a whole chicken). As these pieces simmer there is time to assemble and make ready the other ingredients. The sauce can be made in minutes. Serve with a crusty loaf and a tossed green salad.

Gratin de Volaille Pavillon
(Chicken and noodles baked in cream sauce)

2 cooked whole chicken breasts (see recipe for poaching chicken)	½ cup heavy cream
	Salt and freshly ground pepper
6 ounces medium-width noodles	2 tablespoons finely chopped shallots
5 tablespoons butter	1 cup fresh or canned tomatoes, drained
3 tablespoons flour	
2 cups fresh or canned chicken broth (if desired, use the broth from the poached chicken recipe)	1 egg, lightly beaten
	2 tablespoons freshly grated Parmesan cheese

1. Remove the chicken meat from the bones. Discard the skin and bones and cut the meat into one-and-one-half-inch cubes. There should be about 3 cups or slightly less.

2. Cook the noodles according to package directions. Do not overcook. Drain. Return them to the pot and add 1 tablespoon butter. Toss.

3. Meanwhile, melt 2 tablespoons butter in a saucepan and add the

flour, stirring with a wire whisk. When blended, add the broth, stirring rapidly with the whisk. When the sauce is thickened and smooth, simmer about 5 minutes. Add the cream and let simmer briefly. Add salt and pepper to taste. Set aside.

4. Melt 2 tablespoons butter in another saucepan and add the shallots. Cook briefly, stirring, and add the tomatoes to the shallots. Cook down about 3 minutes.

5. Add the chicken and salt and pepper to taste.

6. Add 1 cup of the cream sauce and stir gently. Taste and adjust seasoning. Set aside.

7. To the remaining cream sauce add the egg. Bring to the boil, stirring rapidly with the whisk. Do not overcook. Remove from the heat.

8. Butter an 11½- by 8- by 2-inch baking dish with the remaining tablespoon butter. Add the noodles and smooth them over.

9. Spoon the chicken and sauce mixture over the noodles. Cover with the cream and egg sauce. Smooth it over. Sprinkle with cheese.

10. Place the dish under the broiler and cook until nicely browned and bubbling on top.

Yield: Four to six servings.

Poulet Poché
(Poached chicken)

2	whole chicken breasts, about 1 pound each	1	bay leaf
			Salt and freshly ground pepper
2	cups water	2	sprigs fresh parsley
1	cup dry white wine	¼	cup carrot rounds
¼	cup thinly sliced onion		

1. Combine all the ingredients in a saucepan and bring to the boil. Cover and simmer about 10 minutes.

2. Uncover and set aside. Let the chicken cool in its own broth.

Yield: Two cooked chicken breasts.

SOME QUESTIONS ARE INEVITABLE IN A PROfessional chef's life and one of them is, "Do you ever invent a dish?" The inevitable reply is, "Yes." In fact, life would be pretty boring if you stuck to the invariable, classic recipes. A very simple, recent "invention" in my home came about simply on a day that I found myself with an oversupply of vegetables that had, the day before, been the basis for a traditional potage garbure, a soup made with vegetables in season: cabbage, turnips, carrots, and onions. The result was the kind of dish most people, on reading the recipe, would be skeptical about, feeling it too simple to be so delicious.

I simply chopped or cubed the vegetables and cooked them with a newly bought chicken, cut into serving pieces. These ingredients, plus a few seasonings, went into a large pot along with wine and water. They were brought to a boil, covered, and cooked for 20 minutes. The food processor is, of course, this generation's greatest boon to hasty cooking. The vegetables and liquid that had been cooked with the chicken were scooped into the processor, puréed quickly and poured back over the chicken in the pot, where all were briefly cooked together. The finished dish, delicate in flavor and substantial in nutrition, was a considerable success. Since the dish included cubed potatoes added toward the end, it was sufficient with a salad to make a complete meal.

The accompaniment was a simple and quickly made salad containing Boston lettuce and Belgian endive. Incidentally, the dressing for this salad contained a slight amount of egg yolk beaten with mustard, oil, and vinegar. The egg yolk binds the dressing together. It is like a very thin mayonnaise and coats the salad greens respectably.

Ragoût de Poulet
(A chicken and vegetable stew)

- 1 chicken, about 3 pounds, cut into serving pieces
- 4 cups chopped cabbage
- 1½ cups white turnips cut into half-inch cubes
- 1 cup carrots cut into half-inch cubes
- 1 cup coarsely chopped onions
- 1 bay leaf
- 2 cups water
- ¾ cup dry white wine
- ½ teaspoon dried thyme
- Salt and freshly ground pepper
- 2 cups potatoes cut into half-inch cubes
- 1 tablespoon Worcestershire sauce

1. Put the chicken pieces into a large, heavy pot. Add the cabbage, turnips, carrots, onions, bay leaf, water, wine, and thyme. Add salt and pepper to taste.

2. Bring to the boil, cover, and cook 20 minutes.

3. Meanwhile, put the potatoes in a saucepan. Add water to cover.

Bring to the boil and simmer about 2 minutes and drain. Set the potatoes aside.

4. When the chicken is ready, remove the pieces. Pour vegetable mixture and the liquid into the container of a food processor. Blend thoroughly.

5. Return the chicken pieces to the pot. Add the puréed vegetable mixture and the drained potatoes. Cover and bring to a boil. Simmer 15 minutes.

6. Add the Worcestershire sauce and serve.

Yield: Four servings.

Salade d'Endive et Laitue
(Endive and Boston lettuce salad)

- 1 small, firm, unblemished head of Boston lettuce
- 2 heads Belgian endive
- 1 teaspoon egg yolk, optional
- 1 teaspoon imported mustard such as Dijon or Düsseldorf
- 1 tablespoon red wine vinegar
- 4 tablespoons olive oil
- Salt and freshly ground pepper
- 2 teaspoons finely chopped parsley

1. Pull off and discard the tough outer leaves of the Boston lettuce. Cut away the core of the lettuce. Pull off the lettuce leaves. Rinse and dry the leaves either by hand or with a spin drier. Set aside.

2. Cut off and discard the base of the endive. Cut the endive into crosswise shreds. Rinse and dry the shreds by hand or with a spin drier. Add the shreds to the lettuce.

3. Put the egg yolk and mustard in a salad bowl and add the vinegar, stirring with a whisk. Add the oil gradually, stirring briefly with the whisk. Add salt and pepper to taste.

4. Add the lettuce and endive and toss. Sprinkle with chopped parsley and serve.

Yield: Four to six servings.

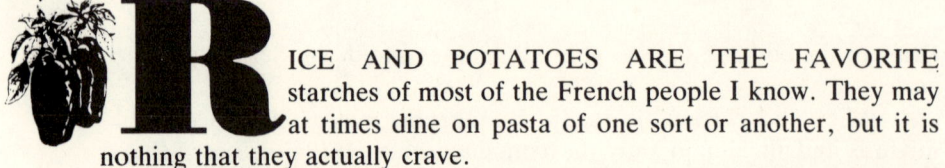

RICE AND POTATOES ARE THE FAVORITE starches of most of the French people I know. They may at times dine on pasta of one sort or another, but it is nothing that they actually crave.

I often resort to rice in many forms of cookery because it blends so well with other foods. I recently wrote about one of my preferred recipes, mussels in a light cream sauce served in a molded pattern with cooked rice top and bottom. I also know that one of the great rice fillings in the French repertory is for squabs Derby, in which the rice is blended with foie gras and truffles before the squab is stuffed and baked.

Of all the cuisines, perhaps it is the Spanish that is best known for its various dishes in which rice is prominently linked with other foods before cooking in the oven or en casserole. I am thinking, of course, of paella, with its various kinds of seafood and chicken that are cooked in a paelleria, and of arroz con pollo or rice with chicken.

Of the two, the arroz con pollo is by far the simpler and least expensive to prepare. Not only is this an uncommonly tasty dish because of its use of sweet green or red peppers, tomato, garlic and olive oil, but it is also one of the most colorful. The peppers give it color and so do the green peas (fresh or frozen may be used) and strips of red pimiento.

At times, this dish is given added flavor with the use of saffron, but it isn't essential. When a touch of saffron (the most expensive spice in the world) is used, the dish is sometimes called arroz amarillo con pollo or yellow rice with chicken. The saffron provides the yellow color.

The dish is of such substance that only a tossed salad is necessary to make a complete meal. You might end it, if you wish, with cheese or perhaps a simple dessert like fresh fruit. As the rice and chicken cook there is more than ample time to prepare the salad.

Arroz con Pollo
(Rice with chicken)

1	chicken, 3 pounds, cut into serving pieces
	Salt and freshly ground pepper
2	tablespoons olive oil
1	cup finely chopped onion
1	teaspoon finely minced garlic
2	cups red or sweet green pepper (preferably one of each), cut into one-inch pieces
½	teaspoon loosely packed stem saffron, optional
1	cup tomato cut into one-inch cubes
½	cup dry white wine
1	cup long-grain rice
1	bay leaf
2	sprigs fresh parsley
1	cup fresh or canned chicken broth
1	tablespoon lemon juice
¼	teaspoon dried hot red pepper flakes
½	cup cooked peas for garnish, optional
1	or 2 canned pimientos, cut into strips for garnish

1. Sprinkle the chicken pieces with salt and pepper to taste.

2. Heat the oil in a heavy skillet large enough to hold the pieces in one layer. Add the chicken pieces skin side down. Cook until golden on one side, about 3 to 4 minutes. Turn and cook until browned on the second side, about 3 minutes.

3. Scatter the onion, garlic, peppers, and saffron over the chicken. Stir the chicken pieces so that the seasonings fall between the pieces. Continue cooking about 3 minutes.

4. Add the tomato and wine and stir. Add the rice and stir to distribute the rice evenly around the chicken. Add the bay leaf and parsley and pour the broth over all. Add salt and pepper to taste, lemon juice, and pepper flakes. Stir and cover closely. Let simmer 20 minutes or until chicken is done.

5. Sprinkle with the peas and stir. Serve piping hot with the pimiento strips arranged over the top.

Yield: Four servings.

Salad with Oregano

6 cups mixed, loosely packed salad greens, such as romaine, arugula, Boston lettuce, and so on, cut into large bite-size pieces	1 tablespoon imported mustard such as Dijon or Düsseldorf
	1 tablespoon finely chopped shallots
	2 tablespoons red wine vinegar
½ cup thinly sliced onion rings	½ cup olive oil
1 teaspoon dried oregano	Salt and freshly ground pepper

1. Rinse the greens well and dry them in a spin dryer or with paper towels. Put the greens and onion rings in a salad bowl. Sprinkle with the oregano.

2. Put the mustard, shallots, and vinegar in a mixing bowl. Gradually beat in the oil. Add salt and pepper to taste.

3. Pour the sauce over the greens and toss well.

Yield: Four servings.

LIKE OMELETS, SOUFFLÉS, AND CREPES, A mousse of one sort or another—sweet or savory—seems to intrigue the average American cook more than any other dish in the French repertory. Whether chocolate or fish, it exerts an enormous appeal to the taste. The name itself means foam, which has to do with the texture of a well-made mousse.

This is not the first time I have noted that the food processor is the greatest kitchen invention of this generation. And when it comes to the preparation of a mousse, it is the ultimate asset. Whenever I make a mousse—and it is often, for I share the public enthusiasm—I am reminded that, with the processor I accomplish in seconds what once required hours of tedious hand work—grinding and pounding fish or chicken or whatever, to produce a fine enough texture. Generally speaking, it was necessary years ago to put the basic mixture through a fine sieve and to place it in a basin of ice to get the proper consistency.

One of the best and quickest mousses I have made recently is of chicken. The procedure is to purée the skinless, boneless breast of chicken in the processor along with seasonings, an egg yolk, and heavy cream. This is an elegant dish and one that you will want to serve on special occasions. The initial preparation takes 15 minutes or less, the cooking time another 15 minutes.

The mousse requires a sauce, and I would propose a simple and easily made mushroom sauce with a little tomato added for flavor and color and a touch of tarragon for subtlety. The dish is best served with plainly cooked rice with a bit of butter stirred in.

Mousse de Volaille
(Chicken mousse)

2 whole skinless, boneless chicken breasts, about 1½ pounds	Pinch of cayenne pepper
Salt and freshly ground pepper	1 egg yolk
⅛ teaspoon freshly grated nutmeg	1¼ cups heavy cream
	Mushroom sauce (see recipe)

1. Preheat the oven to 400 degrees.
2. Pick over the breasts and cut off any membranes or tendons. Cut the chicken into two-inch cubes.
3. Put the chicken into the container of a food processor and add salt and pepper to taste, nutmeg, cayenne pepper, and the egg yolk.
4. Start processing until the flesh is coarse-fine.
5. Continue processing while adding the cream.
6. Butter the insides of four small ramekins or baking dishes. Individual Chinese rice or soup bowls are ideal for this. The volume of each portion is about half a cup. Spoon equal portions of the mixture into the ramekins.

7. Cut out four pieces of wax paper to fit the tops of each mousse.

8. Set the ramekins in a heatproof pan of hot water. Set the pan on the top of the stove. Bring the water to a boil and place the ramekins and the water bath in the oven. Bake 15 minutes. Serve with mushroom sauce (see recipe).

Yield: Four servings.

Sauce aux Champignons
(Mushroom sauce)

¼ pound fresh mushrooms
3 tablespoons butter
2 tablespoons finely chopped shallots
Salt and freshly ground pepper
½ cup dry white wine
½ cup chopped canned tomatoes
¾ cup fresh or canned chicken broth
¼ teaspoon dried tarragon
½ teaspoon arrowroot or cornstarch
1 tablespoon water

1. Slice the mushrooms as thinly as possible. There should be about 1¼ cups.

2. Melt 1 tablespoon of the butter in a saucepan and add the shallots and salt and pepper to taste. Add the mushrooms and cook, stirring often, until they wilt and give up their liquid. Cook until the liquid evaporates. Add the wine and cook until most of the wine evaporates. Add the tomatoes, broth, and tarragon and cook about 5 minutes.

3. Blend the arrowroot and water and stir it into the sauce. Simmer about 10 minutes.

4. Swirl in the remaining butter and serve.

Yield: Four servings.

IF THE DISHES NAMED PROVENÇALE IN French cuisine were eliminated from the cook's repertory, it would be an enormous loss indeed. Provençale—or in the style of Provence—has many different meanings where ingredients are concerned. It may indicate the use of tomatoes and green peppers and capers and numerous herbs of Provence—thyme, fennel, rosemary, and so on. The single indispensable flavor of provençale cooking is, however, garlic, either in slight or pronounced amounts.

One of my favorite dishes in that style is a simple sauté of chicken livers and mushrooms made with more than a touch of garlic and no other seasoning added except a generous, last-minute sprinkling of parsley. Chicken livers must be cooked quickly or they will toughen and become slightly unpalatable. Because of the speed involved, you would be well advised to study the recipe carefully. Note that the dish, start to finish, is cooked over high heat and that each batch of ingredients is drained well after cooking. At the end they are returned to the skillet for a final cooking with a small amount of butter.

A fine accompaniment for chicken livers provençale is eggplant, which is about as characteristic of that southern region of France as tomatoes and garlic. Curiously, eggplant, when cut into small cubes and sautéed, goes exceedingly well with rice.

To hasten the preparation, you would do well to begin with the rice and eggplant dish. Once this is put on to cook (the total cooking time is about 30 minutes), you will have time to concentrate on the main dish.

Foies de Volailles Provençale
(Sautéed chicken livers with garlic)

1¼ pounds chicken livers	2 tablespoons butter
Salt and freshly ground pepper	1 tablespoon finely minced garlic
½ pound mushrooms	3 tablespoons finely chopped parsley
8 tablespoons olive oil	
¾ cup flour	

1. Put the livers, one at a time, on a flat surface. Cut away and discard any tough connecting membranes. Cut the livers into quarters. Put the livers in a bowl and sprinkle with salt and pepper to taste.

2. If the mushrooms are small, leave them whole. If they are large, cut them in half or quarter them.

3. Heat 2 tablespoons of oil in a heavy skillet and add the mushrooms. Add salt and pepper to taste. Cook the mushrooms over high heat, shaking and stirring, until they give up their liquid. Continue cooking and stirring, until they are golden brown all over.

4. Drain the mushrooms in a sieve and set aside. Discard the oil in the skillet.

5. Add the flour to the livers and stir to coat them well.

6. Remove the livers to a baking sheet, separating them.

7. Return the skillet to the heat and add 4 tablespoons of oil. When it is quite hot, add half the livers, one at a time. Cook over high heat, turning the livers as they brown. One batch of livers takes about 4 or 5 minutes to cook. When the livers are cooked, transfer them with a slotted spoon to the mushrooms in the sieve.

8. Add the remaining 2 tablespoons of oil to the skillet and cook the remaining livers, turning once. Drain the livers. Wipe out the skillet.

9. Melt the butter in the skillet. When it is quite hot, add the livers and mushrooms. Cook, shaking the skillet and stirring, until the mixture is piping hot.

10. Sprinkle the garlic over the liver mixture. Sprinkle with parsley. Serve immediately.

Yield: Four to six servings.

Riz à l'Aubergine
(Rice with eggplant)

1 eggplant, about 1 pound	1 bay leaf
2 tablespoons butter	½ teaspoon dried thyme
½ cup finely chopped onion	⅛ teaspoon dried hot red pepper flakes
1 teaspoon finely minced garlic	
Salt and freshly ground pepper	½ cup rice
½ cup crushed canned tomatoes	1 cup chicken broth

1. Trim off the ends of the eggplant. Peel the eggplant with a knife and cut it into one-half-inch-thick slices. Stack the slices and cut them into half-inch strips. Cut the strips into half-inch cubes. There should be about 3½ cups. Set aside.

2. Melt the butter in saucepan and add the onion and garlic. Cook, stirring, until the onion is wilted. Add the eggplant and salt and pepper to taste. Stir. Add the tomatoes, bay leaf, thyme, and pepper flakes.

3. Cook, stirring occasionally, about 3 minutes. Add the rice, broth, and salt to taste.

4. Cover. Bring to the boil and let simmer 20 minutes.

Yield: Four servings.

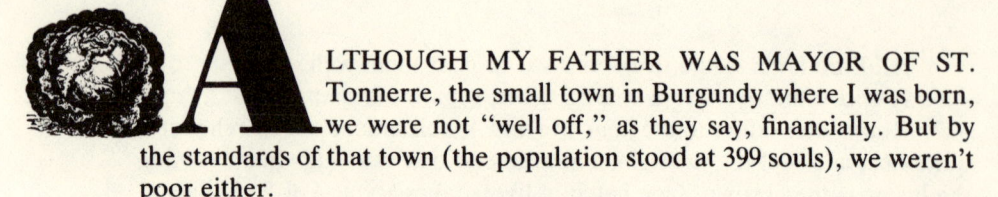

ALTHOUGH MY FATHER WAS MAYOR OF ST. Tonnerre, the small town in Burgundy where I was born, we were not "well off," as they say, financially. But by the standards of that town (the population stood at 399 souls), we weren't poor either.

My parents had just lived through World War I, and we knew the name of economy. If a chicken were brought into the kitchen, almost all parts of it were cooked and eaten, not only the breast, thighs, legs, and so on, but the backs, liver, gizzard, and heart as well.

My favorite food made of chicken, however, was deep-fried livers. My mother simply coated the livers with flour seasoned with salt and pepper and cooked them in a basin of bubbling oil.

I reminisced about this recently when I discovered about a pound and a half of livers that had been left over from a chicken preparation I had made the night before. I decided to make a variation on my mother's recipe. I took a few spices—ground cumin, coriander, and rosemary—and added them to the flour in which I dredged the livers. I deep-fried the livers until they were crisp and crunchy and served them with a hastily made coleslaw, another weekend favorite of my family.

Many home cooks in the United States shy away from deep-frying; I suspect it is because foods tend to spatter when they cook in hot oil. I solve this by covering the kettle in which I deep-fry foods. Once the foods have settled down to a nonspattering simmer, I remove the cover. Uncovered, the foods brown and become crisp.

This menu can be prepared in much less than 60 minutes.

Foies de Volailles aux Aromates
(Deep-fried spiced chicken livers)

1½	pounds fresh chicken livers		Salt
¼	cup milk	¼	teaspoon freshly ground black pepper
¼	teaspoon Tabasco sauce		
5	cups peanut, vegetable, or corn oil	1	teaspoon ground coriander
		½	teaspoon ground cumin
1	cup flour	½	teaspoon ground rosemary

1. Pick over the chicken livers to remove any tough membranes. Soak the livers briefly in milk seasoned with Tabasco sauce.

2. As you prepare the flour, heat the oil in a heavy deep fryer with a lid. It will take about 3 minutes to heat properly. When ready, the oil should be bubbling and almost smoking. The temperature is 350 degrees.

3. Combine the flour, salt to taste, the pepper, coriander, cumin, and rosemary. Blend well.

4. Drain the livers in a colander and toss them in the flour until they are well coated.

5. Add the livers to the hot oil and stir to separate the pieces. Cover closely and cook over very high heat, lifting the cover occasionally to stir with a two-pronged fork. As the livers cook, line a baking sheet with a double layer of paper toweling for draining.

6. Cook the livers about 6 minutes and uncover. Continue cooking, uncovered, over high heat, stirring often, about 2 minutes longer. The total cooking time is about 8 minutes. Drain the livers well on the paper toweling. Strain the fat through a fine sieve or sieve lined with cheesecloth. Let cool and refrigerate for another use.

Yield: Four servings.

Coleslaw

- 1 head cabbage, about 1½ pounds
- 2 medium-size carrots, about ⅓ pound, trimmed and scraped
- 1 egg yolk
- 2 tablespoons distilled white vinegar
- 1 tablespoon imported mustard, preferably Dijon
- Salt and freshly ground pepper
- ¾ cup peanut, vegetable, or corn oil
- 2 teaspoons caraway or poppy seeds

1. Cut the cabbage into quarters. Cut away and discard the core portions.

2. Process the cabbage in the container of a food processor to any desired fineness. The cabbage could alternately be chopped on a flat surface. There should be about 6 cups. Put the cabbage in a mixing bowl.

3. Cut the carrot into quarter-inch rounds. There should be about 1 cup. Put the carrots in the container of a food processor and process. Or chop the carrots to the desired degree of fineness. There should be about 1¼ cups. Combine the carrots and cabbage.

4. Combine the egg yolk, vinegar, mustard, and salt and pepper to taste in a mixing bowl. Start beating with a wire whisk while gradually adding the oil. Beat until thickened and smooth.

5. Pour and scrape the mayonnaise over the cabbage mixture. Add the seeds and blend well.

Yield: Four to six servings.

ALMOST EVERY COOKING UTENSIL HAS A SPEcific shape or form that is designed to produce one finished dish or another. Soufflé dishes, to choose one example, are broader than they are high, because beaten egg whites rise higher when baked in a dish of that shape. An omelet pan is round rather than square and has a smooth bottom to facilitate the tossing and shaping of an omelet.

One rare exception to this rule are the small molds known as darioles. They are small, cylinder-shaped metal molds with a 5-ounce capacity, and they are used for making pastries (known as darioles) for certain vegetable preparations and, for my own purposes, a kind of hot, custard-like pâté made with chicken livers that can be served as a main course.

I have no idea when or how dariole molds came into being and had not given it much consideration when I spotted them recently in some of the pot and pan shops around town.

It was reminiscent of Proust's madeleines in that I was whisked instantly in my memory to that custard-like dish that I so coveted as a child when it was prepared in the home of a favorite aunt, Tante Marie, my mother's sister. It was a dish that inevitably appeared on special occasions, such as my birthday, a hot, delicate food that literally seemed to melt in my mouth. I recall that after she unmolded the dish it was generally garnished with sprigs of parsley and a light tomato sauce.

To prepare this dish it is not essential to use those dariole molds, but in my young mind's eye, the shape seemed to add something to the flavor of the dish. This is, by the way, an extremely easy and hasty dish to make in this age of the food processor.

An excellent accompaniment for it are fine noodles with thin strips of zucchini cooked quickly in butter and tossed together with grated cheese.

Mousse de Foie de Volaille
(Chicken liver mousse)

Butter for greasing the molds
¾ pound chicken livers
1 slice bread, trimmed and cut into one-inch cubes, about ½ cup
¼ cup thinly sliced shallots
1 small clove garlic, finely minced
1 sprig thyme or ¼ teaspoon dried
½ cup loosely packed parsley leaves
1 whole egg
2 egg yolks
⅛ teaspoon finely grated nutmeg
Salt and freshly ground pepper
½ cup heavy cream
2 cups fresh tomato sauce
Fresh basil or parsley sprigs for garnish

1. Preheat the oven to 400 degrees.
2. Butter four dariole molds or other small, round ramekins or baking dishes with a 5-ounce capacity.
3. Pick over the chicken livers to remove all tough connecting membranes. Cut the livers in half.
4. Combine the livers, bread, shallots, garlic, thyme, parsley, whole egg, egg yolks, nutmeg, and salt and pepper to taste in the container of a food processor. Blend thoroughly.
5. Add the cream and blend briefly.
6. Pour the mixture into the prepared molds. Set the molds in a metal or heatproof pan of water. Bring the water to the boil.
7. Place the molds in the pan of water in the oven and bake 20 minutes.
8. To serve, spoon tomato sauce onto each of four small plates. Unmold one mousse in the center. Garnish with fresh basil or parsley sprigs.

Yield: Four servings.

Zucchini aux Nouilles
(Zucchini with noodles)

½ pound zucchini, ends trimmed	Freshly ground pepper
¼ pound fine egg noodles	½ teaspoon finely minced garlic
Salt	1 tablespoon finely chopped fresh basil
2 tablespoons butter	

1. Using a mandolin (vegetable cutter, food processor, or a knife), cut the zucchini into very thin, julienne strips. The strips should be about the same size as the noodles.
2. Drop the noodles into boiling salted water and cook until tender. Drain.
3. Heat the butter in a skillet and add the zucchini. Add salt and pepper to taste. Cook, stirring, just to heat through. Add the garlic and basil. When very hot, add the noodles. Cook, stirring gently to blend well, until hot.

Yield: Four servings.

WHEN I THINK ABOUT THE FOOD I LIKE BEST, I seem to prefer things that are somehow related to my childhood in France or to my early training as a chef. I believe that is why I have a great liking for Rock Cornish game hens. They remind me of the small poussins we admired so much in the small Burgundy town where I grew up. And they can be cooked in precisely the same manner. Needless to say, they do cook quickly because of their size.

Although I am quite happy with the most basic forms of cooked game hens—simply roasted or broiled—I do enjoy them when they are deviled or, as it is known in French, "à la diable."

The technique for cooking game hens à la diable is to have them split for broiling. They are then cooked until done with a brushing of mustard and a sprinkling of bread crumbs. The total cooking time under the broiler and in the oven is about half an hour.

As the birds cook there is plenty of time to prepare a sauce diable or devil sauce. This, of course, is spoken of as deviled because of the spicy nature of the sauce. The flavorings include extra-strong mustard plus a touch of Worcestershire sauce. A dash of cream is added to ameliorate the spicy flavor.

These hens go well with sautéed potatoes or rice and a tossed green salad.

Rock Cornish Game Hens à la Diable
(Deviled breaded Rock Cornish game hens)

4 Rock Cornish game hens, about 1¼ pounds each, split in half for broiling
Salt and freshly ground pepper
¼ cup peanut, vegetable, or corn oil

2 tablespoons imported mustard such as Dijon or Düsseldorf
1 tablespoon dry white wine
½ cup fine fresh bread crumbs
Sauce diable (see recipe)

1. Preheat the broiler to high. If the oven has a separate temperature control, set the oven heat to 450 degrees.

2. Place the split hens on a flat surface and pound them lightly with a flat mallet. Sprinkle the hens on all sides with salt and pepper to taste and the oil.

3. Combine the mustard and wine in a small bowl and set aside.

4. Arrange the halves neatly in one layer, skin side down, on a baking sheet and place under the broiler about 3 inches from the source of heat. Broil about 8 or 9 minutes and turn the halves.

5. Return to the broiler and broil about 3 minutes. Remove the halves and brush the skin side with the mustard and wine mixture. Turn the halves and brush the second side with the mustard mixture. Brush with the pan drippings and sprinkle with bread crumbs.

6. If the oven and broiler have dual heat controls, turn off the broiler and set the oven heat to 450 degrees. Put the hens in the oven and bake 15 minutes. Serve with sauce diable.

Yield: Four servings.

Sauce Diable

1 tablespoon butter	1 tablespoon tomato paste
2 tablespoons finely chopped shallots	½ cup heavy cream
¼ cup dry white wine	1 tablespoon extra strong imported mustard such as Dijon or Düsseldorf
1 teaspoon Worcestershire sauce	Salt and freshly ground pepper
½ cup chicken broth	

1. Melt the butter in a saucepan and add the shallots. Cook briefly, stirring. Add the wine and cook down to about 2 tablespoons.

2. Add the Worcestershire sauce and chicken broth. Stir in the tomato paste and cook down by almost half. Add the cream and stir. Add the mustard, salt to taste, and a generous grinding of black pepper and serve.

Yield: About ¾ cup.

Pommes Sautées au Beurre
(Sautéed potatoes)

6 to 8 new, red-skinned potatoes	1½ tablespoons butter
Water to cover	Freshly ground pepper
Salt	½ teaspoon finely chopped garlic
1½ tablespoons peanut, vegetable, or corn oil	1½ tablespoons finely chopped parsley

1. Wash the potatoes and place them in a saucepan. Add water to cover and salt to taste. Bring to the boil and simmer until tender, about 30 minutes. Drain. When cool enough to handle, peel and slice the potatoes. There should be 3 to 4 cups.

2. Heat the oil and 1 tablespoon of butter in a skillet. Add the potatoes and salt and pepper to taste. Cook, tossing and stirring but avoid breaking up the potato slices. Cook about 10 minutes and when crusty brown, add the remaining butter. Add the garlic and parsley. Toss and stir to blend. Serve.

Yield: Four servings.

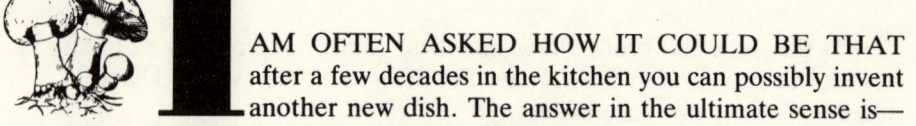

I AM OFTEN ASKED HOW IT COULD BE THAT after a few decades in the kitchen you can possibly invent another new dish. The answer in the ultimate sense is—you can't. Almost any "new" dish that comes off the stove is simply a variation of the rules of cookery that have been set down or known from a couple of centuries back. A good case in point is the dish that I am about to outline here, chicken with tarragon sauce.

There are many ways to prepare a dish that could bear this name. You may sauté your chickens with tarragon, adding a little wine and/or water at the end and the sauce would be a brown sauce. You could make a fricassée of chicken using tarragon as the principal flavor. And, as I have done here, you can use Rock Cornish game hens, simply roasted with tarragon flavor and, at the last moment, add just enough heavy cream so that the "white" sauce that results will coat the chickens.

I think there are three reasons why I have such a high regard for the Rock Cornish game hens in this country. They are the closest approximation that you can find—coast to coast—to the poussins or small chickens of France. It is also true that the quality of the small birds (if you select the best brands and buy them unfrozen) is often superior to that of larger birds to be found in supermarkets. And there is no denying that they are excellent for cookery that is to be done in less than 60 minutes.

I am a great advocate of not wasting foods, and to that end I have used here the livers of the game hens to prepare what I consider the ideal accompaniment for Rock Cornish game hens with tarragon. The livers, along with a few mushrooms, are used to give flavor and texture to a rice dish that is baked at the same temperature and in the same oven alongside the chickens.

Poussins à l'Estragon
(Rock Cornish game hens with tarragon cream sauce)

4 Rock Cornish game hens, about three-quarters of a pound each, with giblets reserved
Salt and freshly ground pepper
1¼ teaspoons dried tarragon
2 tablespoons butter
3 tablespoons finely chopped shallots
⅓ cup dry white wine
½ cup heavy cream
1 tablespoon finely chopped parsley

1. Preheat the oven to 450 degrees.
2. Sprinkle the game hens inside and out with salt and pepper to taste. Add ¼ teaspoon dried tarragon to the cavity of each bird and truss.
3. Melt the butter in a shallow, metal roasting pan that will hold the hens comfortably, bodies touching. Arrange the hens breast side up in the pan and brush them all over with the butter. Scatter the necks and

gizzards around the birds. When the butter starts to sizzle beneath the game hens, transfer the roasting pan to the oven. Bake 15 minutes.

4. Start basting the birds and continue roasting without turning for about 20 minutes.

5. Transfer the game hens to a warm serving platter and cover with foil to keep warm.

6. Spoon out the fat from the roasting pan. Leave the necks and gizzards in the pan. Add the shallots and cook until soft. Add the wine.

7. Cook, stirring to dissolve any brown particles that cling to the bottom and sides of the pan, about 30 seconds. Add any juices that may have accumulated around the chickens.

8. When the wine is reduced by half, add the cream and remaining ¼ teaspoon tarragon.

9. If desired, transfer the gizzards and necks to the cooked hens. Strain the sauce over the hens. Sprinkle with chopped parsley and serve.

Yield: Four servings.

Riz aux Champignons et Foies de Poussin
(Rice with mushrooms and chicken livers)

4 Rock Cornish game hen livers	½ cup finely chopped onion
¼ pound fresh mushrooms, preferably small	1 cup uncooked rice
	1½ cups fresh or canned chicken broth
2 tablespoons butter	
Salt and freshly ground pepper	1 bay leaf

1. Preheat the oven to 450 degrees. If you are preparing the game hens with tarragon, the oven will already be heated.

2. Cut the livers into small cubes and set aside.

3. Cut the mushrooms into quarters. There should be about 2 cups. Set aside.

4. Melt the butter in a saucepan and add the livers. Cook briefly, about 30 seconds, stirring. Add salt and pepper to taste. Add the onion and mushrooms.

5. Cook until the onion wilts. Add the rice and stir to blend ingredients. Add the broth and bay leaf. Bring to the boil. Cover and place in the oven alongside the game hens or on another shelf in the same oven. Bake exactly 17 minutes. Remove the bay leaf and serve.

Yield: Four servings.

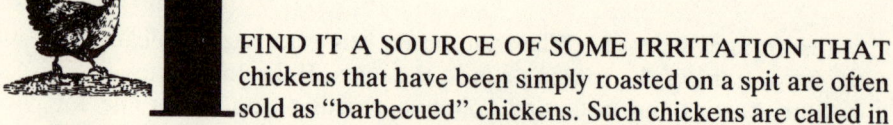

I FIND IT A SOURCE OF SOME IRRITATION THAT chickens that have been simply roasted on a spit are often sold as "barbecued" chickens. Such chickens are called in French "à la broche." To my mind the term "barbecued" should be applied to foods that have been cooked before or over a fire while being basted with a sauce of one sort of another. And, ideally, the foods should be cooked over charcoal.

There are, of course, many kinds of barbecue sauces, the best known in this country being a blend of tomato ketchup and other seasonings such as garlic, soy sauce, honey, and so on. I am not disdainful of this sauce, but it may tend to pall on the palate if it is overused.

Years ago, a friend who had made frequent visits to Missouri told me that one of the great specialties of a barbecue shack in the Missouri "boot heel" region was a secret barbecue sauce, but the owner adamantly refused to divulge it. After several days of experimentation, however, my friend arrived at a formula that his friends declared to be the equal of the barbecue specialists.

I have tried that sauce and it is excellent. It is a blend of cider vinegar, garlic, oil, a touch of chili powder, dry mustard, paprika, and cumin. When I first glanced at the recipe, I was skeptical, believing that the pronounced vinegar flavor would give an unnecessary tartness to charcoal-grilled dishes.

Oddly, the vinegar flavor dissipates to a remarkable degree as the foods cook. I recently used the sauce on one-pound squab chickens that I found at my local poultry market. Cornish game hens, however, would work equally well. Because of the size of the birds, the cooking time is brief.

To complete the menu for these chickens, two kinds of salad are ideal, a sliced tomato and onion salad and a French-style potato salad.

The potato salad I have in mind is made with hot, freshly cooked potatoes sliced with or without the skin, plus a sauce of dry white wine, oil, and vinegar and chopped onions or shallots. A half cup or so of chopped parsley adds a final touch.

Missouri-style Barbecued Chickens

4 squab chickens or Rock Cornish game hens, 1 pound each, split in half for broiling
Salt and freshly ground pepper
2 tablespoons peanut, vegetable, or corn oil
¾ cup cider vinegar
1 teaspoon finely minced garlic
½ teaspoon sugar
1 tablespoon chili powder
1 teaspoon dry mustard
1 teaspoon paprika
½ teaspoon ground cumin

1. Preheat a charcoal grill for barbecuing.
2. Rub the chicken with salt and pepper to taste and oil.

3. Combine the vinegar, ½ teaspoon pepper, garlic, sugar, chili powder, mustard, paprika, and cumin in a mixing bowl and mix well.

4. Place the chickens skin side down on a barbecue grill and cook about 10 minutes on one side, basting often with the sauce. Turn and continue cooking, basting often, on the second side about 10 minutes or until done.

Yield: Four servings.

Salade de Pomme de Terre à la Française
(French potato salad)

16 red, new, waxy potatoes, about 2 pounds	6 tablespoons peanut oil
Salt	3 tablespoons finely chopped shallots or ½ cup chopped red onion
¼ cup dry white wine	
2 tablespoons distilled white vinegar	Freshly ground pepper
	½ cup finely chopped parsley

1. Combine the potatoes, water to cover, and salt to taste in a saucepan. Bring to the boil and cook 20 minutes or until potatoes are tender. Do not overcook. Drain and let stand until ready to prepare. The salad should be made while the potatoes are still hot or warm.

2. Peel the potatoes and cut them into quarter-inch-thick slices. There should be about 6 cups. Put the slices in a mixing bowl and sprinkle them with the wine.

3. Combine the vinegar, oil, shallots, and salt and pepper to taste in a mixing bowl and blend. Add the potatoes and parsley. Blend well. If the salad stands, stir from the bottom before serving.

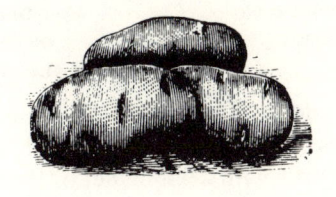

Yield: Four servings.

I AM FREQUENTLY FASCINATED BY THE VARIous condiments or side dishes that are almost invariably served with one dish or another. In Italy, if you have a bollito misto, you almost always get a small serving of mustard fruit on the side, and it is an undeniably great food association. Rarely in France are you served pâtés, terrines, and sliced cold meats, such as salamis, without the pickles known as cornichons—and often mustard—as an accompaniment. In this country, sauerkraut is a perfect liaison for a frankfurter on a bun and cole slaw in many places is the inevitable side dish with hamburgers.

One of the most curious of side dishes, to my mind, is coarse salt, but this is a traditional accompaniment for the boiled beef in France. Along with the mustard and pickles, the salt is to be sprinkled on the meat.

This came to my mind some time ago when I dined with Virginia Lee, the well-known Chinese cooking authority. She served a fantastic platter of fried squab and, as an accompaniment, small dishes of salt that had been seasoned with crushed Szechuan peppercorns, plus wedges of lemon. The seasoned salt gave a nice complementary flavor to the roasted pigeons.

I recently decided to use that same seasoning salt as an accompaniment for broiled squab prepared in my own kitchen. I decided that this would be much simpler than deep frying the squab as Mrs. Lee had done. And the combination of the broiled birds with the salt was equally as felicitous.

I served a fairly un-Chinese vegetable dish based on what I found in the refrigerator. This was a hastily prepared dish of fresh spinach and watercress, cooked together and blended with a little butter and cream. It made a tantalizing and wholly compatible accompaniment for the squab. Incidentally, when warm weather arrives, the squabs could just as easily be cooked over a charcoal grill as under the broiler.

Broiled Squab with Chinese Seasoning Salt

- 2 squabs or Rock Cornish game hens, about 1 pound each
- 1 tablespoon Szechuan peppercorns
- 1 tablespoon salt
- 1 tablespoon peanut, vegetable, or corn oil
- Lemon wedges

1. Preheat the broiler to high.

2. Split the squabs or have them split in half. Place the halves on a flat surface and pound lightly with a flat mallet or the bottom of a clean skillet.

3. Put the peppercorns in a skillet and cook until they are lightly roasted and give off a fragrant scent. Grind the peppercorns in a small spice mill or by hand. Combine them with the salt and blend well.

4. Use about ½ teaspoon of the mixture to sprinkle over all of the squab. Rub the squab all over with the spice mixture and the oil.

5. Arrange the squab halves skin side down on a baking sheet. Place under the broiler about 3 inches from the source of heat. Broil about 5 minutes.

6. Turn the squab skin side up and return to the broiler. Broil about 3 minutes or until nicely browned. Place the squab on the lowest rack of the broiler. Broil 2 to 5 minutes longer, depending on doneness desired.

7. Serve the squab with lemon wedges and the remaining seasoning salt on the side.

Yield: Two servings.

Epinards en Branche et Cresson à la Crème
(Spinach and watercress in cream)

1 pound spinach in bulk, or one 10-ounce cellophane bag	2 tablespoons butter
2 bunches watercress	Salt and freshly ground pepper
½ cup cream	⅛ teaspoon freshly grated nutmeg

1. Pick over the spinach and remove and discard any tough stems and blemished leaves. Rinse and drain well. There should be about 8 cups loosely packed.

2. Cut off the tough ends of the watercress. Rinse and drain well. There should be about 7 cups loosely packed.

3. Combine the spinach, watercress, cream, butter, salt to taste, and a generous grinding of pepper. Sprinkle with nutmeg.

4. Cook, turning the greens in the sauce, about 5 minutes. Serve hot.

Yield: Two to four servings.

A NEIGHBOR, WHILE GLANCING THROUGH MY files, commented that one of her favorite foods was missing from the menus

"Where," she wanted to know, "are the duck recipes?"

It was an interesting question, and the answer, on reflection, was obvious. Duck is one of the most difficult of poultries to cook within an hour's time.

A duck is one of the easiest of roasts to cook, because it is self-basting. You put it in the oven, turn it a couple of times while pouring off fat, and after a given length of time, the duck flesh is tender, the skin is crisp and the duck is ready to serve. Because of the nature of its flesh and skin, the usual roasting time is 90 minutes to two hours.

To accommodate my neighbor I decided to concoct a main course that could be made in less than an hour. The solution was to cut the duck into serving pieces and broil or grill it. The result was excellent. The technique:

Cut the duck into serving pieces and trim all around the pieces to cut away any peripheral skin. Do *not* trim all the skin from the meat, simply the excess at the outer edges. Season the duck pieces and place them skin side up in a baking pan and place under the broiler. When the skin is crisp on both sides, cook the duck in the oven. In this recipe, it is not necessary to pour off the fat as the bird cooks.

Before the duck had finished roasting I rubbed the outer skin with a cut clove of garlic, and it was ready to serve, directly from the oven.

A julienne of winter vegetables goes very well with this dish. There is plenty of time for cutting the vegetables into strips while the duck broils and roasts.

Canard Grillé
(Broiled duck)

1 duck, 4 to 6 pounds, with giblets	Salt and freshly ground pepper
1 bay leaf	2 tablespoons olive oil
	1 clove garlic, peeled and split

1. Cut the duck or have it cut as follows: Cut off the thighs with legs attached. Cut off the wing tips and reserve, along with the carcass, for soup. Cut off the second wing joint. Cut off the two breast portions (with the main wing bones attached) from the carcass. Trim around the breast and thigh portions to cut away all peripheral skin, that is to say the outer edges.

2. Put the breasts, thighs, second wing joints, neck, liver, and gizzard in a large bowl.

3. Chop the bay leaf as finely as possible on a flat surface. Put the chopped bay leaf in a small mixing bowl and add salt and pepper to taste

and the oil. Mix well. Rub the duck pieces with the mixture and let stand until ready to cook.

4. When ready to cook, arrange the breast, thigh and leg, and wing portions skin side up in one layer in a flat baking pan. Add the neck, liver, and gizzard so that they, too, will be exposed to the broiler heat.

5. If the broiler and oven have separate temperature controls, preheat the broiler to high and the oven to 425 degrees. If they have the same temperature control, preheat the broiler to high.

6. Place the duck under the broiler about 3 or 4 inches from the source of heat. Broil about 5 minutes until skin is golden brown. Turn the pieces.

7. Broil duck on second side about 5 minutes or until golden brown.

8. If the broiler and oven have the same temperature controls, turn the oven heat to 425 degrees. Let the duck bake in the oven 10 minutes.

9. Turn the pieces skin side up and continue baking 10 minutes. Rub the outside of the duck skin with the garlic and then put the garlic in the baking dish. Continue baking 5 or 10 minutes and serve.

Yield: Four servings.

Julienne de Légumes
(Vegetables in julienne)

2 small zucchini, about ¾ pound
2 medium-size white turnips, about 6 ounces, peeled
2 carrots, about ½ pound, trimmed and scraped
Salt
3 tablespoons butter
2 tablespoons finely chopped shallots
Freshly ground pepper

1. Cut the ends off each zucchini. Cut the zucchini into quarter-inch-thick slices. Stack the slices and cut them into quarter-inch-wide julienne strips.

2. Prepare the turnips in the same manner, cutting them into julienne strips.

3. Cut the carrots in half crosswise. Prepare them the same way as you did the zucchini and turnips.

4. Put the carrots in a saucepan with water to cover and salt to taste. Bring to the boil and let simmer 2 minutes.

5. Add the turnips and let simmer 1 minute. Drain quickly.

6. Melt the butter in a heavy skillet and add the zucchini, carrots, turnips, and shallots. Season with salt and pepper to taste. Cook, tossing and stirring the vegetables, about 2 to 3 minutes. Do not overcook.

Yield: Four servings.

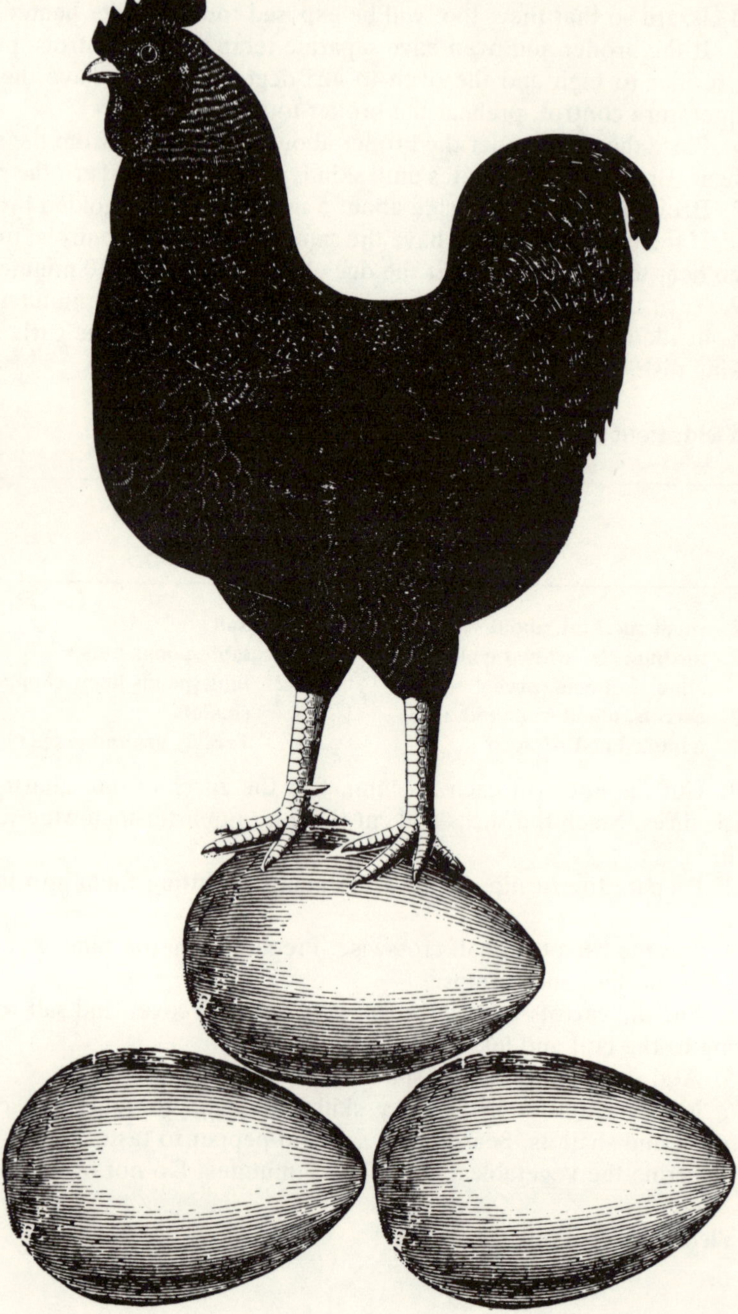

Eggs

THE NOMENCLATURE OF VARIOUS DISHES IS fascinating, for things are, to borrow a phrase, seldom what they seem. There is a crisp puff-pastry dessert called pig's ears; a Mount Blanc is a "mountain" of puréed chestnuts; and eggs in the snow, or les oeufs à la neige, are poached meringues floating in a vanilla custard.

One of my favorite foods with an allusion in its name is oeufs à la tripe, or eggs tripe-style. The dish does not, of course, contain one millimeter of tripe; the name refers to hard-cooked eggs with sliced onions, the combination of which in a light cream sauce gives the illusion (or perhaps gave the illusion to the chef who created it) of strings of tripe such as you find in tripes à la mode de Caën or tripes Lyonnaise. I find this to be one of the most gratifying of luncheon dishes and one that also serves well (with a nice chilled white Burgundy) as a Sunday brunch dish.

It is easy to do and can be ready for the table in far less than 60 minutes. To prepare it, cook onions and mushrooms (the mushrooms are my own addition; they are not basic to the recipe) until wilted, add a sprinkling of flour and then milk and cream plus seasonings. The sauce is allowed to cook for about 15 minutes to meld flavors, during which time the eggs may be cooked, then sliced and gently folded in.

When I prepared this dish recently I found excellent zucchini and tomatoes in the market and assembled a salad with chopped red onion and chopped anchovy fillets. It was something on the order of a modified salade Niçoise, quickly made and an excellent accompaniment to the egg dish. It is recommended that you cook the zucchini briefly for this salad before you begin the eggs in cream sauce. The zucchini slices should be lukewarm before being added to the salad.

Les Oeufs à la Tripe
(Sliced eggs in cream sauce)

8 eggs	1 tablespoon flour
2 cups thinly sliced onions	½ cup milk
1 bay leaf	½ cup heavy cream
¼ pound mushrooms, thinly sliced, about 1½ cups	⅛ teaspoon freshly grated nutmeg
	Salt and freshly ground pepper
1 tablespoon butter	Cayenne pepper

1. Place the eggs in a saucepan and add cold water to cover. Bring to a boil and let simmer about 12 minutes. Drain.

2. Coarsely chop the onion slices.

3. Melt the butter in a saucepan and add the onions and bay leaf. Cook briefly, stirring, until wilted, about 2 minutes. Add the mushrooms and cook, stirring, about 3 minutes.

4. Sprinkle with the flour and stir to blend. Add the milk and cream,

stirring rapidly. Add the nutmeg and salt, pepper, and cayenne to taste. Bring to a boil and let simmer about 15 minutes.

5. Peel and slice the eggs. Add them to the cream sauce and fold them in.

Yield: Four servings.

Salade de Zucchini et Tomates
(Zucchini and tomato salad)

2	zucchini, about ¾ pound	¼	cup finely chopped red onion
	Salt	8	flat anchovy fillets
2	red, ripe tomatoes, cut into quarter-inch-thick slices	2	tablespoons red wine vinegar
		¼	cup finely chopped parsley
	Freshly ground pepper	6	tablespoons olive oil

1. Trim the ends of the zucchini and cut them slightly on the bias into quarter-inch-thick slices. Drop the slices into boiling salted water and let simmer 1½ to 2 minutes. The zucchini must retain a certain resilience.

2. Arrange the zucchini and tomato slices in alternate patterns in a round serving dish. Sprinkle with salt and pepper to taste. Sprinkle with the chopped onion. Arrange the anchovy fillets on top. Sprinkle with the vinegar, parsley, and oil and serve.

Yield: Four servings.

A NEIGHBOR RECENTLY POINTED OUT TO ME what he considers an important omission over the years in my column and that is the lack of dishes tailored especially for Sunday brunch. That is probably because I rarely serve a meal on weekends that I could specifically label as lunch in my own home. As often as not the Sunday meal will consist of a simple fish soup or broiled fish or lobster, depending on the season, and, if there are guests or the children around, a substantial meal that might involve a roast or some sort of ragout.

To my mind, a proper main course for brunch would be almost any egg preparation, such as an omelet or a soufflé or poached eggs on toast with a sauce. Among egg dishes, I have a personal favorite, a method of preparing eggs that is not widely known in this country, and this is eggs en cocotte or eggs baked in ramekins. During my childhood, eggs en cocotte were even more familiar than scrambled eggs.

To make them, the eggs are broken into individual serving dishes and baked until the whites are firm while the yolks remain soft and runny. There are endless variations on this dish, limited only by the imagination of the cook. You can alter the preparation by using a "filling" or base before the eggs are baked. The filling is spooned into the ramekins or individual baking dishes and the eggs are broken over. The fillings or bases might include chicken livers in Madeira sauce, diced ham, or almost any creamed food. I enjoy in particular a filling of creamed chicken, and the name of that dish in French is à la Reine.

To make the filling you may use any leftover cooked chicken. Or you may use freshly cooked chicken that can be hastily made if you use chicken breasts poached in liquid until tender. The chicken is cut into cubes and blended with a cream sauce made with the liquid in which the chicken was cooked. I would serve the dish with croissants, brioches or buttered toast. You might begin with half a grapefruit or a bloody Mary. The eggs should be served with a nice dry white wine. Orange marmalade and more hot brioches, croissants, and so on should be served after the main course with very black coffee.

Les Oeufs en Cocotte à la Reine
(Eggs in ramekins with creamed chicken)

- 1 poached chicken breast (see recipe)
- ¼ pound small mushrooms
- 3 tablespoons butter
- 2 tablespoons flour
- ¾ cup chicken broth
- 1 tablespoon finely chopped shallots
- 2 tablespoons dry sherry
- ½ cup plus 4 tablespoons heavy cream
- ⅛ teaspoon freshly grated nutmeg
- Salt and freshly ground pepper
- 8 eggs

1. Preheat the oven to 400 degrees.
2. Remove the skin and bones of the chicken and discard. Cut the meat into half-inch cubes. There should be about 1½ cups.
3. If the mushrooms are very small, cut them in half. If medium-sized, cut them into quarters. If they are large, slice them. There should be about 1½ cups.
4. Melt 2 tablespoons of the butter in a saucepan and add the flour, stirring with a wire whisk. Add the broth and continue cooking, stirring, until thickened and smooth.
5. Melt 1 tablespoon of butter in a skillet and add the mushrooms and shallots. Cook about 2 minutes. Add the wine and cook about 10 seconds. Add the white sauce and blend. Add ½ cup of the cream and stir. Season with nutmeg and salt and pepper to taste. Let simmer about 1 minute.
6. Rub four one-and-one-quarter-cup individual soufflé dishes with butter. Spoon equal portions of the creamed chicken mixture into each dish. Break 2 eggs on top of each portion. Sprinkle with salt and pepper to taste.
7. Set the soufflé dishes in a pan of water. Bring the water to the boil. Place the pan with the soufflé dishes in the oven and bake 20 minutes. Spoon one tablespoon of cream on top of each serving. Serve hot.

Yield: Four servings.

Poitrine de Volaille Pochée
(Poached chicken breast)

1	chicken breast, about 1 pound	1	bay leaf
2	cups water, approximately	¼	teaspoon dried thyme
¼	cup coarsely chopped carrots		Salt and freshly ground pepper
¼	cup coarsely chopped onion	3	sprigs fresh parsley
¼	cup coarsely chopped celery		

1. Put the chicken breast in a saucepan and add the water to barely cover. Add the remaining ingredients.
2. Cover and bring to the boil. Let simmer 10 minutes. Remove from the heat and let stand until ready to use. Drain and reserve the broth for use in another dish. There should be about 2 cups.

Yield: One poached chicken breast.

I AM ALWAYS FASCINATED BY THE AMERICAN preoccupation with the techniques of omelet making. During my childhood, omelets were as much a commonplace on the home table as bacon and eggs are in this country, and the cook in the family—a mother, an aunt, or a grandmother—was brought up knowing how to hold a fork and tilt a pan so that a perfect omelet came out every time.

My enjoyment of omelets undoubtedly stems from that childhood, for my mother was an expert omelet maker and we had them as a frequent dish for supper, which was almost invariably when the sun went down during my young days in Burgundy.

A particular favorite is one I discovered as an adult and as a chef: a flat omelet with crabmeat simply piled high atop the omelet after it is turned onto a plate. The dish was vastly popular as a luncheon entrée during my days as a chef at Le Pavillon many years ago.

The preparation of the omelet is simpler than most because it is not necessary to tilt the pan and fold the omelet expertly. It is cooked until the eggs are set and then allowed to sit over the heat—increased at the end—so that it browns nicely and quickly on the bottom. The omelet is then turned into a plate bottom side up.

The important thing about this particular dish is the preparation of the crab. Lump crabmeat is preferred and, of course, it is a luxury. The crab is cooked so that the lumps are nicely browned and slightly crunchy on the exterior and then flavored with chopped shallots and just a touch of vinegar, which gives an uncommon sweetness to the crab.

An excellent accompaniment for this dish is a salad made with fresh tomatoes and briefly cooked zucchini.

Omelette Fines Herbes aux Crabes
(Omelet with herbs and crabmeat)

- 3 tablespoons plus 4 teaspoons butter
- 1 pound lump crabmeat
- Salt and freshly ground pepper
- 12 eggs
- 8 teaspoons finely chopped fresh parsley
- 4 teaspoons chopped fresh basil or 2 teaspoons dried
- 2 teaspoons finely chopped fresh tarragon or 1 teaspoon dried
- 2 tablespoons finely chopped shallots
- 2 teaspoons red wine vinegar
- Chopped parsley for garnish

1. Melt 3 tablespoons of butter in large skillet and add crabmeat. Add salt and pepper to taste. Cook over moderately high heat about 1 minute. Stir and continue cooking about 3 minutes or until the exterior of the lumps is nicely browned.

2. Use 3 eggs at a time to make individual omelets. Put 3 eggs in mixing bowl and add 2 teaspoons of parsley, 1 teaspoon basil, and ½ teaspoon tarragon. Add salt and pepper to taste. Beat well.

3. Melt 1 teaspoon of butter for each omelet in an eight-inch Teflon-lined skillet. Add the beaten egg mixture and cook over moderately high heat. As the eggs cook stir with a fork, keeping the tines parallel to the bottom of the skillet. Stir almost constantly until the eggs are set, about 30 seconds. Increase the heat and cook about 30 seconds until omelet is browned on bottom. Turn the omelet out onto a warm serving plate, cooked side up.

4. Add the chopped shallots to the crabmeat and sprinkle with vinegar. Stir to blend well.

5. Spoon one-fourth of the crab mixture onto the serving and sprinkle with parsley for garnish.

6. Continue making omelets until butter, eggs, and crabmeat are used.

Yield: Four servings.

Salade Tomates et Courgettes
(Tomato and zucchini salad)

4	small zucchini, about ¾ pound	1	tablespoon finely chopped fresh basil, optional
	Salt		
2	red, ripe tomatoes, about 1½ pounds	1	tablespoon finely minced fresh parsley
	Freshly ground pepper	1	tablespoon red wine vinegar
1	teaspoon finely minced garlic	¼	cup olive oil

1. Trim off the ends of the zucchini. Cut each zucchini crosswise into thirds. Cut each piece lengthwise into quarters.

2. Drop the zucchini into a saucepan with boiling water to cover. Add salt to taste. Bring to the boil and simmer 2 minutes. Drain well.

3. Core the tomatoes and cut into half-inch-thick slices. Arrange the slices in symmetrical circles on a serving dish. Sprinkle with salt and pepper to taste. Scatter the zucchini over the tomatoes.

4. Blend the garlic, basil, and parsley and sprinkle over the vegetables. Sprinkle with vinegar and olive oil. Serve.

Yield: Four to six servings.

ONE OF THE MOST PERSISTENT MEMORIES OF my life has to do with an omelet. When I was fifteen years old, fresh out of Burgundy and a not-yet-dry-behind-the-ears apprentice, there was a sous-chef at the Restaurant Drouant named Emile Domas. It seemed to my young sensibilities that he chose me for the most menial, tedious work, for jobs that kept me polishing and scrubbing the range while all the other kids had gone off to wander around Paris.

The first dish I was ever asked to cook for a customer was an omelet, specifically an omelet aux fines herbes—with chopped tarragon, parsley, chervil, and chives. I had had a few preliminary sessions in the techniques of omelet-making and, needless to say, I didn't feel all that sure-footed on this occasion.

I made the omelet and, while it was not a total disaster, it was nothing that Monsieur Doamas would want to dispatch to the Drouant dining room. The "skin" of the omelet was wrinkled and brown.

"Alors, Pierre," my superior said, grabbing an ear and twisting it, "I asked you for an omelette fines herbes, not an omelette grand-mère!"

I'd had enough. I took the omelet and threw it at him and ran out of the kitchen into my small room upstairs. He followed me and, naturally, I expected the punishment that I fully deserved.

Instead, he smiled. "You'll have to learn to control your temper," he said, "but someday you may learn to be a good chef."

To this day I never make an omelet without remembering that scene. There are, of course, many kinds of omelets, some flat, some folded like a well-made omelette aux fines herbes, and some "puffed."

In cold weather, one of my favorite omelets is more substantial than most and resembles the Italian frittata—a flat omelet. The frittata I prefer contains a variety of vegetables, including potatoes, that have been cooked in advance. If you make this dish, put the potatoes on to boil while you prepare the remaining ingredients. The omelet itself takes longer to cook than a folded omelet, but its total cooking time can be measured in minutes. It is a complete meal and, with a tossed salad, well rounded.

Frittata

- 1 pound potatoes, preferably red, new potatoes with skins on
- Salt
- 2 cups thinly sliced fresh mushrooms
- ½ cup chopped leeks
- 1 green pepper, cored, seeded, and cut into thin strips, about 1½ cups
- 1 cup thinly sliced zucchini rounds
- 1 cup very thinly sliced onions
- ½ cup diced cooked ham
- 6 tablespoons peanut, vegetable, or corn oil
- 4 tablespoons butter
- 8 eggs
- Freshly ground pepper
- 2 tablespoons red wine vinegar

1. Put the potatoes in a saucepan, add water to cover, and salt to taste.
2. Bring to the boil and cook until tender, about 20 minutes. Drain. When the potatoes are cool enough to handle, peel them. Cut them into half-inch slices. Set aside.
3. Meanwhile, prepare the other vegetables and the ham and set aside.
4. Heat 3 tablespoons oil in a well-cured omelet pan. Add the sliced potatoes and cook, stirring often but gently, until they are golden brown. Using a slotted spoon, remove the potato slices and set aside.
5. To the omelet pan add the remaining oil. Heat and add the mushrooms and cook, stirring often, over high heat until they start to turn brown. Remove and set aside.
6. To the pan, add the leeks, green peppers, zucchini, and onion. Cook, shaking the pan and stirring, about 5 minutes or until the vegetables are wilted.
7. Now add the butter and stir. Add the potatoes, mushrooms, and ham and cook about 2 minutes, stirring to blend.
8. Beat the eggs very well in a bowl and pour them over the ingredients. Add salt and pepper to taste. Cook over high heat, stirring the eggs gently with a spatula. Lift the sides of the omelet and cover. Let cook about 2 minutes. The omelet will remain slightly unfirm on top.
9. Sprinkle with the vinegar.
10. Invert a plate larger than the omelet pan over the pan. Holding the plate tightly over the pan quickly turn the pan upside down, letting the omelet fall into the plate.

Yield: Four to six servings.

YEARS AGO, I KNOCKED ON A NEIGHBOR'S door in the hope of borrowing a flashlight, the batteries of mine being dead. She was in the midst of giving a small dinner for four, and all evidence suggested that the project was not going well. I apologized for my intrusion, but she asked me in for a moment.

The guests were in the living room, and a soufflé was in the oven. Just as I appeared, her young son raced into the kitchen and out of childish curiosity opened the oven door. The hostess panicked. 'STOP!' she screamed.

I was amused by this, but I have since learned that American cooks are generally overly cautious when it comes to soufflés. Soufflés do not fall at the opening of an oven door or the jarring of a kitchen floor. And they will, within reason, "wait" for a guest, although the soufflé must be served the moment it is taken from the oven.

Soufflés are very easy to make. Most of them consist simply of a white or cream sauce to which egg yolks are added to thicken further and egg whites are added to given them their puffed or "souffléed" texture. Actually, the mixture may be made in advance up to the point where the whites are added. The best way to add the whites is in two batches. Add half the whites and beat them in with a wire whisk. Add the remainder and fold them in.

A long time ago I first sampled a Roquefort cheese soufflé at the Taillevent restaurant in Paris. I have adapted this for a main course with the addition of chopped ham. A well-made soufflé can easily be prepared within the space of an hour.

Soufflé au Roquefort et Jambon
(Roquefort and ham soufflé)

4	tablespoons butter plus butter for greasing the soufflé dish	2	tablespoons cornstarch
3	cups milk	1	tablespoon water
7	tablespoons flour	9	egg yolks
	Salt and freshly ground pepper	¾	cup finely diced ham
⅛	teaspoon freshly grated nutmeg	¼	pound Roquefort cheese, finely crumbled
¼	teaspoon Worcestershire sauce	6	egg whites
2	or 3 drops Tabasco sauce		

1. Preheat the oven to 375 degrees.

2. Lightly butter an eight-cup soufflé dish and place it in the refrigerator.

3. Heat the milk in a saucepan.

4. Melt the 4 tablespoons of butter in a saucepan and add the flour, stirring with a wire whisk. When blended and smooth, add the milk, stirring vigorously with the whisk.

5. When thickened, add salt and pepper to taste, the nutmeg, Worcestershire, and Tabasco.

6. Blend the cornstarch and water and add it to the mixture, stirring rapidly. Reduce the heat to low and add the egg yolks, beating vigorously. Continue stirring over very low heat about 30 seconds. Do not let the mixture become too heated or it may curdle.

7. Add the ham and stir to blend. Remove the sauce from the heat and scrape the sauce into a mixing bowl. Add the cheese and fold in. Set aside.

8. Beat the egg whites until quite stiff. Add about half of the egg whites to the basic mixture and beat them in quickly with the whisk. Add the remaining whites and fold them in gently but thoroughly.

9. Pour and scrape the mixture into the prepared soufflé dish. Put the dish in the oven and bake 25 minutes.

Yield: Four to six servings.

Salade de Crudités
(Vegetable salad)

½	pound green beans	1	tablespoon red wine vinegar
3	small zucchini, about ½ pound, trimmed	1	teaspoon finely minced garlic
			Freshly ground pepper
1	medium-size sweet green or, preferably, red pepper, about ¼ pound	¼	cup olive oil
		½	cup coarsely chopped red onion
	Salt	1	tablespoon chopped fresh basil
1	teaspoon imported Dijon mustard		

1. Trim off the ends of the green beans. Rinse and drain. Cut the beans into 2-inch lengths. There should be about 2 cups.

2. Cut the zucchini into 1½-inch lengths. Cut each length into quarters or eighths.

3. Core the pepper and cut away the white inside veins. Cut the pepper into strips. There should be about 1½ cups.

4. Bring enough water to the boil to cover the green beans and zucchini when added. Add salt to taste and the beans. Simmer about 5 minutes.

5. Add the zucchini and pepper strips and cook about 2 minutes. Drain well. Run the vegetables under cold water to chill well. Drain.

6. Mix the mustard, vinegar, garlic, and salt and pepper to taste in a bowl, stirring rapidly with a whisk. Add the oil, beating vigorously.

7. Add the vegetables, onion, and basil to the bowl and toss to blend. Serve at room temperature.

Yield: Four servings.

AS ALL TUTORED OR EVEN NOVICE COOKS know, most soufflés rely upon a white sauce—a blend of flour, butter, and milk—as the foundation. There are also "mock" soufflés made with cubes of bread, but these, which are not technically soufflés at all, also have flour as a base.

Some years ago we discovered a revolutionary "new" soufflé, made in the kitchens of the Girardet Restaurant in Crissier, Switzerland, one of the world's finest dining establishments. This one contained not a speck of flour and was excellent in all respects. The owner-chef had flavored his version with passion fruit, which is a rare commodity in this country. Since that time, we have experimented with numerous, more available flavors for this flour-free type of soufflé. We found that a spinach soufflé made this way will puff as high as its counterpart made with flour, and has a fine texture and flavor.

Soufflé aux Epinards
(Spinach soufflé)

1 pound spinach in bulk, or one 10-ounce package in cellophane	8 eggs, separated
¼ cup water	2 tablespoons heavy cream
Butter for greasing the soufflé dishes	⅛ teaspoon freshly grated nutmeg
	Salt and freshly ground pepper

1. Preheat the oven to 450 degrees.

2. Pick over the spinach and remove and discard any tough stems or blemished leaves.

3. Bring the water to the boil in a saucepan and add the spinach. Stir until the leaves wilt. Cook about 30 seconds. Drain in a sieve, pressing to extract any excess moisture.

4. Butter the bottom and sides of four individual soufflé dishes, each with a 1½-cup capacity.

5. Put the spinach into the container of a food processor and process to a smooth purée. There should be about ½ cup.

6. Spoon the spinach into a mixing bowl and add the egg yolks, cream, nutmeg, and salt and pepper to taste. Beat well.

7. Beat the egg whites until stiff and fold them into the spinach mixture. Spoon the mixture into the prepared dishes. Place the dishes on a baking sheet and bake 7 minutes.

8. Reduce the oven heat to 425 degrees and continue baking 5 minutes. Serve immediately.

Yield: Four servings.

Soufflé au Fromage sans Farine
(Cheese soufflé without flour)

4 ounces cream cheese, softened	Pinch of cayenne pepper
6 eggs, separated	¼ teaspoon freshly grated nutmeg
1¼ cups finely grated cheese, preferably imported Gruyère or Swiss	Salt and freshly ground pepper
	Butter for greasing the soufflé dish

1. Preheat oven to 425 degrees.
2. Combine the cream cheese, egg yolks, cheese, cayenne, nutmeg, and salt and pepper to taste in a mixing bowl. Beat with a wire whisk until smooth.
3. Beat the egg whites until quite stiff and fold them into the cheese mixture.
4. Generously butter the bottom and sides of a 6-cup soufflé dish. Spoon the mixture into the prepared dish. Place the dish on a baking sheet and place in the oven.
5. Bake 10 minutes and reduce the oven heat to 400 degrees. Bake 15 minutes longer. Serve immediately.

Yield: Four servings.

Salade Panachée
(Mixed green salad)

1 bunch watercress	2 tablespoons tarragon vinegar
1 head Boston lettuce	1 clove garlic finely minced
1 red, ripe tomato, cored and cut into eighths	1 tablespoon imported mustard such as Dijon or Düsseldorf
6 radishes, trimmed and thinly sliced	6 tablespoons olive oil
	Salt and freshly ground pepper

1. Trim off the tough stems of the watercress. Core the Boston lettuce and separate the leaves. Rinse the greens and shake off any excess moisture. Put the greens in a mixing bowl and add the tomato and radishes.
2. Blend the vinegar, minced garlic, and mustard in a mixing bowl. Stir with a whisk, gradually adding the oil. Add salt and pepper to taste.
3. Toss the greens with the dressing.

Yield: Four servings.

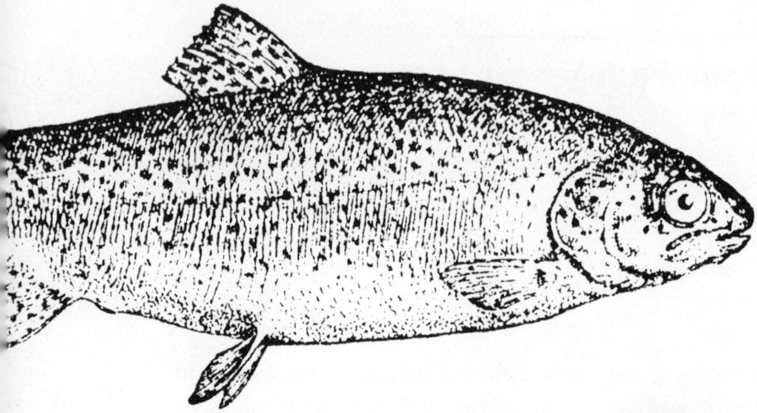
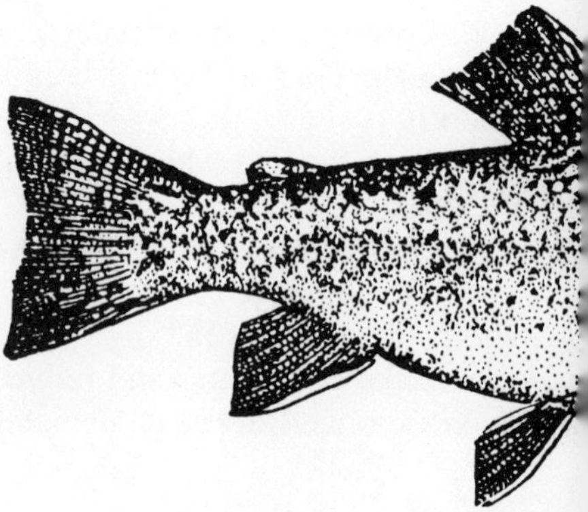
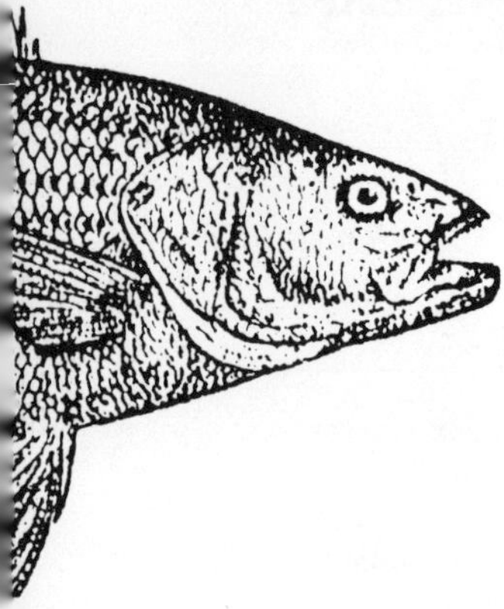
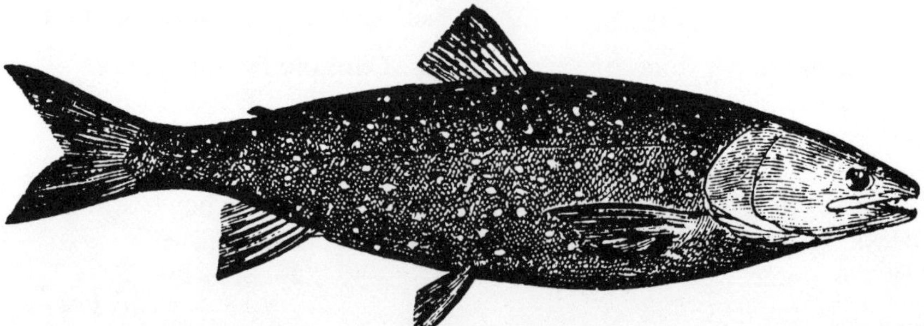

Fish

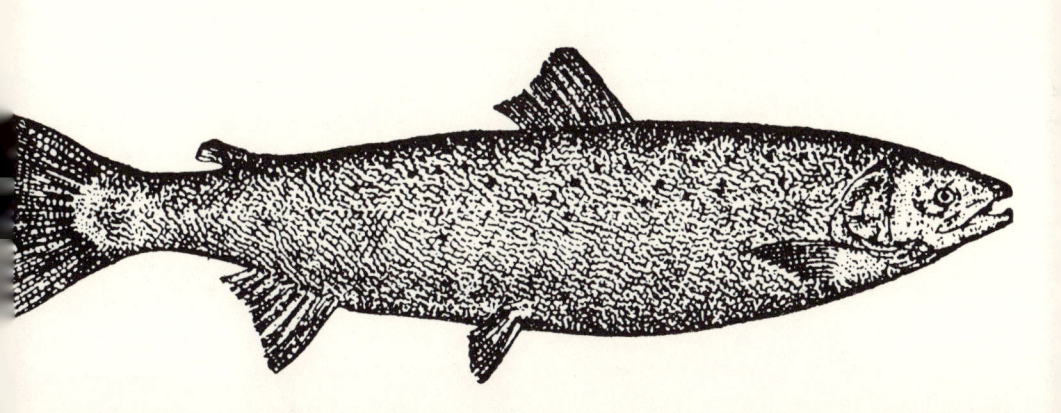

CHINESE INFLUENCE ON THE KITCHENS OF THE world within the past decade has been nothing short of remarkable. The influence is marked in France by the "undercooked" or crisp-tender vegetables to be found in nouvelle cuisine. In America people have taken to cooking with woks and stir-frying by the hordes.

One of the most widely used and admirable techniques employed in Chinese cookery is steaming—meats, fish, vegetables, and so on. And one of the greatest steamed ingredients for hasty cookery or a meal in less than an hour is fish.

By far the best utensil for steaming fish is a fish cooker or a fish poacher. This is the oval implement with a cover. There is a rack with two vertical handles at either end to facilitate lifting the rack out of the cooker.

This utensil was primarily designed for cooking or poaching fish in a court bouillon, that universal liquid made, generally, with water plus aromatics such as leeks, carrots, celery, onions, and so on. This same utensil can be put to excellent use for steaming. In my own kitchen, I simply bend the rack handles forward slightly, just enough so that the lid can be clamped on. The reason for this is that to steam, you must elevate the rack slightly. For this, I use two small, after-dinner coffee cup saucers turned upside down. This elevates the rack and if the rack handles are not bent forward, the cover will not fit snugly on the cooker. Or if you choose not to bend the rack handles forward, simply cover the cooker with aluminum foil.

If you don't own or wish to buy a fish poacher, you can improvise by outfitting a wok or small roaster with a rack. The important thing is that the fish or whatever should not touch the water as it boils.

In the steamed fish recipe here, the cooking time for a two-and-one-half-pound striped bass is only 10 to 12 minutes. You can determine when the fish is done by tugging at the bones along the back. If they come out easily, the fish is cooked. An excellent sauce for steamed fish is a sauce Breval made with shallots, tomato and mushrooms.

Steamed Whole Fish

1   whole fish such as striped bass,
    red snapper, sea bass, haddock,
    and so on, 2½ pounds

1. The best utensil for steaming a fish is a fish steamer. You can improvise, however, by using a Chinese steamer, a small roasting pan and so on. The important thing is to have a rack that can be slightly elevated above a basin of boiling water. As the fish cooks, the steaming utensil should be covered to allow as little steam to escape as possible.

2. If a fish steamer is to be used, place two small plates such as after-dinner coffee cup saucers upside down at each end of the cooker. Add the steaming rack and enough water to come up almost but not quite to the bottom of the rack.

3. Remove the rack and place the fish on it. If you bend the handles of the rack slightly toward the center, the lid of the steamer will fit snugly on top. If you do not bend the handles, you will have to cover the fish closely with heavy-duty aluminum foil.

4. Bring the water to the boil in the steamer. Add rack with the fish on it.

5. Cover closely. Let the fish steam until tender. A 2½-pound fish will steam in from 10 to 12 minutes. Do not overcook. The fish is properly cooked when the bones along the backbone can be pulled out easily with the fingers.

Yield: Four servings.

Sauce Breval

3 tablespoons butter
1 tablespoon finely chopped shallots
2 cups thinly sliced mushrooms
Salt and freshly ground pepper
1 cup chopped, peeled, fresh or canned tomatoes
½ cup dry white wine
½ cup heavy cream
2 tablespoons finely chopped parsley

1. Melt 2 tablespoons of the butter in a small skillet and add the shallots. Cook until wilted.

2. Add the mushrooms and sprinkle with salt and pepper to taste. Cook until they give up their liquid. Cook until the liquid evaporates.

3. Add the tomatoes and cook about 1 minute. Add the wine and cook about 5 minutes.

4. Add the cream and salt and pepper to taste. Let boil about 1 minute. Turn off the heat. Swirl in the remaining tablespoon butter and stir in the parsley.

Yield: Four servings.

THE GOODNESS AND SAVOR OF A DISH CAN never be measured in direct proportion to the time and labor involved in creating it. An expertly executed omelet made with the freshest eggs and a simple filling of, perhaps, a superior cheese can rival beef Wellington or other complicated foods that sometimes require hours to prepare.

One key to success in quick food preparation lies in the freshness of the ingredients. This is particularly true of fish.

The recipe for broiled fish that follows is one that I would most certainly teach a beginner in the kitchen, if teaching was my profession. It is as basic as scrambled eggs and almost as quick and easy to do. Basically, it consists of nothing more than sprinkling skinless, boneless fish fillets with salt and pepper, turning them in melted butter and adding a sprinkling of bread crumbs.

Incidentally, it is best to make your own crumbs from fresh bread rather than use the commercial, seasoned variety. Bread crumbs can be made in seconds in an electric blender or food processor and leftover crumbs keep well for two days or slightly longer if tightly sealed in a jar and kept in the refrigerator.

When ready, the fish will cook under the broiler for two to eight minutes depending on its thickness.

The noodle side dish recommended here, a shortened and greatly simplified version of that popular spaghetti dish called Primavera, will take considerably longer to prepare than the fish, but far less than an hour.

The salad dressing offered here, with Pernod or Ricard, is especially nice with fish. The dressing can be made an hour or two in advance and stirred again at the last moment before the salad is tossed.

Poisson Grillé à l'Anglaise
(Broiled fish)

4 skinless, boneless fish fillets such as flounder, sole, or cod, about 1¼ pounds
Salt and freshly ground pepper

2 tablespoons butter
1½ tablespoons fine fresh bread crumbs

1. Preheat the broiler to high.
2. Sprinkle the fish with salt and pepper to taste. Set aside.
3. Select a flame-proof dish large enough to hold the fish in one layer. Add the butter. Heat under the broiler until the butter melts.
4. Add the fish fillets and turn them over to coat both sides with butter. When ready for broiling, leave the fish pieces skin side down. Sprinkle the top of the fish evenly with bread crumbs.
5. Place under the broiler about five inches from the source of heat.

The cooking time will depend on the thickness of the fish. A very thin fillet such as that of a small flounder will cook in about 2 to 4 minutes. A one-inch-thick slab of boneless skinless cod will require 8 minutes.

Yield: Four servings.

Les Nouilles au Printemps
(Noodles with vegetables)

½ pound noodles	½ cup heavy cream
Salt	¼ teaspoon freshly grated nutmeg
4 tablespoons butter	½ cup freshly grated Parmesan cheese
3 cups thinly sliced mushrooms	
3 cups thinly sliced zucchini	⅓ cup toasted pine nuts
Freshly ground pepper	

1. Bring water to the boil for the noodles. Add salt to taste.
2. Melt the butter in a skillet and add the mushrooms and zucchini. Cook, shaking the skillet and stirring, about 1 minute or until the vegetables are crisp-tender. Do not overcook.
3. Cook the noodles and drain them.
4. Return the noodles to the kettle and add salt and pepper to taste. Add the vegetables, cream, nutmeg, cheese, and pine nuts. Place over low heat. Toss until ingredients are blended and serve.

Yield: Four servings.

Sauce Salade
(Salad dressing)

1 teaspoon of imported mustard, preferably Dijon	1 tablespoon red wine vinegar
	3 or 4 tablespoons olive oil
Salt and freshly ground pepper	1 tablespoon Pernod or Ricard
1 egg yolk	

1. Put the mustard, salt and pepper to taste, egg yolk, and vinegar in a mixing bowl. Blend well with a wire whisk.
2. Gradually add the oil, to taste, stirring briskly with the whisk.
3. Beat in the Pernod or Ricard.

Yield: Dressing for 4 servings.

THERE ARE SPECIALIZED FORMS OF COOKERY or cooking techniques that have always fascinated me. One of these is the technique of cooking foods in paper or, as it is known in French, en papillote. As any Southerner or visitor to New Orleans can tell you, this means wrapping and sealing foods with a sauce or seasonings in parchment and baking until done. The foods generally remain notably moist and the "bag" in which the foods are cooked puffs up. There are, generally speaking, two ways to serve such foods. You either cut a circle from the top of the puffed paper to expose the dish, or you open up the package and transfer the foods to individual dishes.

The most famous en papillote dish in New Orleans—and, therefore, America—is pompano en papillote. I cannot vouch for the legend, but history has it that this dish was originated in 1901 when a French balloonist named Alberto Santos-Dumont visited the city and the chef of Antoine's Restaurant created a dish that would look like a hot-air balloon. Antoine's famous specialty consists of cooking the fish in paper with a cream sauce containing shrimp, crab, and oysters.

I know of a very simple and yet excellent fish creole dish in which the fish (you can use almost any kind of fish fillets) is baked with a creole sauce in a very hot oven. The sauce can be made with onions, garlic, mushrooms, green peppers, and tomatoes in a very short while and the baking period is about ten minutes.

Although parchment is the traditional paper to be used for dishes en papillote (you can buy kitchen parchment in many shops that specialize in baking products) you may substitute heavy-duty aluminum foil. To use either, you cut a length of paper or foil into a heart shape or that of a figure eight. You oil the paper or foil and enclose the fish and sauce, sealing it all around almost hermetically. This package is placed on a baking sheet and ten minutes later after baking it is ready to be served. Steamed or boiled potatoes are an ideal accompaniment for this dish.

Filets de Poisson en Papillote
(Fish fillets baked in paper or foil)

2¼ pounds boneless fish fillets such as striped bass, weakfish, bluefish, flounder, fluke, and so on	2 cups thinly sliced mushrooms
	1 cup peeled, cubed, red ripe tomatoes or use imported canned, drained tomatoes
2 tablespoons olive oil plus oil for brushing	1 bay leaf cut in half
	¼ teaspoon dried thyme
1 cup thinly sliced onions	⅛ teaspoon dried hot red pepper flakes
1 teaspoon finely minced garlic	
1½ cups cored, seeded green pepper cut into thin strips	Salt and freshly ground pepper

1. Preheat the oven to 500 degrees.
2. Cut the fish into four pieces of equal size and weight.
3. Cut four pieces of parchment paper or aluminum foil into the shape of an eight. The eight should be about 24 inches long and 12 inches wide at the widest part of each rounded top and bottom. It should measure about 7 inches where the two rounded halves meet at the center.
4. Heat 2 tablespoons of the oil in a skillet and add the onion, garlic, green pepper, and mushrooms. Cook, stirring until the peppers and onions are wilted. Add the tomatoes, bay leaf, and thyme. Add pepper flakes and salt and pepper to taste.
5. Open up the paper or foil. Brush it all over the inside lightly with oil. Place one fish fillet in the center of the rounded bottom paper cutout. Spoon about one-fourth of the tomato mixture over the fillet. Fold the paper over. Fold and seal the edges of the overlapping paper or foil securely to exclude as much air as possible. Continue adding filling and enclosing the fish until all four are ready for the oven.
6. Arrange the fish packages on one or two baking sheets. Bake in the oven 10 minutes.
7. To serve, place one fish en papillote on each of four dinner plates. Cut a circle around the upper part of the paper or foil. Or open up the packages and transfer the fish to the dinner plates. Serve with steamed potatoes.

Yield: Four servings.

Pommes Vapeur
(Steamed potatoes)

1 pound red, new waxy potatoes	2 tablespoons butter, optional
Salt	Freshly ground black pepper

1. Rinse and drain the potatoes and put them in a small pot or deep saucepan.
2. Cover with water and add salt to taste. Bring to the boil and simmer 20 minutes or until tender. Drain and, when cool enough to handle, peel.
3. Heat the butter in a heavy saucepan and add the potatoes. Sprinkle with salt and pepper to taste. Cover and heat thoroughly.

Yield: Four servings.

AS A PROFESSIONAL COOK, I HAVE BEEN ASKED a thousand times such questions as, "What is your favorite dish?" "What category of food do you like best?" and "What kind of cooking do you prefer?" My answer to all three questions would probably be fish. I like fish and shellfish in almost all its forms, from a simply fried platter of whitebait, a simple plate of broiled sole to the most elaborate fish dishes in still wine or Champagne sauces.

The two fish that I prefer out of American waters are striped bass in summer and fresh codfish in winter. Cod is one of the most versatile of fish—in chowders, in cream sauces, baked, broiled and so on. It has, when freshly caught, some of the sweetest, tenderest, flakiest flesh of anything out of the sea. Its quality and taste has to do with the seasonal coldness of the water in which it swims.

One of the best—and one of the quickest—ways of cooking fresh cod fillets is to batter-fry them. Batter bases, of course, vary enormously—some made with beer and/or beaten egg whites; some with yeast and so on. For cod I heartily endorse what may be the simplest of all, a blend of water, flour, an egg yolk, and only a touch of oil and baking powder. When dipped in this batter and deep fried, the fish emerges from the hot fat with a crisp, fragile coating as thin and delicate as a sugar wafer.

A fine accompaniment for batter-fried cod is a light, noncreamed tomato sauce flavored with horseradish (if you are fortunate enough, use freshly grated horseradish). Since the preparation of the batter for the fish and the deep frying require less than 10 minutes, it is best to prepare the sauce in advance and have it ready. Serve the fish with the sauce, with a boiled potato and a simple tossed green salad.

Filets de Morue Frites
(Batter-fried fresh cod)

1½ pounds skinless, boneless cod fillets, each about 1 inch thick	1 cup plus 2 tablespoons flour
1 cup cold water	1 teaspoon baking powder
2 tablespoons peanut oil	Oil for deep frying
1 egg yolk	Tomato sauce with horseradish
Salt and freshly ground pepper	(see recipe)

1. Cut the fillets into 10 to 12 pieces of more or less equal size.

2. Put the water, oil, and egg yolk into a mixing bowl. Add salt and pepper to taste and the flour. Beat with a wire whisk until blended and smooth.

3. When ready to cook, add the baking powder and stir briskly to blend well.

4. Heat the oil for deep frying. Dip the pieces of cod, one at a time, in the batter and drop them into the hot fat. Cook only as many pieces of cod

at one time as will fit comfortably in the fat without crowding. Cook about 2 to 3 minutes or until the pieces are golden brown. Cooking time for each piece may vary, depending on size. As the pieces are browned, transfer them to paper towels to drain. Continue frying until all the pieces are cooked. Serve with tomato sauce (see recipe).

Yield: Four servings.

Sauce Tomate au Raifort
(Tomato sauce with horseradish)

2 tablespoons butter	2 tablespoons tomato paste
½ cup finely chopped onion	Salt and freshly ground pepper
1 teaspoon finely minced garlic	2 tablespoons horseradish, preferably freshly grated
1 tablespoon red wine vinegar	
1 bay leaf	
1 cup fresh or canned red, ripe tomatoes, chopped	

1. Melt half the butter in a saucepan and add the onion and garlic. Cook until wilted and add the vinegar and bay leaf. Cook until the vinegar is reduced by half.

2. Add the tomatoes, tomato paste, and salt and pepper to taste. Cook, stirring often, about 5 minutes.

3. Stir in the horseradish.

4. Swirl in remaining butter. Serve.

Yield: About 1¼ cups.

ALMOST EVERY COOK AND CHEF I KNOW HAS one favorite fish, one whose flavor and texture he prizes above all others. And it may vary from season to season. In the spring it may be shad, for which I have a craving once the season begins. After a while, however, I find that shad is a little specialized, and my craving diminishes with familiarity.

In the summer when bluefish are plentiful, I never tire of them. It is only as the season passes and the cost is elevated that I reluctantly forego them. To my taste, the greatest fish to be found in the market in the early spring is fresh cod. Fresh cod has a sweetness in flavor and a tender, flaky texture that makes it irresistible. What's more it is an incredibly easy fish to cook whether it is simply simmered in seasoned water with a little milk (the milk helps keep its pure white color) or simply broiled over a good fire.

One of the best cold weather dishes I know is made with fresh cod. This is cod that is blended in a cream sauce with cooked potato slices. Fresh cod complements the simplicity of potatoes and vice versa. The only seasoning for the sauce is a light grating of nutmeg with a touch of cayenne pepper.

This dish is quickly made. The cod and potato slices are cooked separately but simultaneously. And as they cook there is ample time to start making the simple cream sauce that will blend and bind them together. Ideally, the dish should be served as soon as the various elements are combined, although it can be reheated briefly before serving.

Fresh cod in cream sauce with potatoes is sufficient unto itself as a main course. You may, however, wish to serve it with an herbed green salad.

Morue Bonne Ma Man
(Codfish with potatoes and zucchini)

2	pounds fresh, skinless codfish, cut crosswise into 1-inch steaks
1	large onion, cut into quarter-inch-thick slices, about 2 cups
1	bay leaf
4	whole cloves
2	cups milk
½	cup water plus water to cover the vegetables
	Salt
10	peppercorns, crushed
3	large Idaho potatoes, about 2½ pounds, peeled and cut into slices about one-third inch thick
2	large zucchini, about three-quarters of a pound, trimmed and cut into slices about one-third inch thick
3	tablespoons butter
4	tablespoons flour
½	cup heavy cream
	Freshly ground pepper
¼	teaspoon finely grated nutmeg
⅛	teaspoon cayenne
½	cup finely chopped parsley

1. Select a casserole that will hold the codfish in one layer.
2. Arrange the fish pieces in the casserole. Scatter the onion rings over the fish. Add the bay leaf, cloves, milk, ½ cup water, salt to taste, and the peppercorns. Bring to the simmer. Cover and let cook about 5 minutes or just until the fish flakes easily when touched with a fork. Set aside.
3. Meanwhile, put the potatoes and water to cover in a saucepan and bring to the boil. Cook 5 minutes and add the zucchini and cook about 2 or 3 minutes or until they are barely tender. Drain and set aside.
4. Pour off the cooking liquid from the fish. There should be about 2½ cups. Set it aside.
5. Melt the butter in a saucepan and add the flour, stirring with a whisk. When blended, add the reserved cooking liquid, stirring rapidly with the whisk. When blended and smooth, add the cream, salt and pepper to taste, nutmeg, and cayenne.
6. Select an oval dish (a dish measuring about 11 by 17 inches is suitable) and arrange the cod pieces and onions in the center. Arrange the potato and zucchini slices alternately and slightly overlapping around the fish.
7. Strain the sauce over the fish and vegetables. Sprinkle with chopped parsley and serve hot. This dish is best served immediately, but you may set it aside and reheat it in the oven or on top of the stove.

Yield: Four or more servings.

Salade Vinaigrette aux Herbes
(Tossed green salad with herbs)

2 small heads Boston lettuce	Salt and freshly ground pepper
2 tablespoons tarragon vinegar	1 tablespoon finely chopped dill
1 teaspoon finely minced garlic	1 tablespoon finely chopped parsley
1 tablespoon imported mustard such as Dijon or Düsseldorf	1 tablespoon finely chopped chives, optional
6 tablespoons olive oil	

1. Pull off and discard any blemished outer leaves of the lettuce. Cut away the core of the lettuce. Separate the leaves. Rinse in cold water and drain or spin dry. Add to a salad bowl.
2. In another small bowl, combine the vinegar, garlic, and mustard. Using a wire whisk, beat in the oil. Add salt and pepper to taste, the dill, parsley, and chives. Pour the dressing over the salad and toss.

Yield: Four servings.

LIKE MANY PROFESSIONALS IN THE WORLD OF food—and many nonprofessionals, I would suspect—I have occasionally lamented the fact that in this day and age, so few foods can be classified as seasonal. With present-day packaging and transportation, almost any food can be obtained in America year-round, including fresh asparagus, "spring" lamb and every known lettuce.

That is one reason that I cherish the first days and weeks of cold weather. It is then that I can go to my local fish market and buy the first catch of codfish, to my taste one of the most delicately flavored of all fish and one with the finest flesh as well.

It almost goes without saying that I have relished cod in its many forms throughout my lifetime, including in its salted, dried version (the year-end holidays without salt cod in the form of brandade de morue are almost unthinkable). I have eaten cod in soups and chowders and with a variety of sauces including egg, creole and tomato sauces.

But most of all for day-to-day feasting when cod is in season, I prefer it in one of the simplest ways possible—poached in a blend of milk and water and served with a basic cream sauce.

You should count on about half a pound of cod per person. It is imperative that when you simmer codfish, you do not overcook it. Even if the cod steak or fillet is quite thick, only a minute or two in simmering water is sufficient. If you overcook the fish, it becomes tasteless and fibrous.

The reason for the blend of milk and water is to help the cod retain its snowy white texture, and it just may add a touch of flavor and richness to the flesh. Very few seasonings are needed when poaching cod: bay leaf, cloves and thyme. And the liquid used in cooking the fish is also used in preparing the cream sauce in which the fish is served.

Because it must be cooked gently but quickly, codfish in a cream sauce is ideal for a less-than-an-hour menu. The most complementary food to serve with cod is a plain boiled potato. Its bland nature is a perfect foil for such a delicate dish.

Morue Fraîche à la Crème
(Fresh codfish in cream sauce)

1	large fillet of codfish, about 2 pounds	2	sprigs fresh thyme or ½ teaspoon dried
2¼	cups water, approximately	6	sprigs fresh parsley tied into a bundle
2¼	cups milk, approximately	¼	teaspoon cayenne pepper
	Salt	2	tablespoons butter
10	peppercorns	3	tablespoons flour
½	cup thinly sliced small onions	½	cup heavy cream
1	bay leaf	¼	teaspoon freshly grated nutmeg
2	whole cloves		

1. Arrange the fish in an oval or other shaped dish. If necessary, cut the fish in half or into four portions to make it fit compactly in the baking dish.
2. Add the water and milk to barely cover. Add salt to taste and the peppercorns. Add the onion slices, bay leaf, cloves, thyme, parsley, and cayenne. Bring to the simmer and cook slowly about 2 minutes. Remove from the heat and set aside.
3. Melt the butter in a saucepan and add the flour, stirring with a wire whisk. When blended and smooth, add two cups of the liquid in which the fish cooked. Cook, stirring rapidly with the whisk, until thickened and smooth.
4. Add the cream and nutmeg and stir.
5. Drain the fish and pour the thickened sauce over the fish. Reheat gently and serve with boiled potatoes.

Yield: Four servings.

Pommes Bouillies
(Boiled potatoes)

8	small red waxy new potatoes, about 1¼ pounds	Salt

1. If you wish to be fancy, use a small paring knife or swivel-bladed paring knife and remove a thin layer of skin around the middle of each potato. Leave the skin intact top and bottom. Many chefs feel that this makes a more interesting-looking potato. Rinse the potatoes.
2. Put the potatoes into a saucepan with water to cover and salt to taste. Bring to the boil and simmer 25 minutes or until tender. Pommes bouillies are generally served unbuttered and without further garnish. Serve plain or buttered according to your individual preference.

Yield: Four servings.

THE TWO MOST IMPORTANT ELEMENTS IN FINE cooking are, of course, flavor and texture. Naturally, flavor is the more critical of the two, but a lumpy sauce, a "gummy" bread or an undercooked vegetable can mar a fine cook's best efforts. The subtleties of describing a desired texture are at times a bit tricky. That is why you will often encounter the phrase "cook until crisp-tender" in recipes printed here. It usually pertains to vegetables that are to be cooked just until they have lost their raw taste yet retain a crunchy texture.

One of the best examples I know of a dish in which this crunchy texture is desirable is for fish baked with vegetables in a light wine and cream sauce. The recipe for it is printed below. The slightly crisp texture of the chopped vegetables—in this case, carrot, celery, and leeks—is an excellent foil for the softer (but not too soft) texture of the fish.

Most of the preparation could be done a few hours in advance. If the fish is notably fresh, it could be placed in its baking dish in the morning. The vegetables, too, could be sautéed in the morning and refrigerated for several hours. The dish could then be completed in an extremely short time later in the evening.

If you have a choice of fish in making this dish, I would strongly recommend fluke, which has the perfect texture to complement the vegetables.

Like most baked and steamed fish dishes, this one teams remarkably well with steamed or boiled potatoes. The potatoes can be put on to cook during the final preparation of the fish.

Carrelet au Plat
(Fluke baked with vegetables)

2 fillets of fluke or sea bass, about 1¾ pounds	1 small carrot
1½ tablespoons butter	½ cup thinly sliced leeks
Salt and freshly ground pepper	4 sprigs fresh parsley
1 small onion	½ cup dry white wine
2 ribs heart of celery	1 cup heavy cream

1. Preheat the oven to 450 degrees.

2. Select a flame-proof baking dish large enough to hold the fish fillets close together in one layer. Rub the dish with ½ tablespoon of butter. Sprinkle the bottom of the dish with salt and pepper. Arrange the fish in the dish and sprinkle it with salt and pepper to taste.

3. Peel the onion and cut it in half lengthwise. Cut each half crosswise into very thin slices. There should be about ½ cup. Set aside.

4. Trim the celery ribs and cut them crosswise into one-eighth-inch-thick slices. Set aside.

5. Trim and scrape the carrot. Use a lemon peeler to make lengthwise ridges around the carrot. Cut the carrot into thin rounds. Set aside.

6. Pluck off bits of parsley leaves from each sprig. There should be about ½ cup. Set aside.

7. Heat the remaining tablespoon of butter in a saucepan. Add the onion, celery, carrots, leeks, and parsley. Add salt and pepper to taste. Cook, stirring, until vegetables are crisp-tender, about 3 minutes.

8. Add the wine and cook about 2 minutes over high heat.

9. Add the cream and cook over high heat about 3 minutes.

10. Spoon the vegetables and sauce over the fish. Place the dish on top of the stove and heat thoroughly.

11. Transfer the dish to the oven and bake 10 minutes.

Yield: Four servings.

Boiled Potatoes with Parsley

8 to 12 small, new, waxy potatoes or use 3 or 4 medium-size Idaho or Maine potatoes Salt	2 tablespoons melted butter 2 tablespoons finely chopped parsley

1. Peel the potatoes. If the potatoes are small and new, leave them whole. If they are large, cut them into thirds or quarter them.

2. Place the potatoes in a saucepan and add water to cover and salt to taste. Bring to the boil and simmer until the potatoes are tender, about 10 to 15 minutes, depending on size.

3. Drain and pour melted butter over them. Sprinkle with parsley and toss. Serve hot.

Yield: Four servings.

I DOUBT THAT THERE IS ANYTHING MORE confusing in the American kitchen than the various kinds of fish that are sold over the counter as sole. When one speaks of sole in France or England, one almost invariably means that fine fish that comes from the English Channel and is known in England as Dover sole and in France as sole de la Manche. There is, to my mind, no sole found anywhere to equal it.

But consider the kinds of fish sold as sole in this country. In *The Encyclopedia of Fish*, by A. J. McClane (Holt, Rinehart & Winston, 1977), the author lists butter sole, curlfin sole, lemon sole, rex sole, rock sole, sand sole, and so on. Not to mention gray sole and yellow sole.

In the McClane book, there is a special section on flounder, which is also known as sole in the United States. And it was of special interest to me to learn that the fish that is known as fluke in America is actually summer flounder. This fish averages from three to five pounds but sometimes grows to a weight of 15 or 20 pounds.

To my taste, fluke is one of the finest of fish to be found in domestic waters in spring or summer. I was recently able to purchase fluke fillets in one of the best fish markets in the Hamptons. Fluke has an excellent texture and I prefer it when it is slightly thick.

I found two fillets that weighed about one pound each. I cooked them with a provençale sauce, which is the French equivalent of what is known as a Creole sauce in Louisiana. I spooned the quickly made sauce into a baking dish and placed the fillets on top. They fit the dish compactly. The fillets were topped with a blend of bread crumbs, parsley and garlic and the total baking time was 15 minutes.

This is a dish that I would normally serve with buttered rice or a steamed potato, but on this occasion I served it with buttered bulgur, or cracked wheat. It made an excellent accompaniment and cooked in the same time that it took to bake the fish once it was placed in the oven.

Filets de Carrelet Provençale
(Fluke fillets with tomato and green pepper sauce)

2 skinless, boneless fillets of fluke, about 2 pounds	½ cup dry white wine
Salt and freshly ground pepper	1¾ cups skinned, seeded tomatoes cut into half-inch cubes
4 tablespoons olive oil	1 bay leaf
2 cups thinly sliced onions	¼ cup fine fresh bread crumbs
1½ teaspoons finely minced garlic	¼ cup finely chopped parsley
2 cups thinly sliced mushrooms	
1 green pepper, cored, seeded and thinly sliced, about 1 cup	

1. Preheat the oven to 425 degrees.
2. Sprinkle the fish with salt and pepper to taste. Set aside.
3. Heat half of the oil in a deep, small skillet and add the onions and ½ teaspoon garlic. Cook briefly and add the mushrooms and green pepper. Cook about 1 minute.
4. Add the wine, tomatoes, and bay leaf and bring to the boil. Add salt and pepper to taste. Cook, stirring occasionally, about 15 minutes.
5. Select a baking dish large enough to hold the fish in one layer. It may be necessary to split the fish down the center to accommodate them in the dish. We used a dish measuring about 9 by 15 inches that was 2 inches deep. Spoon the tomato sauce over the bottom of the dish. Smooth it over. Arrange the fish fillets on top of the sauce.
6. Brush the fish with the remaining oil.
7. Combine the bread crumbs, parsley, and remaining teaspoon of garlic. Sprinkle this over the fish.
8. Place the fish in the oven and bake 15 minutes.

Yield: Four to six servings.

Bulgur Pilaf
(Cracked wheat pilaf)

2 tablespoons butter	Salt to taste
½ cup finely chopped onion	2 tablespoons finely chopped parsley
1 cup bulgur	
2 cups chicken broth	

1. Melt the butter in a saucepan and add the onion. Cook until wilted.
2. Add the bulgur, broth, and salt to taste. Bring to the boil and cover.
3. Let simmer 15 minutes. Uncover and stir in the parsley.

Yield: Four servings.

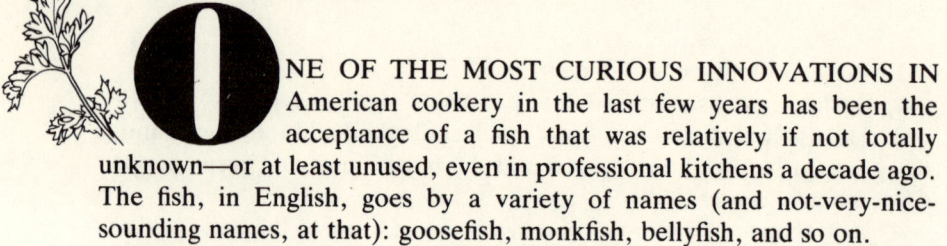

ONE OF THE MOST CURIOUS INNOVATIONS IN American cookery in the last few years has been the acceptance of a fish that was relatively if not totally unknown—or at least unused, even in professional kitchens a decade ago. The fish, in English, goes by a variety of names (and not-very-nice-sounding names, at that): goosefish, monkfish, bellyfish, and so on.

When I grew up in France, this saltwater fish, known in French as lotte, was well known. One of the principal ways of preparing it was in the style called Dugléré, which is with tomatoes, white wine, shallots and cream.

I cannot account for the sudden availability of this fish out of American waters; one reason for its popularity may be that it is relatively inexpensive in comparison with such American fish as striped bass, sea bass, and the like.

In any event, it is a happy discovery, for lotte or monkfish has many excellent qualities. It has a somewhat meaty flesh that is ideal for soups. Whereas many fish, including sole and flounder, tend to fall apart in a soup kettle, monkfish holds up well.

One of the best uses to which I have put it in recent months is in a dish that I choose to call lotte provençale.

The dish came about for an interesting reason. One of my children told me that he was hungry for lobster Américaine, which is, of course, lobster cooked with shallots, tomatoes and a touch of cognac. When we went to the fish market, there were no lobsters to be had. There was an ample supply of monkfish, however, so we took that home, and I cooked it with a sauce Américaine. I thought that one could not properly call it Américaine, which demands lobster, so we called it provençale.

The fish is easy to cook in the tomato sauce in much less than an hour. Rice is the ideal accompaniment, with a dish of cucumber salad.

Lotte Provençale
(Monkfish with tomatoes and tarragon)

1½ pounds skinless, boneless, center-cut section of lotte (also called monkfish, bellyfish, goosefish, and so on)	⅓ cup finely chopped carrots
	1 teaspoon dried tarragon
	1 bay leaf
	¼ teaspoon dried thyme
2 tablespoons olive oil	⅛ teaspoon cayenne pepper
Salt and freshly ground pepper	2 tablespoons cognac
3 tablespoons butter	3 cups diced ripe tomatoes
½ cup finely chopped onion	½ cup dry white wine
2 tablespoons finely chopped shallots	3 tablespoons tomato paste
	½ cup fish broth (see page 119)
½ teaspoon finely minced garlic	1 teaspoon chopped fresh tarragon, optional
¼ cup finely chopped celery	

1. Place the fish on a flat surface and cut it into two-inch cubes. There should be about 3 cups.

2. Heat the olive oil in a large casserole or deep skillet over high heat. Add the fish, and salt and pepper to taste. Cook, stirring, about 1 minute. Pour off the oil from the skillet.

3. Add 1 tablespoon of the butter. When melted, scatter the onion, shallots, garlic, celery, and carrots over the fish. Add the dried tarragon, bay leaf, thyme, and cayenne pepper.

4. Add the cognac and ignite it. Add the tomatoes, wine, and tomato paste. Stir to blend well. Add the fish broth. Cook about 8 minutes.

5. Spoon out the pieces of fish and set aside. Let the sauce continue cooking about 5 minutes.

6. Line a mixing bowl with a sieve and pour the sauce into the sieve.

7. Strain the sauce, pushing down with a spoon to extract as much liquid as possible from the vegetables. Discard the solids.

8. Pour the sauce into a saucepan and add the fish cubes plus any liquid that has accumulated around them. Bring to the boil. Remove from the heat. Swirl in the remaining 2 tablespoons of butter. Stir in the fresh tarragon if available. Serve hot with rice.

Yield: Four to six servings.

Salade de Concombres
(Cucumber salad)

---

2 firm, fresh, unblemished cucumbers	3 tablespoons peanut, vegetable, or corn oil
Salt and freshly ground pepper	2 tablespoons finely chopped fresh dill or parsley
1 tablespoon white vinegar	

1. Use a swivel-bladed paring knife and peel the cucumbers. Split each cucumber in half. Using a melon ball cutter or a spoon, scoop out the cucumber seeds.

2. Slice each half and put in a mixing bowl. Sprinkle lightly with salt. Cover and chill at least half an hour.

3. Line a mixing bowl with cheesecloth and pour the cucumber into it. Squeeze lightly but firmly to extract much of the liquid. Turn the cucumber slices into another bowl and sprinkle with salt and pepper to taste. Add the vinegar and oil and toss. Put in a serving dish and serve sprinkled with chopped dill or parsley.

Yield: Four to six servings.

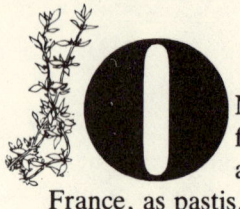

ONE OF THE MOST CURIOUS AND INTERESTING flavors that I have used in my kitchen over the years is an anise—or licorice-flavored spirit, known in Marseilles, France, as pastis.

The best known of these in France are Pernod, Ricard, and Berger.

Pastis was not originally designed for the kitchen but for the bar. It is normally drunk in a small glass and when water is added, it becomes milky or opalescent.

I first tasted pastis as an ingredient of bouillabaisse when I was an apprentice in my teens. Since then I find it gives a haunting flavor to almost any fish soup.

Similar spirits are to be found in most Mediterranean countries. In Italy there is anisette, in Turkey arrack, and in Greece ouzo.

I was fascinated some years ago to dine with Greek friends on a dish called, in Greek, garides me feta or shrimp baked in tomato sauce with feta cheese crumbled on top. At the last minute the cook had added a dash of ouzo and I was immediately reminded of the bouillabaisse of my youth.

Since then I have borrowed the formula for that shrimp dish and adapted it to a platter of red snapper. It is a very simple and delicious dish in which the fish is baked in a tomato sauce flavored with oregano—as characteristic a Greek seasoning as it is Italian—plus a few capers and, my own addition perhaps, a few hot red pepper flakes. There is nothing more Greek, to my mind, than feta cheese which is white, crumbly, and salty, and made of sheep's milk. It comes in three degrees of saltiness—mild, moderate, and sharp. I prefer the moderately salty.

To make the dish, you prepare a quickly cooked tomato sauce, arrange fish fillets in a baking dish and pour the sauce over. The dish is baked for 20 minutes with the feta added for the last five minutes of cooking. To accompany this I like rice cooked with browned broken pasta.

Red Snapper à la Grecque
(Baked red snapper with feta cheese)

- 2 red snapper fillets, about 1¼ pounds each
- 4 tablespoons olive oil
- ¼ cup finely chopped onion
- 2 teaspoons finely minced garlic
- 2 cups canned tomatoes with tomato paste
- 2 tablespoons drained capers
- 1 teaspoon dried oregano
- ¼ teaspoon dried hot red pepper flakes
- ¼ cup plus 2 tablespoons finely chopped parsley
- Salt and freshly ground pepper
- ¼ pound crumbled feta cheese
- 1 tablespoon ouzo (Greek anise liqueur)

1. Preheat the oven to 425 degrees.
2. Wipe the fish fillets with a damp cloth.
3. Heat 2 tablespoons of the oil in a saucepan and add the onion and garlic. Cook, stirring, until onion is wilted.
4. Add the tomatoes with tomato paste, capers, oregano, pepper flakes, ¼ cup chopped parsley, and salt and pepper to taste. Cook 10 minutes.
5. Put the remaining 2 tablespoons of oil in a baking dish, preferably oval, large enough to hold the fish in one layer. Arrange the fish skin side up in the dish. Pour the tomato sauce over all.
6. Place the dish on top of the stove and bring the sauce to the boil. Put the dish in the oven and bake 15 minutes. Sprinkle with feta cheese and bake 5 minutes longer.
7. Sprinkle with ouzo and remaining 2 tablespoons chopped parsley. Serve piping hot.

Yield: Four servings.

Riz au Nouilles
(Rice with browned noodles)

3 tablespoons peanut, vegetable, or corn oil	¾ cup raw rice
¾ cup broken capellini or thin spaghetti	1¼ cups cold water Salt

1. Heat the oil in a saucepan and add the broken capellini. Cook, stirring briefly, until the strands are golden brown. Do not burn.
2. Add the rice and stir. Add the water and salt to taste and bring to the boil. Cover and simmer 17 minutes.

Yield: Four servings.

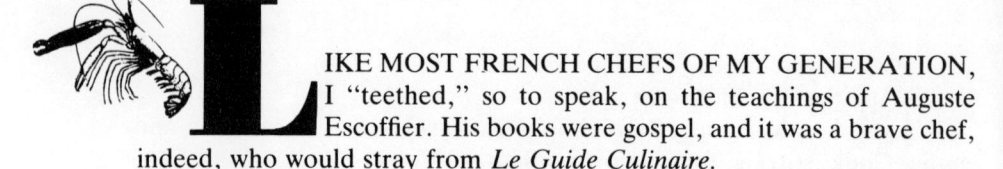

LIKE MOST FRENCH CHEFS OF MY GENERATION, I "teethed," so to speak, on the teachings of Auguste Escoffier. His books were gospel, and it was a brave chef, indeed, who would stray from *Le Guide Culinaire*.

The writings and "school" of Escoffier are still at the foundation of all classic French cookery, and yet his rules are broken. Chefs have learned to adapt and adopt from other cultures. Most of the precepts that I use in the kitchen date back to my early apprenticeship and yet I find pleasure in "borrowing" thoughts from other cultures.

Over a period of time I have spent many hours in East Hampton watching Virginia Lee, the chef and author, chop fresh ginger, add a dash of soy sauce—light or dark—to one preparation or another, sprinkle fresh coriander, sometimes called Chinese parsley, over a dish she was stir-frying in her wok, and so on.

And as a consequence I have gained a hitherto unknown appreciation of ingredients that are "foreign" to the French. One recent dish that I prepared has quite definite overtones borrowed from Virginia. It is a dish of fillets of sole stuffed with chopped shrimp seasoned not only with such Western staples as celery and mushrooms but with chopped fresh ginger and chopped fresh coriander. The sole is baked and at the very end basted with a blend of heavy cream (cream is almost never used in traditional Eastern cookery), soy sauce and chopped scallions.

This is a very easy dish to prepare and the cooking time is relatively brief. It bakes in 20 minutes. An ideal accompaniment for the dish is obvious, a simple dish of rice, which cooks in approximately the same length of time as the sole.

To go about the preparation of this meal, it is best to begin assembling and chopping and otherwise making ready the sole with shrimp stuffing. Once it is in the oven, proceed to the preparation of the rice. A simple tossed salad of Boston lettuce, oil, and vinegar would make an excellent accompaniment.

Limandes Farcies Orientale
(Sole stuffed with shrimp and ginger)

- 8 small skinless, boneless fillets of sole, about 1½ pounds
- ¼ pound fresh shrimp, shelled and deveined
- 3 tablespoons butter
- ¼ cup finely chopped onion
- ¾ cup finely chopped mushrooms
- ½ cup finely diced celery
- Salt and freshly ground pepper
- 1 tablespoon finely chopped fresh ginger
- ½ cup fine fresh bread crumbs
- 1 tablespoon finely chopped fresh coriander leaves
- ¼ cup heavy cream
- 1 tablespoon soy sauce
- ½ cup chopped scallions

1. Preheat the oven to 425 degrees.
2. There is a small fine bone line about half way up the center of each fillet. Cut around it and discard it.
3. Put the shrimp on a flat surface and chop finely. There should be about ½ cup. Set aside.
4. Melt 1 tablespoon of the butter in a saucepan and add the onion. Cook until wilted and add the mushrooms and celery. Cook briefly, stirring often, about 1 minute. Add salt and pepper to taste. Stir in the ginger and remove from the heat. Scrape the mixture into a mixing bowl.
5. Add the shrimp and bread crumbs, salt and pepper to taste, and coriander to the mixture and blend well.
6. Use 1 tablespoon of butter to rub the bottom of a shallow baking dish large enough to hold four of the fish fillets in one layer. Sprinkle with salt and pepper to taste.
7. Arrange four of the fillets, skinned side down, on the baking dish in one layer. Spoon equal amounts of the filling on top of each fillet in the center.
8. Cover each serving with another fillet, skinned side down.
9. Sprinkle with salt and pepper to taste. Brush the top of the fillets with the remaining butter.
10. Put the dish on the stove and heat until the butter in the baking dish starts to bubble. Put the dish in the oven and bake 10 minutes.
11. Combine the cream, soy sauce, and scallions. Spoon equal portions of this over the stuffed fish. Return to the oven and bake 10 minutes, basting occasionally.

Yield: Four servings.

Riz au Carrottes
(Rice with carrots)

---

1 small carrot	Salt and freshly ground pepper
1 tablespoon butter	1 cup long-grain rice
1 tablespoon finely chopped onion	1½ cups water

1. Trim and scrape the carrot. Cut the carrot into one-and-one-half-inch lengths.
2. Cut each length into very thin slices. Stack the slices and cut them into very fine julienne strips. There should be about ½ cup.
3. Melt the butter in a small, heavy saucepan with a tight-fitting lid. Add the onion and carrot. Add salt and pepper to taste. Cook briefly until onion is wilted.
4. Add the rice and water. Bring to the boil and cover closely. Cook 17 minutes.

Yield: Four servings.

OVER THE PAST DOZEN YEARS I HAVE SPENT A good deal of time thinking about and putting into print and into practice various aspects of nouvelle cuisine. One of the most interesting things about nouvelle cuisine in the home is that until the term was coined, there were two basic sauces in common use in American kitchens, a hollandaise (with its variation, a béarnaise) and mayonnaise.

Something that is relatively new was introduced to the public with a simply made sauce that has been common in professional kitchens for a long time, a sauce called buerre blanc, meaning literally "white butter" sauce. This is a melted butter sauce that is thickened by being beaten into a reduction of white wine and shallots. It has an enormously tempting flavor and a thousand uses in French cuisine. Needless to say, it is more prevalent in the practice of nouvelle cuisine than it was in previous years.

The preparation of a buerre blanc requires a minimum of time. In fact, it must be made hurriedly or else it might curdle or separate. An excellent use for the white butter sauce is on grilled fish.

Here is a hastily made main course—a grilled salmon steak with beurre blanc. The fish goes well with steamed, buttered parsley potatoes and a salad.

Darne de Saumon Grillé au Beurre Blanc
(Broiled salmon steak)

1   1½-pound salmon steak, about 1½ inches thick
1   teaspoon peanut, vegetable, or corn oil

Salt and freshly ground pepper
Beurre blanc (see recipe)

1. Preheat the broiler.
2. Brush the salmon on both sides with oil and sprinkle with salt and pepper to taste.
3. Arrange the salmon in a shallow baking dish and place it about 6 inches from the source of heat. Broil about 10 minutes. It is not necessary to turn the steak as it cooks. The fish is done when the center bone comes away easily from the flesh. Serve with beurre blanc.

Yield: Two servings.

Beurre Blanc
(White butter sauce)

6 tablespoons finely chopped shallots	12 tablespoons butter
1½ cups dry white wine	Salt and freshly ground pepper

1. Combine the shallots and wine in a saucepan and bring to a vigorous boil.
2. Let the wine cook down to about ⅓ cup. Continue cooking over high heat, stirring rapidly with a wire whisk, and add the butter about 2 tablespoons at a time.
3. Add salt and pepper to taste.

Yield: About 1¼ cups.

Pommes Vapeur
(Steamed potatoes)

1 pound new, red potatoes	2 tablespoons butter, optional
Salt	Freshly ground black pepper

1. Rinse and drain the potatoes and put them in a small kettle or deep saucepan.
2. Cover with water and add salt to taste. Bring to the boil and simmer 20 minutes or until tender. Drain and, when cool enough to handle, peel.
3. Melt the butter in a heavy saucepan and add the potatoes. Sprinkle with salt and pepper to taste. Cover and heat thoroughly.

Yield: Four servings.

HAVE LONG BEEN FASCINATED BY THE FACT that a number of fine cooks avoid cooking certain foods. Usually the reason is that these cooks do not come from areas where such foods were commonly used. Squid, which is used extensively in Italian and Spanish kitchens, falls typically into such a category. Indeed, squid was relatively unknown in my own kitchen until quite recently.

Our friend Ed Giobbi came over one morning and we went food shopping. He bought squid for a fritto misto that he intended to prepare at my beach house at noon that day. He dipped the squid and other fish into flour and deep fried the whole batch until crisp.

Since then I have often used squid in many ways, including fish soups and stews. Squid are a little tricky to clean, but the preparation is relatively simple. When someone recently asked me the French name for squid, I had to do a good bit of thinking before recalling that it is calmars, which is similar to the Italian word for squid, calamari.

One of my family's favorite versions is stuffed squid. I vary the filling from one preparation to the next. One is made with shrimp and bread crumbs and is cooked in a light wine and tomato sauce. Rice with noodles (Armenian-style) goes well with this dish.

Calmars Farcis
(Stuffed squid)

8 large squid, about 1¾ pounds	Salt and freshly ground pepper
½ pound shrimp, shelled and deveined	¼ teaspoon or more hot dried red pepper flakes
5 tablespoons olive oil	¾ cup diced tomato
½ cup plus ⅓ cup finely chopped onion	¾ cup dry white wine
	1 bay leaf
1 teaspoon finely minced garlic	2 sprigs fresh thyme or ½ teaspoon dried
⅓ cup plus 2 tablespoons finely chopped parsley	3 sprigs parsley
1 cup fine, fresh bread crumbs	2 tablespoons butter
1 egg	

1. Put each whole squid under cold running water and get rid of the mottled outer skin by rubbing and pulling it away. Cut off the tentacles with a knife and set them aside. Discard the ink sacs, the center bones, the eyes, and jaws. Wash thoroughly. What should be left of each squid is the white triangular body with an opening for stuffing, plus the tender parts of the tentacles.

2. Put the tentacles into the container of a food processor and process until coarse-fine. Put in a mixing bowl.

3. Coarsely chop the shrimp. There should be about ¾ of a cup. Add them to the mixing bowl.

4. Heat 3 tablespoons of the oil in a small skillet and add ½ cup chopped onion and the garlic. Cook until wilted. Add this to the bowl. Add ⅓ cup of chopped parsley, bread crumbs, egg, salt and pepper to taste, and pepper flakes. Blend well.

5. Spoon an equal amount of the stuffing into each of the squid bodies. Do not overstuff for the squid will shrink. Sew up the openings.

6. Heat the remaining 2 tablespoons of oil in a heavy skillet and add the stuffed squid. Cook, turning the pieces often, about 5 minutes. Add the remaining ⅓ cup chopped onion and stir. Add the tomatoes, salt and pepper to taste, wine, bay leaf, thyme, and parsley sprigs. Cover closely and bring to the boil. Let cook 30 minutes.

7. Transfer the squid to a platter and remove the strings.

8. Cook down the sauce by half. Swirl in the butter. Return the squid to the sauce and reheat briefly. Serve sprinkled with remaining chopped parsley.

Yield: Four servings.

Riz Arménien
(Armenian rice)

1	tablespoon peanut, vegetable, or corn oil		Salt and freshly ground pepper
¼	cup fine egg noodles	2	tablespoons butter
1	cup raw rice	1½	cups chicken broth
1	teaspoon finely chopped garlic	¼	cup finely chopped parsley

1. Heat the oil in a saucepan and add the noodles. Cook, stirring, until browned.

2. Add the rice and garlic and stir. Add salt and pepper to taste, butter, and the broth.

3. Cover and cook over low heat exactly 17 minutes. Stir in the finely chopped parsley and serve.

Yield: Four servings.

IT HAS LONG BEEN MY CONTENTION THAT IF home cooks exercised a little foresight, they could save themselves time and money. Essentially, this would include the basic preparation and freezing of such stocks as chicken, beef, and fish. For example, if you found an especially good buy on chicken parts (necks, backbones, wings, and so on), you would benefit by buying them and throwing them into a stock pot with a little water and a few vegetables to make the basis for countless stews and sauces. You might ask your fish dealer to throw in a few fish bones and, preferably, fish heads along with your purchase. These, too, should be cooked, strained, and frozen for future use. You should clearly label these various stocks.

I recently prepared a quickly cooked fish dish that, for want of a better term, I chose to call Mediterranée. Mediterranée, Côte d'Azur, and so on are simply broad terms to indicate fish or seafood generally cooked with tomatoes and various seasonings—usually garlic, bay leaf, and thyme.

Even if you must start from scratch in preparing the stock, the dish, with an accompanying combination of vegetables, could easily be prepared within an hour. The cooking time for a basic fish stock or broth is much less than that of a chicken or beef broth. It does not need long simmering to extract the goodness from the bones. The bones, with water and seasonings, require only 10 minutes to reach a totally acceptable degree of flavor (for chicken or beef, it's an hour longer). The dish that I propose here was originally made with two one-pound striped bass fillets. But weakfish (or sea trout, its fancy name) would also be good, as would blackfish or red snapper. This fish dish is a bit savory, with a touch of hot pepper flakes.

An ideal accompaniment is a dish of buttered potatoes with cucumbers.

Bar Rayé Mediterranée
(Striped bass with tomato sauce)

- 2 skinless, boneless fish fillets such as striped bass or weakfish, about 1 pound each
- 1 carrot
- 2 tablespoons peanut, vegetable, or corn oil
- ½ cup finely chopped onion
- 1 cup finely chopped leeks
- ½ cup finely chopped celery
- 1 cup crushed canned tomatoes
- 1 cup fish broth (see recipe)
- 1 bay leaf
- ⅛ teaspoon dried hot red pepper flakes
- ¼ teaspoon dried thyme
- Salt and freshly ground pepper
- 2 tablespoons finely chopped parsley

1. Cut each fish fillet in half crosswise. Set aside.

2. Trim and scrape the carrot. Cut it into 1½-inch lengths. Cut each length into quarter-inch slices. Stack the slices and cut them into quarter-inch strips. There should be about ¾ of a cup.

3. Heat the oil in a skillet large enough to hold the four fish pieces in one layer and add the onion and leeks. Cook, stirring, until the onion wilts. Add the carrot and celery and cook briefly.

4. Add tomatoes, fish broth, bay leaf, pepper flakes, and thyme. Add salt to taste and a generous grinding of pepper. Stir. Bring to the boil, simmer 10 minutes.

5. Add the fish fillets and spoon the sauce over. Cover and let cook about 5 minutes. Sprinkle with chopped parsley and serve.

Yield: Four servings.

Fumet de Poisson
(Fish broth)

2½ pounds fish bones, preferably including a fish head, gills removed	½ cup dry white wine 2 cups water Salt to taste

Chop the fish bones into pieces so that they will fit into a saucepan. Combine all the ingredients in a saucepan. Bring to the boil and simmer about 10 minutes. Strain. Discard solids.

Yield: About 2¼ cups.
Note: Leftover broth can be frozen.

Pommes et Concombres Doria
(Potatoes and cucumbers with parsley)

2 potatoes, about ¾ pound 1 cucumber, about ¾ pound 1 tablespoon butter	1 tablespoon finely chopped parsley Salt and freshly ground pepper

1. Peel the potatoes. Split them in half lengthwise, then cut into quarters.

2. Put the potatoes in a small skillet with water to cover. Bring to the boil and cook about 10 minutes.

3. Meanwhile, scrape the cucumber. Cut it into 1½-inch lengths. Cut each length in half.

4. When the potatoes have cooked 10 minutes, add the cucumbers. Cook about 4 minutes. Drain.

5. Add the butter to the vegetables and toss. Sprinkle with parsley and salt and pepper to taste and serve.

Yield: Four servings.

ONE OF THE GREATEST ADVANCES IN THIS nation's taste during the past decade has been the adoption of European or European-style mustards. There is, of course, nothing wrong with the standard American version, the so-called ball park mustard. It is excellent on hot dogs and cold meat sandwiches, but it doesn't work as well when it is used in the preparation of sauces. The reason, I suspect, is the predominant flavor of turmeric, which gives the mustard its rich yellow hue.

It also seems to me that more and more French chefs are using mustard in food preparation. One of the best new dishes that I have sampled in recent years was a quick sauté of veal chops with imported mustard and mustard seeds, the creation of Jean Troisgros when he visited my kitchen in East Hampton, L.I.

Mustard has, of course, been a basic ingredient for all deviled dishes or dishes à la diable, be they made with meat, poultry or shellfish. One of the best and most easily and quickly made dishes of my own experience is a platter of swordfish, smeared lightly with mustard before broiling. Swordfish is, to my taste, one of the best fish in American or European waters and comes closest, I think, to resembling an incredibly delicate meat. For this dish, it is only necessary to brush swordfish steaks previously sprinkled with salt and pepper with a little mustard and melted butter. When placed under the broiler for 15 minutes, the results are admirable.

The cooking time is so brief, in fact, that it would be best to start preparing the side dish—in this case a simple but excellent combination of carrots and turnips—before the main item.

Broiled Swordfish with Mustard

1   swordfish steak, about 1¼ pounds and about 1 inch thick
    Salt and freshly ground pepper
2   tablespoons butter
2   teaspoons mustard such as Dijon or Düsseldorf

1   teaspoon mustard seeds
    Lemon wedges
    Melted butter, optional

1. Preheat the broiler to high.
2. Sprinkle the swordfish with salt and pepper to taste.
3. Melt the butter in a baking dish large enough to hold the swordfish steak. Brush the steak on both sides with mustard and sprinkle with mustard seeds.
4. Place the steak in the dish and place in the oven about 4 or 5 inches from the source of heat. Broil about 3 or 4 minutes.
5. Turn the fish and broil on the second side about 4 or 5 minutes. Do

not overcook. Serve with lemon wedges and, if desired, melted butter poured over.

Yield: Two to four servings.

Carrottes et Navettes
(Carrots and turnips)

1¾ cups carrots cut into very thin rounds	Salt and freshly ground pepper
2 tablespoons butter	2 cups white turnips cut into half-inch cubes
¼ cup water	

1. Combine the carrots, half the butter, water, and salt and pepper to taste in a shallow skillet. Cover closely and bring to the boil.
2. Add the turnips and cook about 5 minutes or slightly longer until turnips are crisp tender. Do not overcook. Stir in the remaining butter and add salt to taste.

Yield: Four servings.

TO ANYONE WITH AN IN-DEPTH KNOWLEDGE of cooking, professional or not, it is obvious that all or almost all foods fall into individual categories. And if you learn the basic techniques for making one category, you, therefore, know approximately how to go about making the rest of the related dishes in that sector.

It is as simple as this: If you can make a hollandaise, you can easily proceed to something like a béarnaise through the use of peppercorns and tarragon, or a maltaise with the addition of an orange flavor, or a mousseline with the addition of whipped cream.

To my mind, one of the most basic and best of all main courses falls into the category of what is known as meunière, and if I were teaching beginning cookery, this is one of the dishes that I would demonstrate within the first couple of weeks.

To prepare it, take a fish such as trout or fish fillet and dip it into a small amount of milk. Remove it without drying and coat it all over with flour seasoned with salt and pepper. Heat a very light layer of unflavored oil such as peanut or corn in a skillet and cook the fish quickly, first on one side and then the other.

Remove the fish, wipe out the skillet and add butter. Heat this briefly until it starts to turn brown and pour it over the fish. A variation of this is a great personal favorite—trout grenobloise, which is meunière with lemon and capers. Serve it with boiled potatoes, a classic accompaniment, and a salad.

Truite Grenobloise
(Trout with lemon and capers)

4	fresh or frozen trout, about 10 ounces each	1	lemon, peeled and cut into very small cubes
½	cup milk	6	tablespoons butter
½	cup flour	⅓	cup drained capers
	Salt and freshly ground pepper	2	tablespoons finely chopped parsley
½	cup peanut, vegetable, or corn oil		

1. Rinse the trout inside and out in cold water and pat dry. Using a pair of kitchen shears, cut off the fins.

2. Put the trout in a dish and add the milk. Turn the fish to coat with the liquid.

3. Remove each trout and dredge in flour seasoned with salt and pepper to taste. Shake to remove excess.

4. Heat the oil in a skillet and add the trout. Cook over moderately high heat about 4 to 5 minutes or until golden brown on one side. Turn and cook until golden brown on the other side. Let cook until the trout are

cooked throughout. As the fish cook, baste with the oil in the skillet. The total cooking time is about 10 to 15 minutes.

5. Transfer the fish to a warm serving dish. Sprinkle with the cubed lemon.

6. Pour off the fat from the skillet and wipe it out. Heat the butter until it starts to brown. Add the capers. Cook about 15 seconds and pour the butter sauce over the fish. Serve sprinkled with chopped parsley.

Yield: Four servings.

Pommes Vapeur
(Steamed potatoes)

1	pound new, red potatoes	2	tablespoons butter
	Salt		Freshly ground black pepper

1. Rinse the potatoes, drain, and put in a deep saucepan.
2. Cover with water and add salt to taste. Bring to the boil and simmer 20 minutes or until tender. Drain, and when cool enough to handle, peel.
3. Melt the butter in a heavy saucepan and add the potatoes. Sprinkle with salt and pepper to taste. Cover and heat thoroughly.

Yield: Four servings

Salade Panachée
(Mixed green salad)

1	bunch watercress	2	tablespoons tarragon vinegar
1	head Boston lettuce	1	clove garlic, finely minced
1	ripe tomato, cored and cut into eighths	1	tablespoon imported mustard such as Dijon or Düsseldorf
6	radishes, trimmed and thinly sliced	6	tablespoons olive oil
			Salt and freshly ground pepper

1. Trim off the tough stems of the watercress. Core the Boston lettuce and separate the leaves. Rinse the greens and shake off any excess moisture. Put the greens in a mixing bowl and add the tomato and radishes.

2. Blend the vinegar, garlic, and mustard in a mixing bowl. Stir with a whisk, gradually adding the oil. Add salt and pepper to taste. Toss the greens with the dressing and serve.

Yield: Four servings.

IT SEEMS TO ME THAT MOST CHEFS THAT I know are hard put to name one particular category of cookery that they prefer above all others. Although I am fascinated by all aspects of cooking, from scrambling eggs to an elaborate preparation like a coulibiac of salmon, I know full well that the form of cookery that I enjoy most is fish cookery. This always struck my mother as a bit odd in that we lived in Burgundy, a few hundred miles from the nearest salt water. From my childhood on, however, I always had access to freshly caught fish, most of it brought from the coast on a fast train.

The fish that I prefer to cook is one that I have hooked myself and, happily, during the summer months when I often find myself with a load of stripers and other fish from my neighboring waters on Long Island.

When I go fishing, which may be several times a day on weekends, I generally come home and feed guests with the day's haul. One thing that fascinates me is that my guests seem to marvel at nothing so much as a simple fish soup with mussels or clams that I have also harvested myself. Fortunately, I can also purchase very fresh fish from a local dealer.

The only important thing in preparing a fish soup—and it almost goes without saying, since it is a dish that must be prepared quickly—is the timing at which the ingredients are added. You should not add cubed fish, which cooks in seconds, at the same time that you add, let us say, clams, which may require five minutes or so to open. You time the addition of each ingredient so that when the soup is finished, the various components retain a good texture and none is overcooked.

When I want to vary the fish soup, I often serve a sauce rouille (which literally translates as rust sauce because of its color), which is an easily made mayonnaise-type preparation with potatoes and garlic. Serve the fish soup with a crusty loaf of French bread and a salad.

Soupe de Poissons
(Fish soup)

1¼ pounds skinless, boneless, sea bass, striped bass, or belly fish (also known as monkfish and angler fish) fillets	2 cups finely chopped leeks
	1 teaspoon loosely packed stem saffron, optional
	1 pound red, ripe tomatoes
1 pound skinned, cleaned eel	Salt and freshly ground pepper
2 squid, about ½ pound total weight	2 tablespoons tomato paste
	1 cup dry white wine
6 shrimp	½ bay leaf
12 littleneck clams	2 sprigs fresh thyme or ½ teaspoon dried
¼ cup olive oil	
1 cup finely chopped onion	Finely chopped parsley for garnish
2 tablespoons finely minced garlic	
¾ cup finely diced heart of celery	Sauce rouille (see recipe)

1. Cut the fish fillets into one-and-a-half-inch cubes. Set aside.
2. Cut the eel into 12 pieces of more or less the same size. Set aside.
3. Clean the squid, removing the outer skin and inner parts. Rinse well. Cut it into two-inch pieces. Set aside.
4. Peel and devein the shrimp.
5. Rinse the clams well and set aside.
6. Heat the oil in a large saucepan. Add the onion, garlic, celery, and leeks. Sprinkle with saffron. Cook, stirring, about 3 minutes.
7. Add the tomatoes, salt and pepper to taste, tomato paste, wine, bay leaf, and thyme. Let cook about 5 minutes.
8. Add the fish, eel, and squid. Cook, stirring often, about 5 minutes.
9. Add the clams and cook until they open, about 5 minutes. Add the shrimp and cook until they lose their raw look. Serve in soup bowls garnished with chopped parsley and sauce rouille on the side.

Yield: Four to six servings.

Sauce Rouille
(A potato and garlic mayonnaise)

- 1 large potato, about ¼ pound
- 1 teaspoon finely minced garlic
- 1 egg yolk
- 1 teaspoon paprika
- 1 teaspoon cold water
- Salt and freshly ground pepper
- ½ cup olive oil

1. Peel the potato and cut it crosswise into quarter-inch-thick slices. Put the slices in a saucepan and add cold water to cover. Bring to the boil and simmer three to five minutes or until the slices are tender.
2. Drain the potato and put it through a food mill or potato ricer.
3. Scrape the potatoes into a mixing bowl and add the garlic, egg yolk, paprika, water, and salt and pepper to taste. Start beating with a wire whisk. Gradually add the oil to make it like a mayonnaise.

Yield: About ¾ cup.

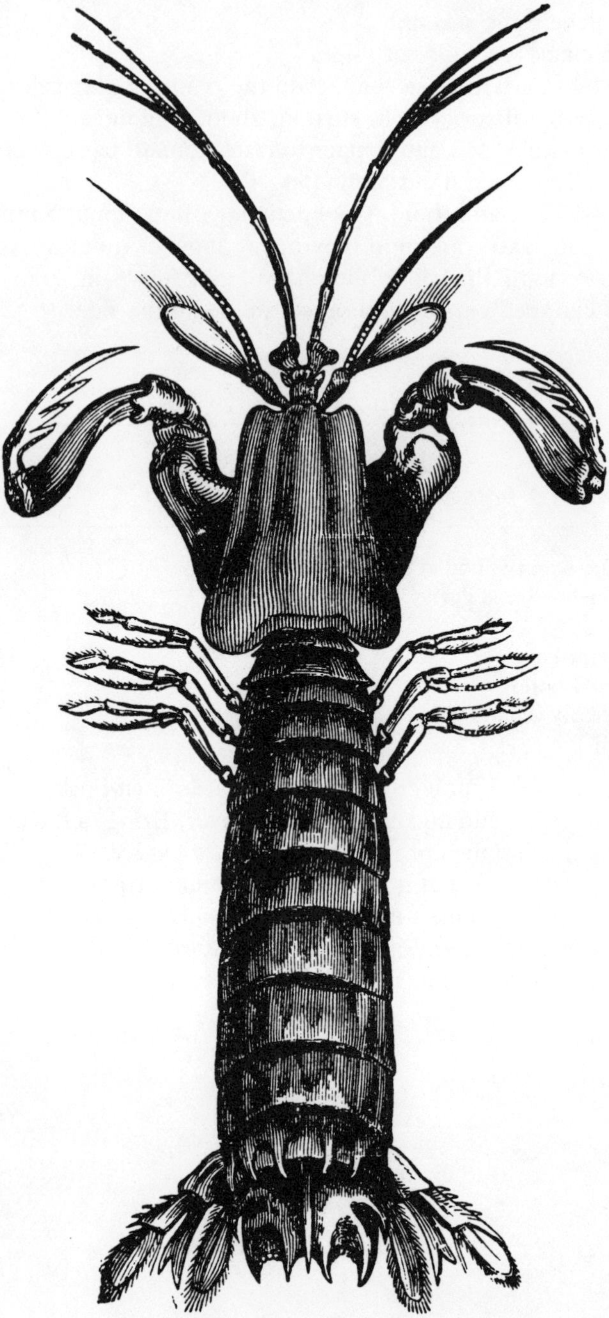

Shellfish

THE MOST CHRONICLED OUTLINE OF THE beginnings of classic French cookery has to do with Catherine de Medici, who, when she came from Florence as the wife of King Henry II, brought with her an entourage of Florentine cooks who impressed the nobility with their techniques for making soups, sauces, aspics, and desserts. This is a theory that I have heard hotly contested since my youth, but one that I, personally, have never felt all that feverish about.

One week recently I was thinking about the differences in national and regional flavors. Until a short while ago basil was not much used in French kitchens. And I have been told by Italian colleagues that tarragon is not all that common in Italian kitchens.

The reason these thoughts arose had to do, oddly enough, with two clam preparations that I put together when I found myself the recipient of several dozen littlenecks offered by a neighbor and fellow clam digger.

I decided to use part of the batch for a plate of clams marinières, following almost precisely the same technique as used for moules or mussels marinières. Incidentally, the clams used here are not identical with the clams or palourdes of France. The clams marinières were steamed with butter, white wine plus shallots, garlic, and parsley.

On a succeeding evening I found in my refrigerator the leftovers of a large can of Italian tomatoes with tomato paste. Thus, I decided to prepare another soup, this time Italian-style—or, more precisely, perhaps, Neapolitan-style, a zuppa di vongole. For this I used olive oil, anchovies, oregano, garlic, basil, and red pepper flakes.

Both dishes were hastily made and equally praised by guests who sat around my table. And it occurred to me that the clams marinières might easily have been prepared in Northern Italy; the seasonings in zuppa di vongole would not have been out of place in Provence.

Soupe de Palourde Marinière
(Clam soup)

- 3 dozen littleneck clams
- 6 tablespoons butter
- 6 tablespoons finely chopped shallots
- 2 teaspoons finely chopped garlic
- 2 cups dry white wine
- 12 tablespoons finely chopped parsley
- 2 cups heavy cream
- Salt and freshly ground pepper

1. Scrub the clams well and drain.

2. Melt the butter in a kettle and add the shallots and garlic. Cook, stirring briefly, about 30 seconds.

3. Add the wine and 8 tablespoons of the parsley and bring to the boil. Add the clams. Cover closely and cook until the clams start to open. Add the cream and salt and pepper to taste. Cover and continue cooking until

all the clams open, about 5 to 10 minutes. Serve sprinkled with the remaining chopped parsley.

Yield: Four servings.

Zuppa di Vongole
(Italian clam soup)

3 dozen littleneck clams	1 tablespoon chopped fresh or 1½ teaspoons dried basil
⅓ cup olive oil	½ cup finely chopped parsley
2 tablespoons finely minced garlic	½ teaspoon dried hot red pepper flakes or to taste
6 flat fillets of anchovies, chopped	Freshly ground pepper
1 cup dry white wine	8 garlic croutons (see recipe)
4 cups canned tomatoes with tomato paste	
2 teaspoons dried oregano	

1. Scrub the clams well and drain.
2. Heat the oil in a large pot and add the garlic. Cook briefly, stirring, and add the anchovies. Cook briefly until the anchovies become a paste.
3. Add the wine and simmer about 1 minute. Add the tomatoes with tomato paste, oregano, basil, parsley, pepper flakes, and ground pepper to taste. Do not add salt. The anchovies are salty.
4. Add the clams and cover the pot closely. Cook until all the clams open, 5 minutes or longer. Serve in soup bowls with two garlic croutons on each serving.

Yield: Four servings.

Croutons

Brush 8 slices of French or Italian bread with olive oil, about ½ teaspoon for each. Run under a broiler until golden brown on one side. Turn and broil until brown on the second side. Rub each crouton with a cut clove of garlic.

Yield: Eight croutons.

SOME TIME AGO A READER ASKED ME WHY I never printed a recipe for frogs' legs. There are two reasons. The first is that frogs' legs, which are relatively scarce, are a premium and generally costly item in America; the second is because, for some reason, frogs' legs fall into the food prejudice category. It is hard for me to understand why the latter is true, for frogs' legs are as tasty and tender as chicken (and the diet of frogs is equally if not more clean than that of chickens).

A short while back, courtesy of one of my neighbors, I found myself with several dozen frogs' legs, and I turned them into a veritable feast while preparing them in numerous fashions. That is one of the nicer things about frogs' legs—they are highly adaptable to so many ways of cooking.

Frogs' legs are particularly prized in the southern states, notably Louisiana, where more often than not they are simply coated with a batter and deep-fried. Two of my favorite preparations are provençale (served with a tomato sauce) and poulette, in which the legs are served in a cream sauce. Both are quickly cooked. You can find frogs' legs in almost every fish store that has high quality and varied merchandise.

Cuisses de Grenouilles Provençale
(Frogs' legs with tomato sauce)

8 pairs frogs' legs, about 2 pounds	⅓ cup milk
	½ cup flour
6 red, ripe, unblemished tomatoes, about 2 pounds, or use 3 cups drained, imported canned tomatoes	¾ cup peanut, vegetable, or corn oil, approximately
	Juice of half a lemon
	4 to 6 tablespoons butter
2 tablespoons olive oil	1 tablespoon finely minced garlic
Salt and freshly ground pepper	2 tablespoons finely chopped parsley
1 bay leaf	

1. Pat the frogs' legs dry. Cut off and discard the bottom end of each leg.

2. Peel the tomatoes. Cut in half and squeeze them to extract the seeds. Chop them. There should be about 3 cups.

3. Heat the olive oil in a heavy skillet and add the tomatoes. Add salt and pepper to taste and the bay leaf. Cook, stirring often from the bottom, about 20 minutes or until the sauce is quite thick.

4. Pour the milk onto the frogs' legs.

5. Season the flour with salt and pepper. Drain the frogs' legs and dredge them one at a time in the flour.

6. Heat the peanut oil in one or two large skillets, adding more oil as necessary. Add the frogs' legs and cook over moderately high heat about 3

or 4 minutes or until golden brown. Turn and cook about 3 to 4 minutes on the second side or until golden brown.

7. As the frogs' legs cook, transfer them to a warm serving platter.

8. Spoon the tomato sauce in the center or over the frogs' legs. Sprinkle with lemon juice.

9. Melt the butter in a skillet and when it is hot and starting to brown add the garlic. Cook briefly, swirling it around. Pour the butter over the frogs' legs and serve sprinkled with chopped parsley.

Yield: Four servings.

Cuisses de Grenouilles Poulette
(Frogs' legs in cream sauce)

8	pairs' frogs legs, about 2 pounds	½	cup of dry white wine
4	tablespoons butter	1	cup heavy cream
2	tablespoons finely chopped shallots	2	teaspoons flour
		1	egg yolk, lightly beaten
			Juice of half a lemon
½	pound mushrooms, cut into quarters, about 3 cups	⅛	teaspoon cayenne pepper
	Salt and freshly ground pepper	2	tablespoons finely chopped chives

1. Pat the frogs' legs dry. Cut off and discard the bottom end of each leg.

2. Melt 2 tablespoons of the butter in a skillet large enough to hold the frogs' legs in one layer. Add the shallots and cook briefly.

3. Add the frogs' legs, mushrooms, and salt and pepper to taste. Cook, stirring the ingredients around, about 1 minute. Add the wine and cook for 5 minutes. Transfer the frogs' legs to a warm serving platter.

4. Bring the cooking liquid to the boil over high heat and cook down to ⅓ cup. Add the cream and cook about 1 minute.

5. Blend the flour with the remaining 2 tablespoons butter. When thoroughly mixed, add this gradually to the simmering sauce. Add the egg yolk. Remove the sauce from the heat and stir rapidly. Add the lemon juice and cayenne pepper.

6. Pour and scrape the sauce over the frogs' legs. Serve sprinkled with chopped chives.

Yield: Four servings.

ALTHOUGH LOBSTERS ARE AMONG THE EASiest of all sea creatures to cook, almost every professional chef I know has a "different" technique for steaming or boiling them. One European chef uses a large quantity of vinegar plus water, but it is my theory that vinegar in the liquid tends to toughen the meat.

Professionals agree that the best liquid in which to cook lobsters is fresh sea water that has been taken from deep water, a good distance from the shore. Unfortunately, fresh sea water for most home cooks is hard to come by. On occasion I use this technique, but usually I prepare an easily made and well-seasoned court bouillon.

The time it takes to cook a lobster, of course, depends on the size. A one-pound lobster requires about seven minutes; a one-and-a-half-pound lobster about 10 minutes, and a three-pound lobster about 15 minutes. For all these lobsters, you should remove the kettle from the heat and let the lobster rest in the cooking liquid for five minutes more.

The finest cold lobster dishes that I know are those in which the lobster meat is combined with or served with a well-seasoned mayonnaise. The cold lobster dish here is made with a mayonnaise seasoned with capers, tomato, and cognac. It is served on a bed of finely shredded Boston lettuce.

Chiffonade de Homard
(Lobster mayonnaise with shredded lettuce)

4	cooked lobsters weighing from 1 to 1½ pounds each (see instructions for cooking)	1	cup peanut, vegetable, or corn oil
1	firm, unblemished head of Boston lettuce	¼	cup finely chopped celery
		3	tablespoons capers
1	egg yolk	1	teaspoon finely chopped basil
1	teaspoon Dijon mustard	1	tablespoon finely chopped parsley
2	teaspoons white wine vinegar	1	teaspoon finely chopped tarragon
2	teaspoons tomato paste		
	Salt and freshly ground pepper	2	hard-cooked eggs, optional
2	or 3 drops Tabasco sauce	1	sprig fresh basil or parsley for garnish
1	tablespoon cognac or Pernod		

1. Crack the claws, tail, and body of the lobsters.

2. Remove the meat from the claws and set aside. Remove the meat from the body and tail and cut it into bite-size cubes. There should be about 3 cups of cubed lobster meat.

3. Pull off the large outer leaves from the lettuce. Arrange them on the outer rim of a large platter. Finely shred the center of the lettuce. There should be about 4 cups. Pile the shredded lettuce in the center of the platter.

4. Pile the cubed lobster meat over the shredded lettuce. Use the claw meat as a decorative garnish around the cubed meat.

5. Put the yolk in a mixing bowl and add the mustard, vinegar, tomato paste, salt and pepper to taste, Tabasco, and cognac. Start beating vigorously with a wire whisk. Gradually add the oil while beating.

6. Add the celery, capers, basil, chopped parsley, and tarragon. Blend well.

7. If desired, put the eggs through a sieve and add them to the sauce.

8. Spoon the sauce over the lobster meat. Garnish with the sprig of fresh basil or parsley.

Yield: Four to six servings.

Timetable

Plunge a lobster or lobsters into boiling unseasoned sea water if available. Or plunge them into a boiling court-bouillon (see recipe).

Cook one-pound lobsters exactly seven minutes and drain. Cook one-and-a-half-pound lobsters exactly 10 minutes and drain. Cook a three-pound lobster for 15 minutes and a five-pound lobster for 25 minutes.

When the lobsters have cooked, you may remove the kettle from the heat and let the lobsters stand in the cooking liquid for five minutes more.

Court Bouillon
(For four lobsters)

12	cups water	12	peppercorns
¾	cup chopped celery	1	bay leaf
¾	cup chopped carrots	2	sprigs fresh thyme or ½ teaspoon dried
1	cup chopped onion		
6	parsley sprigs		

1. Combine all the ingredients in a kettle large enough to hold four lobsters. Cover and bring to the boil.

Yield: Cooking liquid for up to four lobsters.

THE MORE I HAVE THOUGHT ABOUT IT OVER the years, the more I have been amused by the notion that most people believe fine French cookery demands many hours in the kitchen and tedious preparation.

One of the finest foods that I know—it is certainly a great personal favorite—is a pilaf of mussels bonne femme. This consists of mussels in a wine and cream sauce, served either with rice on the side or with the mussels packed inside a rice mold. When I worked as chef at Le Pavillon, it was a dish that was asked for as often as not by such visitors as the Duke and Duchess of Windsor, Cole Porter, and Ludwig Bemelmans, the writer.

It happens to be one of the simplest of all dishes to prepare, requiring little more than steaming mussels with parsley, shallots, onions, and a little dry white wine. When the mussels open, they are shucked and set aside. The cooking liquid is made into a light white wine sauce to which quickly cooked fresh mushrooms are added.

There are two refinements that I always used when I served this dish at Le Pavillon. Mussels, as you know if you know your shellfish, have what resembles a tough-tender "string" around them when they are removed from the shell. It is similar to a rubber band. It is not essential that these be removed, but the mussels are a bit more elegant without them.

Then, when the mussels are combined with a little of the cream sauce, I would pack them into a rice mold, simply for the sake of presentation.

To do it, select a suitable bowl in which the rice and creamed mussels fit snugly. Pack in half of your cooked rice and make a well in the center, pressing the rice around the inside bottom of the mold. Add the mussels and pack in more rice. Invert this over a plate and serve quickly with the remaining sauce on the side. This makes a fine luncheon or supper dish. Add only a well chilled bottle of white Burgundy, a tossed salad, and a simple dessert.

Pilaf des Moules Bonne Femme
(Mussels with rice)

6 pounds mussels, about 4½ quarts	½ cup dry white wine
4 tablespoons butter	Freshly ground pepper
¼ cup finely chopped parsley	½ pound mushrooms, thinly sliced, about 3 cups
4 tablespoons finely chopped shallots	3 tablespoons flour
2 tablespoons finely chopped onion	¾ cup heavy cream
	2½ cups cooked rice (see recipe)

1. The mussels should be thoroughly washed in cold water and scrubbed. Drain well.

2. Put the mussels in a large, heavy pot and add 2 tablespoons of the butter, the parsley, half of the shallots, the onion, wine, and pepper to taste. Cover closely and cook about 5 minutes or longer, until the mussels are open.

3. Reserve the juice in a saucepan. There should be about 3½ cups of liquid.

4. Remove the mussels from the shells and set aside. It is good to remove the "rubber band" around each mussel.

5. Melt the remaining 2 tablespoons of butter in a saucepan and add the remaining shallots and mushrooms. Cook, stirring, until mushrooms are wilted. Add the flour, stirring rapidly with a wire whisk.

6. Add the reserved mussel liquid, stirring rapidly with the whisk until thickened and smooth. Cook about 5 minutes, stirring often. Add the cream.

7. Put the reserved mussels in a saucepan and add about ½ cup of the mussel sauce. Heat briefly.

8. There are two ways to serve this dish. You can serve the rice on individual plates with the mussels in sauce in the center and more sauce on the side. Or, if you want to be fancy, add about half of the rice to a round-bottomed five-cup mold and make a cavity in the center. Press the rice firmly to the sides of the mold. Put the mussels in the center of the cavity. Add the remaining rice. Press down to make the whole compact. Invert the mold onto a round serving dish. Spoon half of the sauce around it. Serve the remaining sauce on the side.

Yield: Four to six servings.

Riz Pilaf
(Rice pilaf)

2 tablespoons butter	Salt and freshly ground pepper
3 tablespoons finely chopped onion	1 bay leaf
1 cup long-grain rice	2 sprigs fresh parsley
1½ cups water	3 sprigs fresh thyme
	Tabasco sauce to taste

1. Melt butter in saucepan and add the onion. Cook, stirring, until wilted.

2. Add the rice and stir. Add the water, salt and pepper to taste, bay leaf, parsley, thyme, and Tabasco. Bring to a boil.

3. Cover and cook exactly 17 minutes. Remove the bay leaf and sprigs of parsley and thyme before serving.

Yield: About 2½ cups.

IT IS A WELL-KNOWN FACT THAT CHEFS AND professional cooks in the kitchen have a language—some people call it a code—that is all their own. Various names are given to some dishes—sauces, for example—and if you mention one dish (they run into the thousands), it is unnecessary to go into detail as to how that dish is prepared. There is a word for it.

If you speak of a sauce mousseline, it is not necessary to add that this is a hollandaise to which whipped cream has been added. If you speak of an omelette Agnes Sorel, it is not necessary to elaborate that this is an omelette with mushrooms, chicken purée, and truffles.

In rare cases there may be some indecision as to one dish or another, as happened recently when Roger Fessaguet, one of America's finest chefs and one of the owners of La Caravelle, came into my kitchen in East Hampton.

The subject of a dish called "mouclade" came up. Both he and I were familiar with the name, but we could not recall the contents on the spur of the moment. Shortly thereafter, Mr. Fessaguet came up with three methods for making the dish, and I had found one in a yellowed and battered book on regional French cooking. A mouclade is from an area near Charente where cognac is produced. It is made with mussels taken from a coastal bay in the region.

Subsequently I prepared a mouclade that is excellent and quickly made. Basically, it is little more than steamed mussels served in a sauce that is generally thickened with a little butter and flour and enriched with egg yolk and cream. There are numerous variations on a basic mouclade. Some recipes call for the addition of curry powder, but you would never find this in the original.

A mouclade, I discovered recently, is a fine idea for a Sunday night supper served with a crusty loaf of French bread that had been stuffed with herbs in melted butter.

La Mouclade
(Steamed mussels Charentaise)

5 pounds mussels, about 4 quarts	1 tablespoon butter
1 cup dry white wine	1 tablespoon flour
3 tablespoons coarsely chopped shallots	¾ cup heavy cream
	1 egg yolk
1 bay leaf	Juice of ½ lemon
½ teaspoon dried thyme	¼ cup finely chopped parsley
Freshly ground pepper	

1. Scrub the mussels thoroughly and remove their beards.
2. Put the wine and shallots in a heavy casserole large enough to hold

the mussels. Bring to the boil and cook over high heat until the liquid is reduced to ½ cup.

3. Add the bay leaf, thyme, and pepper to taste. Add the mussels and cover closely with a tight-fitting lid. Cook, shaking the casserole occasionally to redistribute the mussels, about 4 to 6 minutes or until the mussels are opened.

4. Meanwhile, blend the butter and flour to a smooth paste.

5. Using a large scoop, transfer the mussels to a platter. When cool enough to handle, remove the top shell of each mussel. Arrange the mussels in two or three layers in an oval baking dish.

6. There will be about 2 cups of liquid left in the casserole. Cook this down to 1 cup. Add the cream and bring to the boil.

7. Add the butter-flour mixture, a little at a time, while stirring rapidly with a wire whisk. Add the egg yolk and stir rapidly. Remove from the heat.

8. Preheat the broiler.

9. Line a bowl with a sieve and pour the sauce into it. Rub the inside of the sieve with a rubber spatula to extract as much juice as possible from the solids. Add the lemon juice.

10. Spoon the sauce over the mussels and place them under the broiler close to the source of heat. Heat briefly and sprinkle with parsley. Serve in bowls with hot parsley bread.

Yield: Four servings.

Pain Persillé
(Parsley bread)

1 crusty loaf French bread	¼ cup finely minced parsley
6 tablespoons butter	Salt and freshly ground pepper
1 teaspoon finely minced garlic	

1. Preheat the oven to 375 degrees.

2. Using a sharp knife, split the loaf of bread in half lengthwise.

3. Melt the butter in a saucepan and add the garlic, stirring. Stir in the parsley and salt and pepper to taste and remove from the heat. Spoon and brush one half of the bread with the mixture. Cover with the second side, sandwich fashion.

4. Wrap the bread in a sheet of heavy-duty aluminum foil and bake 10 minutes or until piping hot throughout.

Yield: Four servings.

THE PSYCHOLOGY OF EATING IS A CURIOUS thing. Throughout my youth I was taught that oysters were to be eaten during months that had an "r" in them (the months in French with an "r" are identical to those in English). Later we learned that as long as the oysters are briny fresh there is no reason on earth why they can't be eaten from spring until fall. Somehow, however, oysters never taste as good in midsummer as they do when the warm weather passes.

Recently, friends came up from Florida and brought with them a couple of pints of oysters from Apalachicola. They were of exceptional quality—tender and sweet and quintessentially fresh. We dined on them twice, once with a simple mignonette sauce—good vinegar plus finely chopped shallots and coarsely ground black pepper.

For the second meal I cooked them with mushrooms in a quickly made sauce of the oysters' liquid plus shallots, a little white wine and a substantial amount of heavy cream. The name of the sauce is Bercy. The name derives from a quarter of Paris once celebrated as the center of the wine trade.

There are several possible accompaniments for the creamed oysters and mushrooms. They could be served with buttered noodles, over toast points, or with a dish of hot, fluffy cooked rice. On the evening in question I prepared the rice with chopped fresh dill.

The preparation of the oysters is expeditious once the mushrooms and shallots are chopped, so if you intend to serve rice, it is probably best to get it on the stove and cooking before turning your attention to the oyster dish. The rice can stand for up to half an hour without damage once it is cooked. Serve this meal with a salad of tossed greens.

Huîtres et Champignons Bercy
(Oysters and mushrooms Bercy)

2 cups fresh oysters	2 cups thinly sliced mushrooms
½ cup oyster liquor	½ cup dry white wine
3 tablespoons butter	1 cup heavy cream
1 tablespoon flour	Salt and freshly ground pepper
3 tablespoons finely minced shallots	Cayenne pepper to taste
	1 tablespoon chopped parsley

1. Drain the oysters and set the oysters and liquor aside in separate containers.

2. Melt 1 tablespoon of the butter in a saucepan and add the flour, stirring with a wire whisk. Add the oyster liquor, stirring rapidly with the whisk, until smooth and thickened. Set this sauce aside.

3. Melt the remaining two tablespoons of butter in a small skillet and

add the shallots. Stir briefly and add the mushrooms. Cook until the mushrooms are wilted.

4. Add the wine and bring to the boil. Cook down about 5 minutes or until the wine is almost completely reduced.

5. Add the oyster sauce to the skillet. Add the cream and bring to the boil. Cook the mixture about 5 minutes or until the sauce is reduced to 2 cups.

6. Add salt and pepper to taste and a touch of cayenne. Add the oysters and cook just until the sauce is bubbling and the oysters are piping hot. Cook as briefly as possible or the oysters will toughen. Stir in the parsley. Serve with rice or noodles or over buttered toast.

Yield: Four servings.

Riz à l'Aneth
(Rice with dill)

3 tablespoons butter	Salt and freshly ground pepper
⅓ cup minced onion	2 tablespoons finely chopped dill
1½ cups uncooked rice	½ bay leaf
2¼ cups water	Tabasco sauce to taste

1. Preheat the oven to 400 degrees.

2. Melt half the butter in an ovenproof casserole and add the onion. Cook, stirring, until wilted. Add the rice and stir to blend.

3. Add the water, stirring to make certain there are no lumps in the rice. Add all of the remaining ingredients except the butter. Cover with a close-fitting lid, and when the water boils, place the casserole in the oven.

4. Bake exactly 17 minutes. Remove the cover and discard the bay leaf. Using a two-pronged fork, stir in the remaining butter. If the rice is not to be served immediately, keep covered in a warm place.

Yield: Four to six servings.

IT WAS PART OF MY TRAINING, WHEN I WAS A young boy in a Burgundy town about 15 miles from Chablis, that you didn't waste food. Leftover ends of bread were saved for toasting or turning into bread crumbs; leftover scraps of cheese were scraped into a crock to age and blend with garlic and white wine (it was my family's version of a dish called cancoillotte from another region of France), and leftover cooked meat was always turned into a hachis, which is where the English word "hash" comes from.

That is undoubtedly why, to this day, I hesitate to discard any food that can be salvaged for a second meal. I enjoy improvising and creating dishes with whatever happens to be left in the refrigerator. My children have told me that there is nothing that I could not or would not use as a filling for an omelet.

On a recent occasion I found myself with two very fancy leftovers. As often happens, I had entertained my guests with a sort of bouillabaisse with fish and seafood that I had purchased from my local fish market. The contents included monkfish or angelfish, shrimp, eels, clams, and mussels. I had also purchased a small amount of bay scallops and shucked oysters to toss into the soup at the last moment.

Somehow these last ingredients had become hidden in the back of the refrigerator at the time I made the soup, and I happily discovered them two days later, carefully packed and as fresh as the day I had bought them.

With guests coming for dinner that night, I decided against going out for additional scallops. Instead, by blending the two remaining ingredients there would be sufficient food for a party of four.

The dish that I set before my guests that evening required something less than 15 minutes to prepare. I cooked the scallops and oysters with wine, cream, butter, and shallots and it was apparently a success. Not a scrap remained. The dish was served with another hastily made dish, fine buttered noodles and sliced mushrooms.

Coquilles St. Jacques aux Huitres
(Scallops with oysters)

- 2 tablespoons butter
- 2 tablespoons finely chopped shallots
- ½ cup dry white wine
- 1 pint (2 cups) bay scallops
- ½ pint (1 cup) shucked oysters with a little of their natural liquid
- ½ cup heavy cream
- Salt and freshly ground pepper
- 4 tablespoons cold butter, cut into 8 pieces
- 2 tablespoons finely chopped parsley

1. Melt the 2 tablespoons butter in a casserole and add the shallots. Cook, stirring briefly, and add the wine. Cook until the wine evaporates almost entirely.

2. Add the scallops and oysters. Cook, stirring occasionally, about 1½ minutes.

3. Line a saucepan with a strainer and add the scallops and oysters, reserving their juice. Return this juice to the original casserole and cook down about 2 minutes to about ¼ cup.

4. Add the cream and any liquid that has accumulated from the drained scallops and oysters. Add salt and pepper to taste. Cook over high heat about 2 minutes. Add the cold butter bit by bit, stirring. Add the parsley, scallops, and oysters. Serve with noodles.

Yield: Four servings.

Les Nouilles aux Champignons
(Noodles with mushrooms)

½ pound fresh mushrooms	Salt and freshly ground pepper
4 tablespoons butter	½ pound fine noodles
2 tablespoons finely chopped shallots	1 tablespoon finely chopped parsley
1 tablespoon Port wine	

1. Slice the mushrooms thinly and set aside.

2. Melt half the butter in a large saucepan and add the shallots. Cook briefly and add the mushrooms. Cook until the mushrooms give up their liquid. Continue cooking until the liquid almost evaporates. Add the wine and salt and pepper to taste and heat thoroughly. Set aside.

3. Cook the noodles according to package directions and drain. Add the noodles, remaining butter, and parsley to the mushrooms. Stir to blend well and serve.

Yield: Four servings.

THERE IS, IN MY OPINION, ONE SINGLE RAW food which, more than any other, best lends itself to hasty cooking: shellfish.

It is not shrimps, lobsters, oysters, nor clams, for these, more often than not, have to be opened, before or after cooking. Scallops, once purchased at the market, are simply ready to be tossed into a skillet or saucepan for sautéeing or another preparation. They can also be blended with other ingredients, of course, and eaten raw as seviche.

I have on occasion been taken to task by one reader or another when I have printed recipes that call for blending scallops with herbs and spices for, they say, "Scallops are so delicious in themselves, why complicate matters?"

I do understand the point. And at the beginning of the scallop season each year, I generally begin the season by only broiling them or sautéeing them quickly in butter. And yet, to my palate, there is a good deal to be said for scallops meunière, floured, cooked quickly in oil and then with a little melted butter and chopped parsley poured over.

I also greatly enjoy such a preparation as a gratin of scallops, blending them with mushrooms, garlic, bread crumbs, and parsley and cooking them briefly when stuffed in a shell.

However they are cooked, it is essential they be cooked as quickly as possible. If scallops are subjected to a prolonged cooking time they become dry, tough, and unpalatable.

Coquilles St. Jacques Meunière
(Scallops quick-fried in butter)

2 cups (1 pint) bay scallops	4 tablespoons butter
¼ cup milk	Juice of half a lemon
Flour for dredging	2 tablespoons finely chopped parsley
Salt and freshly ground pepper	
5 tablespoons peanut, vegetable, or corn oil	

1. Empty the scallops into a bowl and add the milk, stirring to coat. Let stand briefly.

2. Place the flour in a dish and add salt and pepper to taste. Blend well. Drain the scallops. Dredge them in the flour and put them into a large sieve. Shake to remove any excess flour. Scatter the scallops onto a sheet of foil or wax paper so that they do not touch or they might stick together.

3. The scallops must be cooked over high heat without crowding. Heat 3 tablespoons of the oil and 1 tablespoon of the butter in a large skillet. When the mixture is quite hot but not smoking, add half of the scallops, shaking and tossing them in the skillet so that they cook quickly and evenly until golden brown on all sides.

4. Using a slotted spoon, transfer the scallops to a hot platter. Add the remaining 2 tablespoons of oil to the skillet, and when it is quite hot add the remaining scallops, shaking and tossing them in the skillet as before. When brown, transfer them to the platter with the other scallops. Wipe out the skillet and add the remaining butter and cook until lightly browned or the color of hazelnuts. Sprinkle over the scallops. Then sprinkle the scallops with the lemon juice and chopped parsley.

Yield: Four servings.

Gratin de Coquilles St. Jacques
(Breaded scallops in shells)

8 tablespoons butter at room temperature	1 tablespoon finely chopped garlic
1 cup thinly sliced mushrooms	2 cups (1 pint) fresh bay scallops
3 tablespoons finely chopped shallots	½ cup bread crumbs
	½ cup finely chopped parsley
	Salt and freshly ground pepper

1. Preheat the oven to 450 degrees.
2. Melt 4 tablespoons of butter in a small skillet and add the mushrooms. Cook, stirring often, until the mushrooms are wilted and give up their liquid. Add the shallots and garlic and cook briefly.
3. Spoon the mushroom mixture into a serving bowl. Let cool briefly. Add 2 tablespoons soft butter, the scallops, bread crumbs, parsley, and salt and pepper to taste to the mushrooms. Blend well.
4. Use the mixture to fill six seafood shells.
5. Arrange the filled shells on a baking dish. Melt the remaining butter and pour it over the scallops and place in the oven. Bake 10 minutes. Run the scallops under the broiler until nicely browned on top, about 1 minute.

Yield: Six servings.

I WAS REMINISCING RECENTLY ABOUT THE number of flavors and ingredients that have been introduced within a relatively recent period into my kitchen. They include basil (and pesto sauce); arugula, which goes into numerous salads in my home; scungili or conch, which I have grown to enjoy in cold salads with oil, lemon, and garlic, and, most interestingly, perhaps, fresh ginger.

It almost goes without saying, of course, that I have been exposed to ginger in one or more of its various forms all my life—candied ginger, ginger in syrup and even ginger powder. My first acquaintance with fresh ginger came about, I believe, when I spent many hours in the kitchen with my friend Virginia Lee, who visits me once in a while to "cook Chinese."

I have put fresh ginger to many uses, adapting it to the French stove, over the past few years. One of the best soufflés I know is a ginger soufflé served with a ginger sauce.

One of my most recent forays into ginger territory came about when I was cooking fresh scallops. I was preparing them for guests, using various winter vegetables such as carrots, zucchini, and leeks, plus butter and cream, when it suddenly occurred that a touch of fresh ginger would give a welcome Oriental flavor to the meal. It did. I am also fascinated with the thought that I can buy fresh ginger in my local supermarket in East Hampton.

Coquilles St. Jacques au Gingembre
(Scallops with fresh ginger)

1 large or 2 small carrots, trimmed and scraped	2 tablespoons finely chopped fresh ginger
1 small zucchini, ends trimmed	½ cup dry white wine
1 small leek, trimmed	½ cup heavy cream
10 tablespoons butter	Salt and freshly ground pepper
2 tablespoons finely chopped shallots	1¼ pounds bay scallops

1. Cut the carrot into 1½-inch lengths. Cut each length into quarter-inch-thick slices. Cut each slice into quarter-inch-wide bâtonnets, which is to say small, match-like sticks. There should be about ¾ of a cup.

2. Cut the zucchini into bâtonnets of the same size as the carrots. There should be about 1 cup.

3. Cut the leek into 1½-inch lengths. Cut the lengths into thin slices. Shred the slices. There should be about ¾ of a cup.

4. Melt 2 tablespoons of the butter in a skillet and add the shallots. Cook briefly, stirring, and add the carrots. Cook, stirring, about 30 seconds and add the ginger. Cook, stirring briefly, and add the wine. Let

the wine reduce almost completely and add the cream and salt and pepper to taste. Cook down over high heat until the sauce is reduced by half.

5. Add the scallops, zucchini, and leeks. Cook, stirring, about 1 minute and swirl in the remaining butter.

Yield: Four servings.

Boiled Rice

4 cups water	**1 tablespoon butter**
Salt	**Freshly ground pepper**
1 cup long grain rice	**1 teaspoon lemon juice**

1. Bring the water to a boil in a saucepan and add salt to taste and the rice. When the water returns to the boil, let the rice cook in the vigorously boiling water for exactly 17 minutes. Drain in a colander and run hot water over the rice. Drain again.

2. Put the drained rice into a serving dish and add the butter, salt and pepper to taste, and the lemon juice. Toss until the rice grains are coated.

Yield: Four servings.

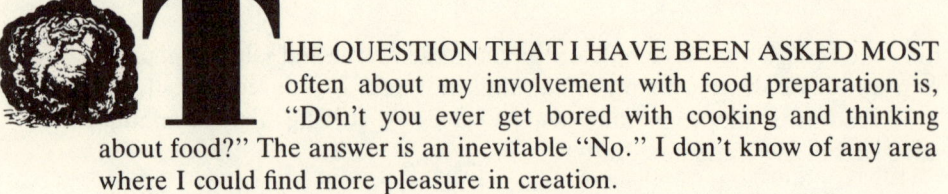

THE QUESTION THAT I HAVE BEEN ASKED MOST often about my involvement with food preparation is, "Don't you ever get bored with cooking and thinking about food?" The answer is an inevitable "No." I don't know of any area where I could find more pleasure in creation.

There are many ways to create recipes, of course: change the flavor of a food by altering the herbs and spices, or change a dish by altering what the food is served on. Recently I prepared scallops provençale, and varied the dish by cooking a half-pound of spinach noodles and turning the meal into a pasta affair.

A provençale sauce is one of the easiest and quickest of all tomato sauces to prepare. And the scallops must be cooked as hastily as possible to avoid overcooking.

For those reasons, it is best, if you intend to serve the scallops with spinach noodles or any other pasta, to have a kettle of boiling water ready to accept the pasta simultaneously with the cooking of the scallops.

Spinach Noodles with Scallops Provençale

1 pint bay scallops	¾ cup flour
¼ cup milk	½ cup peanut, vegetable, or corn oil
1½ pounds red, ripe tomatoes, or use 3 cups partly drained canned tomatoes	½ pound spinach noodles
	3 tablespoons butter
1 bay leaf	1 tablespoon finely minced garlic
Salt and freshly ground pepper	2 tablespoons chopped parsley

1. Put the scallops in a mixing bowl and add the milk. Set aside.

2. If fresh tomatoes are used, peel them and cut them into one-inch cubes. There should be about 3 cups.

3. Put the tomatoes in a skillet and heat thoroughly. Place a sieve in a mixing bowl and pour the tomatoes into the sieve. Return the juice from the tomatoes to the skillet and cook down until reduced by half. Add the tomato pulp, bay leaf, and salt and pepper to taste. Set aside.

4. Drain the scallops well. Toss them in the flour.

5. Heat the oil in one large or two medium-sized skillets.

6. When the oil is very hot and almost smoking, add a few of the scallops. It is important that the scallops be cooked a few at a time. They must not touch, or they will not brown. Cook the scallops over very high heat, shaking the skillet or skillets so that they brown evenly. Use a slotted spoon and, as the scallops brown, transfer them to another dish. Continue adding the scallops to the skillet or skillets and cooking until all the scallops are browned.

7. Combine the scallops and tomato sauce.

8. Meanwhile, cook the noodles according to package directions and drain.

9. Melt the butter in a clean skillet until it is nut brown. Add the garlic and cook briefly.

10. Combine the noodles, scallops in tomato sauce, and garlic butter. Toss well. Sprinkle with parsley and serve.

Yield: Four servings.

Salade avec Croûtons à l'Ail
(Romaine lettuce with garlic croutons)

1 small head romaine lettuce	2 teaspoons imported mustard such as Dijon or Düsseldorf
3 very thin slices white bread	Salt and freshly ground pepper
3 tablespoons olive oil	2 teaspoons red wine vinegar
2 cloves garlic, peeled but left whole	¼ cup olive oil

1. Trim the ends off the lettuce. Pull the leaves apart and rinse well. Pat dry.

2. Trim the bread of crusts. Cut the bread into ½-inch cubes or smaller. There should be about 1 cup.

3. Heat the oil in a skillet, and when hot add the bread and garlic cloves. Cook, shaking the skillet and stirring, until the cubes of bread are golden brown. Drain in a sieve. Discard the garlic cloves or not, as you wish.

4. Cut or tear the lettuce leaves into bite-size pieces. There should be about 8 cups loosely packed. Put the leaves in a salad bowl and sprinkle the croutons over the leaves.

5. Put the mustard in a small mixing bowl with salt and pepper to taste. Add the vinegar and beat with a wire whisk. Add the oil, beating briskly with the whisk. Pour the dressing over the salad and toss.

Yield: Four servings.

We live in an age when almost any comestible can be purchased and cooked almost any season of the year. Foods that were once culinary treasures of spring or summer can now be bought in the middle of winter: asparagus, strawberries, even, at times, corn on the cob. As a consequence, the foods that I treasure most are those that are available at the precise moment of harvest. Perhaps the greatest of foods in this category are bay scallops. There is nothing that can be cooked with greater speed to produce more elegant and tasty results.

The name for scallops is, in French, coquille St. Jacques, and, as often as the season for scallops rolls around, someone inevitably asks me the origin of that name. Coquille St. Jacques translates as the shell of St. James, and the origin of the name dates to the Middle Ages. A shrine built to the memory of St. James the Apostle is at Santiago de Compostela in Spain. Years ago, pilgrims who visited the shrine wore the scallop shell in their hats as a symbol. Thus the name. There is another name for scallops in French, petoncles, but it is seldom used on menus.

Scallops, because of their delicate, subtle nature, make a fine marriage with any number of other foods and seasonings. One of the most interesting combinations is scallops in a cream sauce with a touch of mustard. The mustard must be used sparingly so as not to overpower the dish. But used with discretion, it has great merit.

Ideal dishes to accompany scallops in a mustard cream sauce are noodles enhanced with a few sliced mushrooms and a cucumber and dill salad.

Coquilles St. Jacques Sauce Crème et Moutarde
(Scallops in a cream and mustard sauce)

- 1 pound scallops, preferably bay scallops
- 1 tablespoon butter
- 1 tablespoon finely chopped shallots
- 2 tablespoons red wine vinegar
- 1 cup heavy cream
- Salt
- 1 tablespoon imported prepared mustard such as Dijon or Düsseldorf
- 1 tablespoon finely chopped parsley

1. If sea scallops are used, cut them into quarters and set aside. If bay scallops are used, leave them whole.

2. Heat 1 tablespoon butter in a skillet and add the shallots. Cook briefly, stirring. Add the vinegar. Cook until almost all the vinegar is evaporated.

3. Add the cream and cook down over high heat until reduced by half. Add the scallops and salt to taste.

4. Cook, shaking the skillet so that the scallops cook evenly, about 1

minute. Remove from the heat and swirl in the mustard. Serve sprinkled with chopped parsley.

Yield: Four servings.

Noodles with Mushrooms

- ½ pound egg noodles
- 2 tablespoons butter
- ½ pound fresh mushrooms, thinly sliced, about 2½ cups
- 1 tablespoon chopped parsley
- Salt and freshly ground pepper

1. Bring enough water for the noodles to the boil.
2. Melt the butter in a skillet and add the mushrooms. Cook until mushrooms give up their liquid. Continue cooking until the liquid evaporates.
3. Cook the noodles until tender and drain quickly. Return them to the hot pot and add the mushrooms, the remaining tablespoon butter, and parsley. Add salt and pepper to taste and toss.

Yield: Four servings.

Cucumber and Dill Salad

- 1 to 3 cucumbers, depending on size
- 1 tablespoon sugar
- Salt
- ¼ cup white vinegar
- 2 tablespoons chopped fresh dill
- Freshly ground pepper, preferably white pepper

1. Peel the cucumbers and split them in half. Scoop out the seeds with a melon-ball cutter. If so-called "gourmet" cucumbers are used, it is not necessary to cut them in half or to remove the seeds.
2. Slice the cucumbers crosswise. There should be about 4 cups. Put the slices in a mixing bowl. Add the remaining ingredients and toss to blend. Add more seasonings, such as vinegar, sugar, and so on to taste, if desired.

Yield: Four servings.

ONE OF THE MOST DELICATE AND COVETED deep-fried foods is Coquilles St. Jacques panées à l'Anglaise, that is, scallops breaded and deep fried. The essential factor is speed, to which this book is dedicated. The scallops should be cooked as briefly as possible, just until they lose their "raw" look in the center. If overcooked they become chewy and tasteless.

The breading technique is simplicity itself. You put flour in one dish, beaten egg in another, and fine fresh bread crumbs in a third. You coat the scallops in that order—first in flour, then in an egg wash and finally in bread crumbs. You don't need a great deal of oil (from as little as one cup to twice that, depending on the skillet's size) but it must be piping hot.

It is best to cook the scallops in two or three batches. Don't crowd them or they will not brown properly. Shake the skillet and stir the scallops when they are added. The total cooking time for each batch is two minutes or less. Each batch should be drained after cooking and must be served quickly.

The classic accompaniment is a tartar sauce. But not, heaven forbid, that dreadful concoction served in some American restaurants consisting of bottled mayonnaise with pickle relish and chopped onions. The greatest tartar sauce is made with fresh mayonnaise, chopped pickles—preferably small imported gherkins—capers and chopped onions.

An excellent side dish is a cold salad of shredded carrots and celery with a light vinaigrette sauce flavored with a touch of ground cumin.

Coquilles St. Jacques Panées à l'Anglaise
(Deep-fried breaded scallops)

1½ pints fresh bay scallops	Salt and freshly ground pepper
½ cup flour	2 cups fine, fresh bread crumbs
1 egg	Peanut or vegetable oil for deep frying
2 tablespoons water	
1 tablespoon peanut or vegetable oil	

1. If the source of the scallops is uncertain, rinse in cold water and drain.

2. Put flour in a flat, shallow dish.

3. Put the egg in another flat, shallow dish. Beat lightly and add the water, 1 tablespoon oil, and salt and pepper to taste. Blend well.

4. Put the bread crumbs in another flat, shallow dish.

5. Put the scallops in the dish with the flour and toss to coat well.

6. Transfer the coated scallops to the egg dish and toss to coat.

7. Transfer the scallops to the bread crumbs and toss to coat thoroughly. Put the coated scallops in another dish, separating them so they do not touch.

8. Heat the oil for deep frying in a skillet. There should be slightly less

than an inch of oil. When it is hot but not quite smoking, add about one-third of the scallops. Do not overcrowd. Cook the scallops, shaking the skillet and stirring the scallops so that they brown evenly. Use a slotted or perforated spoon. It will take about 2 minutes until they are golden brown.

9. Transfer the scallops to paper toweling to drain.

10. Add another batch of scallops and continue cooking until all the scallops are done. Serve hot with tartar sauce (see recipe).

Yield: Four to six servings.

Sauce Tartare

- 1 egg yolk
- 2 teaspoons mustard such as Dijon or Düsseldorf
- 2 teaspoons red wine vinegar
- 1 cup peanut or vegetable oil
  Salt and freshly ground pepper
- ¼ teaspoon Worcestershire sauce
- 2 tablespoons finely chopped onion
- 2 tablespoons finely chopped cornichons (imported French sour pickles)
- 1 tablespoon chopped capers

1. Put the yolk in a mixing bowl and add the mustard and vinegar.

2. Stir with a wire whisk and gradually add the oil. Beat briskly until all the oil is added.

3. Add salt and pepper to taste, Worcestershire sauce, onion, cornichons, and capers. Blend well.

Yield: About 1¼ cups.

Carrotte et Celeri Salade
(Carrot and celery salad)

- 4 cups grated or shredded carrots, about 1 pound
- 1 cup finely shredded celery, about ½ pound
- ¼ cup finely chopped onion
- 1 teaspoon ground cumin
- 3 tablespoons white vinegar
- 6 tablespoons peanut or vegetable oil
- 1 teaspoon sugar
  Salt and freshly ground pepper
  Tabasco sauce to taste

1. You may grate or shred the carrots and celery by hand, but they will be prepared more quickly if they are shredded using a food processor.

2. Put carrots and celery in a bowl.

3. Add the remaining ingredients and toss to blend.

Yield: Four to six servings.

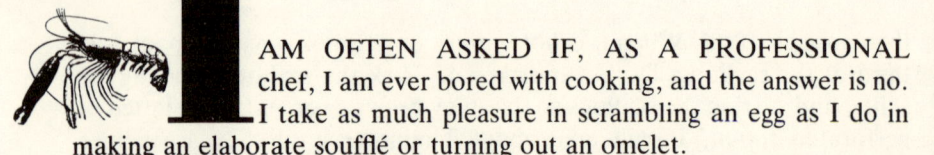

I AM OFTEN ASKED IF, AS A PROFESSIONAL chef, I am ever bored with cooking, and the answer is no. I take as much pleasure in scrambling an egg as I do in making an elaborate soufflé or turning out an omelet.

There is one form of cookery that fascinates me as much as any, however, and that is barbecuing. That is because it is probably the most inexact "science" of any form of cookery. There are so many factors involved: the intensity of the heat, the direction of the wind, the placement of the grill in relation to the source of heat, the nature of the food to be grilled and so on.

Theoretically, grilling or broiling over charcoal should demand more care than most forms of cooking, and yet the latitude allowed the charcoal cook is greater than in more serious forms of cookery. If the surface of a grilled food is a bit charred, that is forgivable. If the leg of lamb turns out to be a bit rare or the chicken a bit overcooked, that's acceptable, too. Within reason.

It almost goes without saying that fish and shellfish are the most delicate of foods that are cooked over charcoal. And woe to the cook who produces an overcooked fillet of fish. In summer I enjoy cooking shrimp on the grill and, preferably, with grilled vegetables cooked alongside.

The base for my marinade is a simple dressing of oil and vinegar or oil and lemon that can be varied a dozen or a thousand different ways. It generally depends on the flavors I find in my herb garden or refrigerator. On a recent occasion these turned out to be fresh ginger root, fresh thyme, and parsley. You can take the oil and lemon base in the recipe outlined here and make your own substitutions. Substitute fresh rosemary for the ginger and parsley, or fresh tarragon or vinegar for the lemon juice and so on.

This is one of the simplest and hastiest of summer meals to prepare. The cooking time for the shrimp is about 5 minutes; the cooking time for the vegetables—in this case zucchini and tomatoes—is 10 minutes. The foods are cooked, of course, simultaneously.

Scampi Grillées
(Charcoal-broiled shrimp)

24 large shrimp, about two pounds
   Salt and freshly ground pepper
1 tablespoon finely chopped fresh ginger
¼ teaspoon dried hot red pepper flakes
2 tablespoons finely chopped parsley

1 bay leaf
½ teaspoon chopped fresh thyme or ¼ teaspoon dried thyme
2 tablespoons olive oil
   Juice of half a lemon
6 tablespoons butter
1 clove garlic, crushed

1. Preheat a charcoal broiler.
2. Using a pair of kitchen shears, cut along the upper rim of the shrimp. You may peel the shrimp or not, according to taste. If you peel them, leave the last tail segment intact. Whether you peel them or not, run the shrimp under cold running water and remove the black vein along the back. Pat the shrimp dry.
3. Combine the shrimp, salt and pepper to taste, ginger, pepper flakes, parsley, bay leaf, thyme, olive oil, and lemon juice in a mixing bowl. Let stand at room temperature for 30 minutes.
4. Put the shrimp on the broiler and cook about 1 or 2 minutes. Turn and cook 2 to 3 minutes on the other side. Transfer the shrimp to a warm serving dish.
5. Melt the butter with the garlic in a saucepan. When bubbling, discard the garlic. Pour the butter over the shrimp and serve.

Yield: Four servings.

Légumes Grillés
(Grilled vegetables)

4 medium-size zucchini, about 1¼ pounds	4 tablespoons olive oil
4 red, ripe, firm tomatoes	2 tablespoons finely chopped fresh basil
Salt and freshly ground pepper	

1. Preheat a charcoal broiler.
2. Trim off the ends of the zucchini. Split the zucchini lengthwise in half.
3. Using a sharp paring knife, score the flesh of each zucchini half without cutting into the skin. Arrange them scored side up.
4. Cut neatly around the core of each tomato and remove it. Cut each tomato in half crosswise. Arrange the tomato halves cut side up.
5. Sprinkle the zucchini and tomatoes with salt and pepper to taste and brush with the oil.
6. Put the tomatoes and zucchini cut side down on the broiler. Cook about 3 to 4 minutes. Turn and cook about 6 minutes on the second side. Transfer to a serving dish. Sprinkle with basil and serve.

Yield: Four servings.

THERE ARE CERTAIN FOODS IN THE WORLD that, for economy-minded cooks, are destined for special occasions. Some of the more obvious examples are two-inch-thick porterhouse steaks, racks of lamb, and dishes with truffles.

In recent years, unfortunately, it has been necessary to include shrimp in that category. Shrimp rarely figure in my repertoire for the simple reason that today they are one of the world's luxury foods, a dish for special occasions.

The adaptability of shrimp to hasty cookery is obvious and often stated. They must be cooked in seconds for maximum flavor and texture. Overcooking renders them tough and chewy. This recipe for shrimp with vegetables in a cognac-scented sauce would fall into the category of nouvelle cuisine. There is no flour used in the sauce, and the vegetables are cut into fine julienne strips, or are chopped or thinly sliced. They are cooked as briefly as possible, just until they lose their raw taste while retaining an al dente texture.

The initial preparation of the various vegetables is more time consuming than the actual cooking. The total cooking time, in fact, is 10 minutes or less.

The ideal accompaniment for this dish—in its light cream sauce flavored with cognac—is rice. And broiled tomatoes. To prepare such a menu, it is best to make all the preparations for the shrimp in advance. Peel them, chop or slice the vegetables and so on. Get the tomatoes ready for broiling. And then start the rice, which takes less than 20 minutes. Once the tomatoes are under the broiler, start cooking the shrimp.

Crevettes Jardinière
(Shrimp and vegetables cognac)

1½ pounds raw shrimp	1 cup sweet pepper, red or green, cut into thin, julienne strips
5 tablespoons butter	
Salt and freshly ground pepper	2 cups thinly sliced mushrooms
3 tablespoons finely chopped shallots	3 tablespoons cognac
	½ cup heavy cream
1 cup finely chopped celery	

1. Peel and devein the shrimp. Rinse well in cold water and pat dry.

2. Melt 2 tablespoons of the butter in a skillet and add the shrimp. Salt and pepper to taste. Cook, stirring the shrimp over high heat so that they cook evenly, for about 2 minutes. Cook only until the shrimp turn pink and lose their raw look.

3. Using a slotted spoon, remove the shrimp and put in a bowl. Add one more tablespoon butter to the skillet and add the shallots. Cook briefly, stirring.

4. Add the celery, pepper strips, and mushrooms. Cook about 2 minutes.

5. Sprinkle with cognac and add the cream. Bring to a boil. Add any liquid that has accumulated from the shrimp. Cook about 30 seconds and add the shrimp. Cook until shrimp are thoroughly heated. Swirl in the remaining 2 tablespoons of butter.

Yield: Four servings.

Riz Persillé
(Parsleyed rice)

3 tablespoons butter	Salt and freshly ground pepper
2 tablespoons chopped onion	Tabasco sauce to taste
1 cup raw rice	2 tablespoons finely chopped parsley
1½ cups water	
1 bay leaf	

1. Melt 2 tablespoons of the butter in a saucepan and add the onion. Cook until wilted. Add the rice and stir briefly.
2. Add the water, bay leaf, salt and pepper to taste, and Tabasco.
3. Bring to a boil. Cover and simmer 20 minutes.
4. Add the remaining tablespoon of butter and parsley. Stir to blend.

Yield: Four servings.

Tomates Grillées
(Broiled tomatoes)

2 ripe tomatoes	Salt and freshly ground pepper
2 tablespoons olive oil	2 cloves garlic, peeled

1. Preheat the broiler. Spread 1 tablespoon of oil on the inside of a baking dish.
2. Cut the tomatoes in half and arrange them in the oiled baking dish. Sprinkle with salt and pepper to taste.
3. Cut the garlic in about 16 thin slivers. Stud the tomato halves with the slivers and sprinkle with the remaining oil.
4. Place under the broiler and broil about 5 minutes or until garlic slivers start to burn. Discard the garlic and serve.

Yield: Four servings.

ONE OF THE MOST CELEBRATED LEGENDS IN French cooking has to do with dishes named imam bayeldi. It seems that the imam married a beautiful young woman whose dowry was copious vats of pure olive oil. Shortly after the wedding, she came to him and asked him to order more oil. He asked what had happened to her dowry and she replied that she had used it all in cooking his favorite food, eggplant. The imam, the story goes, fainted, which is what imam bayeldi, roughly translated, means.

Eggplants are notorious for their absorbent quality when fried in oil and, therefore, many dishes made with eggplant or aubergines in French cookery are labeled imam bayeldi. But I recently concocted a dish of fresh, shelled shrimp on a bed of eggplant and tomato—eggplant marries well with nothing so much as tomatoes—and I found a quarter of a cup of oil quite sufficient for browning four slices of eggplant.

Crevettes Imam Bayeldi
(Shrimp with tomatoes and eggplant)

24 raw shrimp in the shell, about 1¾ pounds	4 tablespoons butter
1 medium-size eggplant, about 1 pound	2 teaspoons finely minced garlic
¼ cup flour	3 tablespoons freshly grated Parmesan cheese
Salt and freshly ground pepper	2 tablespoons finely chopped parsley
¼ cup olive oil	
1 cup well-drained canned tomatoes	

1. Preheat the broiler to high.
2. Shell and devein the shrimp and set aside.
3. Cut a thin slice off the top and bottom of the eggplant. Cut the eggplant into four lengthwise slices, each slice of more or less the same width.
4. Dredge the eggplant slices on both sides in flour seasoned with salt and pepper to taste.
5. Heat the oil in a skillet and when it is quite hot, brown the eggplant on both sides, about 1 or 2 minutes to a side. As the slices are browned transfer them to paper toweling to drain.
6. Arrange the eggplant slices in a baking dish in one layer. Top each slice with ¼ cup of drained tomatoes, distributing the tomatoes evenly over the slices.
7. Melt 2 tablespoons of the butter in a large, heavy skillet and add the shrimp. Cook, stirring often so that they cook evenly, about 1½ to 2 minutes or just until they lose their raw look.
8. Arrange six shrimp over each eggplant slice.

9. Melt the remaining 2 tablespoons of butter in a skillet and add the garlic, swirling it around until it starts to change color and is slightly browned. Do not let the butter burn. Pour an equal part of butter over each portion. Sprinkle with cheese.

10. Run the dish under the broiler about 3 minutes. Sprinkle with parsley and serve.

Yield: Four servings.

Riz au Four
(Baked rice)

2½	tablespoons butter	3	sprigs parsley
2	tablespoons minced onion	1	sprig fresh thyme or ¼ teaspoon dried thyme
½	teaspoon minced garlic		
1	cup uncooked rice	½	bay leaf
1½	cups chicken broth		

1. Preheat the oven to 400 degrees.

2. Melt half the butter in a heavy saucepan. Add the onion and garlic and cook, stirring with a wooden spoon, until the onion is translucent. Add the rice and stir briefly over low heat until the grains are coated with butter.

3. Stir in the stock, making sure there are no lumps in the rice. Add the parsley, thyme, and bay leaf. Cover with a close-fitting lid and bake for exactly 17 minutes. Remove the cover and discard the parsley, thyme, and bay leaf.

4. Using a two-pronged fork, stir in the remaining butter. If the rice is not to be served immediately, keep it covered in a warm place.

Yield: Four servings.

Note: Like most dishes, this rice is best if served as soon as it is baked, but it may be made as much as half an hour in advance as long as it is kept tightly covered and warm.

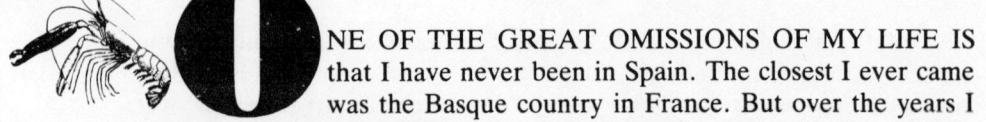

ONE OF THE GREAT OMISSIONS OF MY LIFE IS that I have never been in Spain. The closest I ever came was the Basque country in France. But over the years I have dined with friends who are excellent cooks in the Spanish tradition. One of the most memorable "Spanish" dishes I've ever sampled was in San Juan, Puerto Rico. Now, it's an established fact that San Juan is, unfortunately, not all that celebrated as a restaurant mecca, but on the evening in question we dined at a small, unpretentious place called La Fragua in the Caprice Hotel. The food, overall, was excellent, but the triumph of the evening was a dish of fish in a green sauce. The chef explained to me that the fish was called "mero," which, I believe, is grouper and is not available at my local fish markets.

One recent evening I found myself with a generous amount of shrimp, and suddenly the memory of that meal in San Juan came back to me. It occurred to me that the same sauce I had dined on there would be as admirable on shrimp as it would be on fish. The sauce is a fine, robust concoction, heavily spiced with garlic and containing white wine, clam juice, a good deal of fresh parsley, and green peas. And one of the benefits of the dish is, of course, that it is easily and quickly made in the home kitchen. As a matter of fact, in my modification, I have eliminated an ingredient or two. The sauce in Puerto Rico also contained asparagus, clams, and was garnished with hard-cooked eggs.

The ideal accompaniment for shrimp in green sauce is rice with pine nuts. The best way to accomplish this meal in less than an hour is to prepare and have ready for cooking all the ingredients for both dishes. Get the rice dish going and then start cooking the shrimp. It can be cooked and ready for the table almost simultaneously with the rice.

Crevettes en Salsa Verde
(Shrimp in green sauce)

- 1 pound raw shrimp
- Salt and freshly ground pepper
- 2 tablespoons plus 4 teaspoons flour
- ⅓ cup olive oil
- ¼ cup chopped green onions
- 1 tablespoon finely chopped garlic
- ¾ cup fish broth or clam juice (bottled clam juice may be used)
- ½ cup dry white wine
- ¼ teaspoon dried hot red pepper flakes
- ½ cup finely chopped parsley
- ½ cup green peas, preferably fresh, cooked briefly in boiling salted water and drained

1. Peel and devein the shrimp but leave the last tail segment intact.

2. Sprinkle with salt and pepper to taste and coat on all sides with 2 tablespoons flour. Shake off any excess flour.

3. Heat the oil in a skillet large enough to hold the shrimp in one layer.

4. Add the shrimp and cook about 45 seconds on one side. Turn and cook about 45 seconds on the second side. Quickly transfer the shrimp to another skillet. Leave the oil in the original skillet.

5. To the oil in the skillet add the remaining 4 teaspoons of flour, stirring with a whisk. Add the chopped green onions and garlic, stirring. Add the fish broth and wine and stir. Cook over moderately high heat, stirring often, for about 1 minute and add the pepper flakes.

6. Add the parsley and stir to blend.

7. Spoon the sauce over the shrimp and add the peas. Stir. Bring to the boil. Simmer about 2 minutes. Serve piping hot with rice.

Yield: Four servings.

Rice with Pine Nuts

¼ **cup pine nuts**	1 **cup raw rice**
3 **tablespoons butter**	1½ **cups chicken broth**
¼ **cup finely chopped onion**	**Salt and freshly ground pepper**
½ **teaspoon finely minced garlic**	

1. Put the pine nuts in a skillet and cook, shaking the skillet and stirring, until the nuts are nicely browned. Take care not to overcook and burn. Pour the pine nuts into a saucer and set aside.

2. Melt 2 tablespoons of butter in a heavy saucepan and add the onion and garlic. Cook, stirring, until the onion wilts

3. Add the rice and stir. Add the broth and salt and pepper to taste. Bring to the boil and cover. Cook over low heat for 17 minutes.

4. Stir in the remaining butter and the pine nuts and serve.

Yield: Four servings.

SINCE THE TERM NOUVELLE CUISINE WAS first coined more than a dozen years ago, I have spent many hours in the company of numerous chefs from America, France, Switzerland, and Germany, all of them practitioners of this so-called "new" form of cookery. One of several things that I find considerably interesting is that they take pride in their salads. The unusual aspect of this is that, until nouvelle cuisine came into being, salads rarely played an important role in traditional menus.

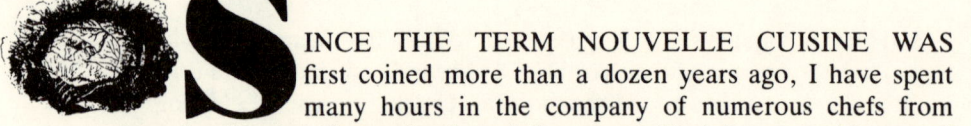

Of course, there have been salads in French cuisine since long before Escoffier, but they never gained much prominence. There was the traditional salad made with tossed greens plus oil and vinegar and perhaps a bit of mustard. But this served primarily as an accompaniment for cheese. There were other salads like a combination of endive and beets; salade russe with a complicated blend of vegetables such as string beans, green peas, turnips, and so on blended with mayonaise; and salads with names like Rachel, consisting of julienne of celery, truffles, artichoke bottoms, and black olives with an anchovy vinaigrette. And, of course, salad niçoise.

But salads as a substantial matter of pride were rare if they existed at all. Now crisp greens blended with hot or lukewarm meats on the order of sliced, freshly roasted breast of squab, or grilled beef or hot, freshly poached lobster are very much in vogue.

One of the simplest of these, a salad of recent creation in my kitchen, consists of various greens such as endive, Boston lettuce, and spinach tossed at the last minute with hot shrimp that have been cooked briefly in oil with Chinese pea pods, a dash of pepper-flakes, and deglazed with red wine vinegar. The vinegar makes a nice foil for the shrimp and actually gives them a meaty, slightly sweet flavor that they might not otherwise possess. This is an excellent salad for a hastily made and elegant summer luncheon, although it could easily serve as a first course for a more complicated meal. A fine accompaniment for it as a luncheon dish would be a hot Parmesan cheese bread made with a loaf of French bread split in half and baked until crisp on top.

Salade de Crevettes Chaudes
(Salad with warm shrimp)

1¼	pounds medium-size shrimp	1	small head Boston lettuce, trimmed and cut into bite-size pieces, about 3 to 4 cups
16	large, firm, unblemished spinach leaves, trimmed of tough stems, rinsed well and patted dry	¾	cup olive oil Salt
16	white, trimmed unblemished endive leaves		Freshly ground pepper Trimmed green pea pods, optional

¼ teaspoon dried hot red pepper flakes	¼ cup red wine vinegar
4 thin slices red onions, broken into rings	2 tablespoons finely chopped fresh dill
	3 tablespoons finely chopped chives

1. Peel and devein the shrimp and set aside.
2. Arrange 4 lettuce leaves on each of the four individual serving dishes. Dinner plates are recommended. Arrange alternate leaves of endive between the spinach leaves.
3. Arrange equal portions of Boston lettuce in the center of each serving.
4. Heat the oil in a skillet and add the shrimp. Cook, stirring, about 30 seconds. Add the pea pods and pepper flakes. Cook, stirring, about 1½ minutes.
5. Add the wine vinegar and cook about 30 seconds. Add the dill and toss. Spoon the shrimp and the sauce over the salad greens. Sprinkle with chopped chives and serve.

Yield: Four servings.

Parmesan Cheese Bread

1 large, crusty loaf French or Italian bread	½ teaspoon finely minced garlic, optional
⅓ cup olive oil	
⅓ cup freshly grated Parmesan cheese	

1. Preheat the oven to 450 degrees.
2. Split the loaf of bread in half lengthwise.
3. Brush the split sides with equal quantities of oil. Sprinkle with cheese. If the garlic is to be used, add it to the oil before brushing the bread.
4. Arrange the halves split side up in a baking dish. Place in the oven and bake 10 minutes.

Yield: Four servings.

IT SEEMS TO ME THAT ONE OF THE GREAT lacks in American cooking is a dictionary or encyclopedia that catalogues in a protracted and definitive sense the foods of this nation. There are several volumes that pretend to do so, but there are dozens, if not hundreds, of gaps in each of them. There is clearly no volume in this country that has done for the nation's kitchens what *Larousse Gastronomique* has done for the French.

This came to mind for the umpteenth time when a guest and I got into a discussion about the components of dishes known as impérial, most notably crab impérial. It was my guest's contention that it is prepared by making a very spicy mayonnaise containing mustard, Worcestershire sauce, and Tabasco. The seafood is blended with this, stuffed into shells, and baked.

I remembered dining with a chef from Louisiana who prepared the dish with sautéed green peppers, onion, and celery in a cream sauce to which a touch of sherry had been added. And this is the version that I admire the most. The chopped vegetables give the dish a nice crunchy contrast to the seafood.

This raises the question in my mind of whether there is such a thing as a "definitive" version of crab or seafood impérial. I am also curious to learn the origin of the dish and whether it is southern, as some people say, eastern, western, or northern.

Whatever its origin, my version of the dish falls neatly into the category of foods that can be prepared in 60 minutes or less. Incidentally the last time I made seafood impérial, the seafood consisted of shrimp and crabmeat because these two simply were the ones to be found in my refrigerator. You could, of course, use all crab or all shrimp or, if you desired, cooked lobster meat. Serve with parsleyed rice.

Shrimp and Crab Impérial

1	roasted sweet red pepper (see recipe)	½	cup heavy cream
4	tablespoons butter		Salt and freshly ground pepper
⅓	cup finely chopped onion		Tabasco sauce to taste
⅓	cup finely chopped celery	¼	cup dry sherry
⅓	cup finely chopped sweet green pepper	⅛	teaspoon freshly grated nutmeg
3	tablespoons flour	1½	pounds raw shrimp, shelled and deveined, or use half shrimp and half crabmeat (the proportions may vary but the weight should remain the same)
1	cup milk		

1. Roast the pepper; seed and cut into small cubes. Set aside.
2. Melt 2 tablespoons of butter in a saucepan and add the onion, celery,

green pepper, and the red pepper. Cook, stirring, about 1 minute. Cover and cook about 5 minutes longer. Set aside.

3. Melt the remaining 2 tablespoons of butter in another saucepan and stir in the flour, using a wire whisk. When blended, add the milk, stirring rapidly with the whisk. When thickened and smooth, continue cooking about 5 minutes, stirring often. Add the cream and blend well. Add salt and pepper to taste, the Tabasco, wine, nutmeg.

4. Add the shrimp to the vegetable mixture. Cook, stirring, until they change color. If crabmeat is used, add it after the shrimp have changed color. Stir briefly. Add the cream sauce and stir gently to blend. Serve with rice on the side.

Yield: Four servings.

How to Roast a Sweet Pepper

Spear a large sweet red or green pepper in the stem end with a two-pronged fork. Hold the pepper over a gas flame, turning it often until charred all over and on the end. Hold the pepper under cold running water and peel off the skin. Trim off the stem end and clean out the seeds and inner veins. The pepper might be roasted, turning often, under a broiler or over charcoal.

Parsleyed Rice

2 tablespoons butter	Salt and freshly ground pepper
2 tablespoons chopped onion	Tabasco sauce to taste
1 cup raw rice	2 tablespoons finely chopped
1½ cups water	parsley
1 bay leaf	

1. Melt 1 tablespoon of butter in a saucepan and add the onion. Cook, stirring, until wilted. Add the rice and stir briefly.
2. Add the water, bay leaf, salt and pepper to taste, and the Tabasco.
3. Bring to the boil. Cover and simmer exactly 17 minutes.
4. Remove the cover and discard the bay leaf. Using a two-pronged fork, stir in the remaining butter and chopped parsley.

Yield: Four servings.

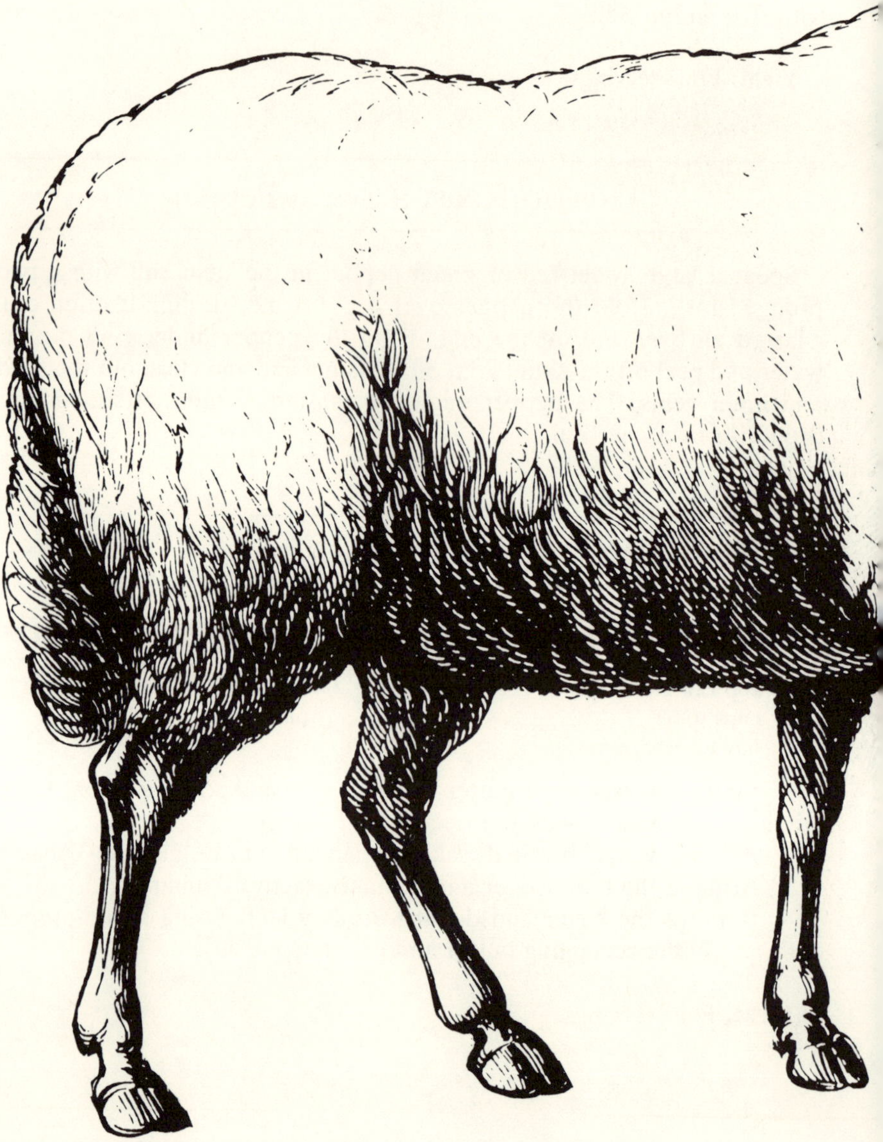

Lamb

IT IS INEVITABLY TRUE THAT ANY FOOD column will inherently reflect the taste and cravings of the author. It is certainly true in my column. I have often noted that some of the foods presented are those directly related to my childhood in Burgundy, or dishes that impressed me mightily when I was only a practicing chef many years ago.

There is one dish of which I never tire, one I first sampled while still an apprentice at the Drouant Restaurant in Paris. I was 16 years old at the time. The name of the dish is côtes d'agneau champvallon, and it consists of lamb chops baked with potatoes and onions. It is not elegant in the sense that a mousse or quenelles might be. And, although it is a dish that might be served in luxury restaurants, it is basically bourgeois.

A friend of mine has pointed out that it bears a close resemblance to the Irish stew that Sean Kinsella of the Mirabeau Restaurant in Dublin once prepared for us in East Hampton. And it is true. The lamb is, preferably, made from rib chops that have been trimmed; there is not an excess of vegetables such as carrots and turnips, and the seasonings are simple. A major difference is that the chops are browned before they are added to the dish and, naturally, the dish is not a stew, but rather a casserole. Speaking of that, this is a dish that can be reheated without damage to flavor.

If you are working within the confines of 60 minutes, you will find that you will need almost all of that time to prepare the dish. The preparation time of the ingredients is about 10 minutes; the baking time is 40. As the dish bakes there is ample time to go about doing other things for the accompanying dish, brussels sprouts with caraway, which requires a very short time to prepare.

One thing about the main dish puzzles me, incidentally, and that is the origin of the name champvallon. It seems nowhere to be found.

Côtes d'Agneau Champvallon
(Lamb chops with potatoes and onions)

8   rib lamb chops, about 2½ pounds
    Salt and freshly ground pepper
1   pound onions
2   pounds potatoes
3   tablespoons butter
4   sprigs fresh parsley
1   bay leaf

2   sprigs fresh thyme or 1 teaspoon dried
1½ cups fresh or canned chicken broth
2   whole cloves garlic, unpeeled
¾   cup water
¼   cup finely chopped parsley

1. Preheat the oven to 425 degrees.

2. Trim away and discard most of the fat around the rim of each chop. Sprinkle the chops with salt and pepper to taste.

3. Peel the onions and cut them in half. Slice each half as thinly as possible. There should be about 4 cups.

4. Peel the potatoes. Cut them into the thinnest possible slices. There should be about 7 cups.

5. Melt the butter in a heavy skillet large enough to hold the chops in one layer. Add the chops and brown quickly on one side, about 2 minutes. Turn the chops.

6. Sprinkle the onions over the chops and continue browning on the second side, about 2 minutes.

7. Tie the parsley, bay leaf, and thyme in a bundle and add this to the skillet. If dried thyme is used, sprinkle it over the onions. Add the whole garlic cloves.

8. Scatter the potatoes over the onions. Sprinkle with salt and pepper to taste. Pour the broth and water over all. Bring to the boil and cook about 3 minutes on top of the stove.

9. Transfer the dish to the oven. As the dish bakes, dip a spoon into the dish and baste the top occasionally with some of the cooking liquid. Bake 40 minutes. Serve sprinkled with chopped parsley.

Yield: Four servings.

Choux de Bruxelles au Karvi
(Brussels sprouts with caraway)

| 1 quart brussels sprouts | 2 tablespoons butter |
| Salt | 1 teaspoon caraway seeds |

1. Pull off any tough outer leaves of the sprouts. Using a paring knife, make a couple of crossed gashes in the base of each sprout.

2. Put the sprouts in a saucepan and add water to cover and salt to taste. Bring to the boil and cook 10 to 15 minutes or until tender.

3. Drain well and add the butter and caraway seeds. Stir until the sprouts are coated with butter and caraway seeds.

Yield: Four to six servings.

WHEN VISITED BY COLLEAGUES FROM FRANCE one thing that has impressed me is their universal praise of American lamb, which they consider equal, if not superior, to European lamb. Lamb is one of the finest of meats grown in this country and is, to my taste, superior to beef both in flavor and texture.

Lamb chops are, of course, a luxury item—not quite as expensive as veal but certainly more costly than chicken. It is the sort of food that is generally served on special occasions.

I like my lamb with or without sauce. Given a choice, it should be broiled with a hastily made noisette butter with a touch of minced garlic poured over. I have a cousin, however, who, when he comes for a visit, generally asks for lamb chops broiled with a béarnaise.

In recently serving grilled lamb chops to guests, I served them surrounded by sautéed mushrooms and spinach—a fine combination of foods. After the chops were cooked I arranged them on a dish, surrounded them with the mushroom mixture and poured over them the noisette butter, which had not only a touch of garlic but also a quick deglazing with a touch of red wine vinegar.

Here is a recipe for that preparation plus a recipe for a béarnaise sauce, which is not all that difficult to make and certainly does not require much time.

Côtes d'Agneau Grillés
(Broiled lamb chops)

4 double loin lamb chops, about ½ pound each	1 teaspoon finely minced garlic
Salt and freshly ground pepper	1 tablespoon red wine vinegar
2 tablespoons butter (see note)	1 tablespoon finely chopped parsley

1. Preheat the broiler.

2. Sprinkle chops with salt and pepper to taste. Arrange the chops on a broiler rack. Place the chops under the broiler, the top of the chops about four to five inches from the source of heat.

3. Broil until nicely browned on one side, about 5 minutes. Turn and continue broiling 5 minutes or until nicely browned on the second side.

4. Meanwhile, heat the butter in a skillet and when it is foaming add the garlic. Cook briefly, swirling the skillet, and add the vinegar. Cook about 10 seconds and stir in the parsley. Pour this sauce over the chops.

Yield: Four servings.

Note: If you prefer to use béarnaise sauce, do not use the butter with garlic, vinegar, and parsley as indicated in the recipe.

Epinards Sautés aux Champignons
(Sautéed spinach with mushrooms)

1 pound fresh spinach in bulk or one 10-ounce package fresh spinach	½ pound mushrooms cut into quarter-inch-thick slices
3 tablespoons butter	Salt and freshly ground pepper
	1 teaspoon finely minced garlic

1. Bring enough water to the boil to cover the spinach when it is added. Add the spinach and cook about 1 minute. Drain well. When cool enough to handle, squeeze the spinach between the hands to extract most of the moisture. Chop coarsely.
2. Melt 2 tablespoons of the butter in a skillet. Add the mushrooms and salt and pepper to taste. Cook, stirring often, over high heat until the mushrooms are browned.
3. Add the remaining butter and add the spinach. Cook, stirring, about 30 seconds. Sprinkle with garlic and stir. Serve hot.

Yield: Four servings.

Sauce Béarnaise

¾ cup butter	2 tablespoons red wine vinegar
1 tablespoon finely chopped shallots	1 tablespoon water
¼ teaspoon freshly ground pepper	1 egg yolk
2 tablespoons finely chopped fresh tarragon or 1 teaspoon dried	

1. Melt the butter and set it aside.
2. Combine shallots, pepper, half of the tarragon, and all of the vinegar in a saucepan. Bring to the boil and cook until vinegar is evaporated.
3. Remove the saucepan to a cool or cold surface and let stand about 5 minutes. The mixture should not become cold, but it should cool down a bit or it will scramble the egg yolk.
4. Add the water and egg yolk and start beating with a wire whisk.
5. Return the saucepan to the stove over very low heat. Start stirring with a whisk. The mixture should increase in volume and become thickened. Do not boil or the egg yolk will curdle.
6. Off heat, stirring vigorously, add the butter gradually. Beat in the remaining tarragon and serve.

Yield: About ¾ cup.

NOT LONG AGO I HAD PLANNED TO SERVE four fairly small lamb chops to another member of my family and myself. There were only the two of us. But shortly before dinner a young couple of long-standing acquaintance stopped by for a drink, and as time passed it became obvious that a dinner invitation was almost if not wholly inevitable.

The problem was how to stretch those four modest chops into a meal for four people. The solution was, naturally, to forage around in the refrigerator and find a means to stretch them. There are some staples that are almost always to be found in my refrigerator—Parmesan cheese and mushrooms.

Mushrooms are one of the grandest ingredients to act as extenders of other foods because the flavors blend so easily in almost any dish. I decided to blend the mushrooms into a duxelles, cooking them with a few chopped shallots and a touch of cream. Using this mixture as a topping for the sautéed lamb chops (the mushrooms could be chopped and cooked after the lamb chops had been placed in a hot skillet), I need simply add a hastily made cheese sauce as a final coating before a brief baking in the oven.

This is one of those dishes that does require almost the limit of 60 minutes to negotiate from the raw state to the cooked, but it can be done with a bit of dexterity on the part of the cook. And it is worth the effort. The mushroom-coated chops are substantial enough to require only a simply grilled tomato and a tossed salad to complete a meal.

About halfway through the preparation that evening, I reflected that what I had created was in reality a variation of a classic preparation known as Maintenon.

Côtes d'Agneau Maintenon
(Lamb chops with mushroom purée)

4 loin lamb chops, about ½ pound each
Salt and freshly ground pepper
1 teaspoon peanut, vegetable, or corn oil
1 cup cooked chopped mushrooms (see recipe)
1¼ cups Mornay sauce (see recipe)
1 tablespoon finely grated Parmesan cheese

1. Preheat the oven to 400 degrees.
2. Put each lamb chop on a flat surface. Using a sharp, heavy knife, trim away most if not all of the fat from the outer edge of the chops. Curl the tail of each chop and skewer with a toothpick. Sprinkle the chops with salt and pepper to taste.
3. Heat the oil in a heavy skillet and add the chops. Cook about 7 to 8 minutes over moderately high heat or until nicely browned on one side. Turn and reduce the heat. Cook on the second side about 8 minutes.

4. Transfer the chops to a baking dish. Top each with an equal portion of the mushroom mixture. Spoon an equal portion of the Mornay sauce over each serving. Sprinkle with the cheese.

5. Place in the oven and bake 15 minutes. Serve.

Yield: Four servings.

Duxelles
(Cooked chopped mushrooms)

½ pound fresh mushrooms	Salt and freshly ground pepper
1 tablespoon butter	2 tablespoons heavy cream
2 tablespoons finely chopped shallots	2 tablespoons finely chopped parsley
Juice of ½ lemon	

1. Rinse the mushrooms well and drain. Put the mushrooms on a flat surface and chop with a knife. Or slice the mushrooms by hand and then chop them fine using a food processor. If you do not slice the mushrooms first, they will become mushy when processed.

2. Put the mushrooms into a clean napkin or dish towel. Bring up the edges and twist to make a bag. Twist the napkin or dish towel over the sink to extract most of the liquid from the mushrooms. Discard the liquid.

3. Melt the butter in a saucepan and add the shallots. Cook briefly and add the mushrooms and lemon juice. Stir to blend. Add salt and pepper to taste. Cook until most of the liquid evaporates, about 3 minutes. Add the cream and stir. Cook about 1 minute and stir in the parsley.

Yield: About 1 cup.

Sauce Mornay
(Cheese sauce)

1 tablespoon butter	1 egg yolk
1 tablespoon flour	1 tablespoon finely grated Parmesan cheese
Salt and freshly ground pepper	
1 cup milk	Pinch of cayenne pepper

1. Melt the butter in a small saucepan and add the flour and salt and pepper to taste, stirring with a wire whisk.

2. Add the milk, stirring rapidly with the whisk. When thickened and smooth, remove from the heat and add the egg yolk, stirring rapidly with the whisk. Stir in the cheese and cayenne pepper.

Yield: About 1¼ cups.

I HAVE ALWAYS REGARDED THE PREPARAtion of my column as similar to menu planning. You try for a proper balance in the foods suggested. A bit of ground beef here, a bit of pork, lamb and fish. And by far the predominant food to be found here is chicken, not only because it is so versatile and tasty, but also because it is priced the lowest of almost all foods.

Generally speaking, I have stayed away from lamb and veal recipes because they are so costly. However, this menu will concern itself with one of the finest and, at times, most expensive meats—boneless loins of lamb.

The dish—noisettes of lamb with tarragon—is most assuredly in the luxury category, but it is the sort of dish found in fine restaurants. When you consider what the dish would cost on a professional menu, making it at home does not seem all that astronomical.

When I made this dish in my own kitchen, I prepared it in the classic fashion. I started with two racks of lamb and boned them. When one of my children complained that I was tossing out the best part—that is to say the bones—I lit the oven and, instead of discarding the bones, I simply roasted them with salt and pepper. They came out crisp and delicious.

You needn't do the boning yourself; your butcher should be happy to do this for you. Ask for boneless loin of lamb with all surface fat removed.

The rest of the preparation is simplicity itself. You simply cook the loins in a little butter for about 10 minutes. You remove the lamb, pour off all the fat from the skillet and add shallots and tarragon and a bit of dry white wine. You cook that down quickly and add chicken broth.

When that cooks for one minute, you are ready to carve the lamb and serve it with the pan liquid. Potatoes with thinly sliced cooked onions go well with this; it is best to prepare the potatoes before you start cooking the lamb.

Noisettes d'Agneau à l'Estragon
(Boneless loin of lamb with tarragon)

- 2 skinless, boneless loins of lamb, about 1 pound (cut from two racks of lamb weighing about 1½ pounds each)
- Salt and freshly ground pepper
- 2 tablespoons butter
- 2 tablespoons finely chopped shallots
- 2 teaspoons finely chopped fresh tarragon or 1 teaspoon dried
- ⅓ cup dry white wine
- ¼ cup chicken broth

1. Sprinkle the lamb with salt and pepper to taste.

2. Melt 1 tablespoon butter in a skillet and add the lamb pieces. Brown quickly on all sides and cook over relatively high heat about 10 minutes.

3. Remove the pieces of lamb to a warm platter. Pour off the fat from the skillet.

4. Add the shallots and cook briefly, stirring, until wilted. Add the tarragon and wine. Cook until the wine is reduced by half and add the broth. Cook about 1 minute.

5. Swirl in the remaining butter. Add any juices that have accumulated around the lamb.

6. Pour the sauce over the lamb. Serve the lamb carved on the bias with the sauce spooned over.

Yield: Four servings.

Pommes Boulangères
(Potatoes with onions)

5 large potatoes, about 2 pounds	1 sprig fresh thyme or ⅛ teaspoon dried
3 tablespoons butter	
1¾ cups thinly sliced onions	2 sprigs fresh parsley
1 teaspoon finely minced garlic	1¼ cups fresh or canned chicken broth
Salt and freshly ground pepper	
1 bay leaf	

1. Peel the potatoes and drop them into cold water. Cut the potatoes in half lengthwise. Cut each half crosswise into eighth-inch-thick slices. There should be about 5 cups.

2. Melt the butter in a large, heavy saucepan and add the onions and garlic. Cook, stirring, until wilted, about 5 minutes.

3. Add the potatoes, salt and pepper to taste, bay leaf, thyme, parsley, and broth. Cover closely and bring to the boil. Let cook about 12 minutes or until potatoes are almost but not quite tender. Uncover and cook over moderately high heat about 10 minutes. Remove the bay leaf, parsley, and thyme sprigs and serve.

Yield: Four servings.

THERE ARE MANY SAUCES IN FRENCH COOKing that are more or less uniform in the minds of well-trained chefs and, generally speaking, do not differ greatly from one professional kitchen to another, sauces such as béchamel, soubise, and américaine.

An exception, however, is curry sauce. A curry sauce, French-style, is considerably different from the sauces you will find in an Indian kitchen. I have no recollection of where the recipe for my basic curry sauce came from. It is something that I have made since I was an apprentice in Paris many years ago and consists of diced apples and bananas cooked with onion and celery and garlic with curry powder sprinkled over. Its degree of hotness depends on how much curry powder is added.

My version is what might be called an all-purpose curry sauce: It can be blended with quickly sautéed shrimp, chicken or meat. On the most recent occasion, I used a very good and tender loin of lamb. That meal was destined for two, and one loin of lamb was just ample for two reasonably hungry people.

The important thing about preparing the lamb, which is cut into thin slices, is that it must be cooked quickly in order to assure its best flavor and texture. If the lamb is cooked too long before it is added to the sauce, it is apt to become dry and less tasty. And once it is added to the basic still-simmering sauce, it should be removed from the heat to prevent further cooking.

Volumes could be written, I suppose, on why rice seems to be the ultimate accompaniment for certain foods, and it is certainly the ideal choice for curried dishes.

This is a meal that would be complemented by a tossed green salad or with a variety of yogurt sauces such as cucumber and dill. The recipe printed here is for two or three servings. For four, double all the ingredients and proceed as indicated.

Emince d'Agneau au Cari
(Curried cubed lamb)

- 1 loin of lamb, 2½ pounds, boned and with fat removed to yield about ¾ pound of meat
- ½ cup golden or dark raisins
- 3 tablespoons butter
- ½ cup finely chopped onion
- ¼ cup finely chopped celery
- ¾ cup finely diced peeled apple
- ½ cup finely diced banana
- 1 teaspoon finely minced garlic
- 2 to 3 tablespoons curry powder
- ½ cup imported peeled Italian tomatoes
- 1 cup rich chicken broth
- 1 bay leaf

1. Place the loin on a flat surface and cut on the bias into quarter-inch-thick slices. Set aside.

2. Soak the raisins in warm water to cover for about 30 minutes.

3. Melt 2 tablespoons of butter in a saucepan and add the onion. Cook, stirring, until wilted. Add the celery, apple, banana, garlic, and curry powder. Cook briefly and add the tomatoes, chicken stock, and bay leaf. Pour and scrape the sauce into the container of a food processor. Blend until smooth. There should be about 2 cups.

4. Return the sauce to the saucepan and heat. Drain the raisins and add them.

5. Melt the remaining tablespoon of butter in a skillet and when it is quite hot and starting to brown, add the meat. Cook over high heat, stirring constantly to separate the pieces and cook them evenly. Cook about 1 or 2 minutes, no longer. Add the meat to the simmering sauce and remove from the heat. Do not let the meat cook in the sauce but serve immediately. Serve with rice or buttered fine noodles.

Yield: Two or three servings.

Riz au Four
(Baked rice)

2½	tablespoons butter	3	sprigs parsley
2	tablespoons minced onion	1	sprig fresh thyme or ¼ teaspoon dried
½	teaspoon minced garlic		
1	cup uncooked rice		Salt and freshly ground pepper
1½	cups chicken broth	½	bay leaf

1. Preheat the oven to 400 degrees.

2. Melt half of the butter in a casserole and cook the onion and garlic, stirring with a wooden spoon, until the onion is translucent. Add the rice and stir briefly over low heat until the grains are coated with butter.

3. Stir in the broth, making sure there are no lumps in the rice. Add the parsley, thyme, salt and pepper to taste, and bay leaf. Cover with a close-fitting lid and place in the oven.

4. Bake the rice exactly 17 minutes. Remove the cover and discard the parsley and thyme sprigs and bay leaf. Using a two-pronged fork, stir in the remaining butter. If the rice is not to be served immediately, keep covered in a warm place.

Yield: Four servings.

THIS BOOK, OF COURSE, IS DEDICATED TO THE proposition that good cooking can be produced within the confines of 60 minutes. Most of the menus have been tailored for the span of time from when a cook walks into the kitchen to the moment the meal is placed on the table.

On rare occasions, I have taken a certain license: that is, to show the preparation of one food or another that can be prepared and made ready for the oven within the space of an hour.

The dish outlined here is one of them. It is a less traditional moussaka à la Grecque, one of the best of all international creations. It is a dish made with ground lamb or beef, eggplant, tomato, a dash of cinnamon, and a splash of red wine. The blend of ingredients is topped with a white sauce containing ricotta or cottage cheese and baked.

A moussaka is a fine dish for entertaining. It can be served hot or lukewarm and can be reheated. It is also good when served cold.

A moussaka requires three separate food treatments—the preparation of the meat moussaka, the cooking of the eggplant slices, and the making of the cream sauce with cheese. By the time you prepare and combine these elements, it will require the better part of 60 minutes. On the other hand, at the end of that time you simply put the dish in the oven, close the door, and wait until it is ready.

This is the kind of dish that requires only a simple salad—lettuce with oil and vinegar—to complete a meal. If you want to be a little more elaborate, you could work in a quickly made Greek salad with feta cheese.

Moussaka à la Grecque

1 eggplant, 1½ pounds	¼ cup tomato paste
Salt and freshly ground pepper	¼ cup dry red wine
¼ cup olive oil, approximately	¼ cup chopped parsley
6 tablespoons butter	3 tablespoons flour
1 cup finely chopped onion	2 cups milk
1 teaspoon finely minced garlic	2 eggs, lightly beaten
1½ pounds ground lean lamb or beef	⅛ teaspoon freshly grated nutmeg
⅛ teaspoon ground cinnamon	1 cup ricotta cheese
½ cup crushed tomatoes	¼ cup freshly grated Parmesan cheese

1. Preheat the oven to 400 degrees.

2. Peel the eggplant. Cut it into five or six half-inch-thick slices. Sprinkle with salt and pepper to taste. Heat half the oil and cook the eggplant slices, a few at a time, turning to brown the slices on both sides. Remove and drain on paper towels. Add more oil as necessary to prevent burning. Set aside.

3. Melt 2 tablespoons of the butter in a heavy skillet and add the onion.

Cook, stirring, until wilted. Add the garlic and meat and cook, stirring and chopping down with the side of a heavy metal spoon to break up the lumps. Cook until meat loses its raw color. Add the cinnamon and salt and pepper to taste, and stir.

4. Add the tomatoes and tomato paste and stir, then add the wine and parsley and let simmer until most of the wine is evaporated.

5. Melt 3 tablespoons of butter in a saucepan and add the flour and salt and pepper to taste, stirring with a wire whisk. When blended and smooth, add the milk, stirring rapidly with the whisk. Cook, stirring often, about 5 minutes.

6. Beat the eggs with a whisk and add the nutmeg and ricotta. Beat to blend well.

7. Add the cheese mixture to the white sauce. Beat well without cooking.

8. Butter a rectangular baking dish (a dish that measures about 12 by 9 by 2½ inches is ideal) with the remaining tablespoon of butter. Add a layer of eggplant slices and spoon the meat sauce over. Smooth it on top. Sprinkle with half the Parmesan cheese. Add the cheese sauce and smooth it over. Sprinkle with the remaining Parmesan cheese.

9. Place the dish in the oven and bake 30 minutes.

Yield: Six or more servings.

Greek Salad

- 2 heads romaine lettuce, cored and coarsely shredded, 4 to 6 cups
- 1 bunch scallions, trimmed and chopped
- 1 small onion, peeled and sliced into rings
- 4 radishes, sliced
- 12 imported black olives
- ½ cup crumbled feta cheese
- ¼ teaspoon dried oregano
- 12 cherry tomatoes, cut in half
- Juice of 2 lemons
- 6 to 8 tablespoons olive oil
- Salt and freshly ground pepper

1. Combine the lettuce, scallions, onion, radishes, olives, feta cheese, oregano, and tomatoes in a salad bowl.

2. Add the lemon juice and toss. Add the olive oil and salt and pepper to taste and toss again.

Yield: Six or more servings.

I HAVE LONG SINCE LOST MY PAROCHIAL FEELing that there is no other worthwhile cuisine in the world except that of my native France. I have learned to cook, with some degree of adeptness, or have been exposed to, many kinds of food in this country, including Chinese, Japanese, Italian, and Thai.

One of my favorite borrowings from the English is that combination specialty called the mixed grill. This has, to my knowledge, no translation on a French menu. It is simply stated mixed grill, and there is no doubt that the bulk of my compatriots know precisely what to expect when they order it.

In its own way it is both the most easily made and simplest of "dishes"—and one of the best. I am often asked to propose good solid menus for summer dining and I consider a mixed grill to be ideal. Although it consists of numerous meats (chops, liver, kidneys, and, sometimes, sausages), the seasonings are most basic: simply salt and pepper plus a light brushing of oil.

The important factor in the preparation of a well-made mixed grill is that of timing. There is nothing more unpalatable to my taste than overcooked livers and kidneys and, worse, perhaps, overdone lamb chops. In the recipe for mixed grill here, which is easily done in less than 60 minutes, my own cooking times are indicated for each ingredient. Serve with potatoes sautéed with garlic. Prepare the potatoes and cook them slightly before or simultaneously with the grilled foods.

Mixed Grill

4 thin slices calf's liver, about ¾ pound
4 lamb chops, about 1¼ pounds, each about 1½ inches thick
4 lamb kidneys
4 large mushrooms
2 large tomatoes, about ¾ pound total weight
¼ cup peanut, vegetable, or corn oil
Salt and freshly ground pepper
Melted butter

1. Preheat a charcoal or gas grill to the desired degree of heat for grilling.

2. Trim away the tough veins or arteries from the pieces of liver.

3. If desired, trim away much of the fat from the chops. Skewer the tail ends of each chop to the chops.

4. Split each kidney in half to make two round medallions. Cut away the white center core of each kidney half.

5. Cut away the stems from each mushroom.

6. Trim away the core of each tomato. Cut each tomato in half to make two rounds.

7. Put the lamb chops, liver, and kidneys in a flat dish large enough to hold them in one layer. Sprinkle with oil and salt and pepper to taste.

Turn the meats and season on the other side. Cover with foil and set aside until ready to cook.

8. Place the tomatoes cut side down on the grill. Place the mushrooms stem side up on the grill. Cook about 1 minute and add the chops.

9. After about 4 minutes, turn the tomatoes and mushrooms. Continue cooking. When the chops have cooked about 5 minutes turn them.

10. When the tomatoes and mushrooms have cooked about 4 minutes on the second side, transfer them to a warm platter and keep warm.

11. When the chops have cooked about 5 minutes on the second side, turn once more and continue cooking to the desired degree of doneness.

12. Meanwhile put the liver and kidneys on the grill. Cook the liver 1 or 2 minutes and turn. Cook 1 or 2 minutes on the second side, or even longer, according to taste.

13. When the kidneys have cooked 2 or 3 minutes, turn them. Cook 2 or 3 minutes or to the desired degree of doneness on the second side.

14. The important thing about a mixed grill is timing. Each food should be cooked to the desired degree of doneness and then transferred to a warm platter. When all foods are cooked, brush the tops with the melted butter.

Yield: Four servings.

Pommes Parmentier
(Potatoes sautéed with garlic)

4 large Idaho potatoes, about 1½ pounds	Salt and freshly ground pepper
¼ cup peanut, vegetable, or corn oil	½ teaspoon finely minced garlic
1 tablespoon butter	1 tablespoon finely chopped parsley

1. Peel the potatoes and cut them into slices slightly more than half an inch thick.

2. Cut each slice into strips slightly more than a half an inch thick.

3. Cut the potatoes into cubes. Rinse in cold water and drain.

4. Heat the oil in a heavy skillet and add the potatoes. Cook, shaking the skillet and turning the potatoes so that they cook evenly. Cook over high heat 8 to 10 minutes or until golden brown.

5. Drain the potatoes in a colander.

6. Return the potatoes to the skillet and add the butter and salt and pepper to taste. Cook about 1 minute, shaking the skillet and stirring often. Add the garlic and blend. Pour the potatoes into a serving dish. Sprinkle with chopped parsley and serve.

Yield: Four servings.

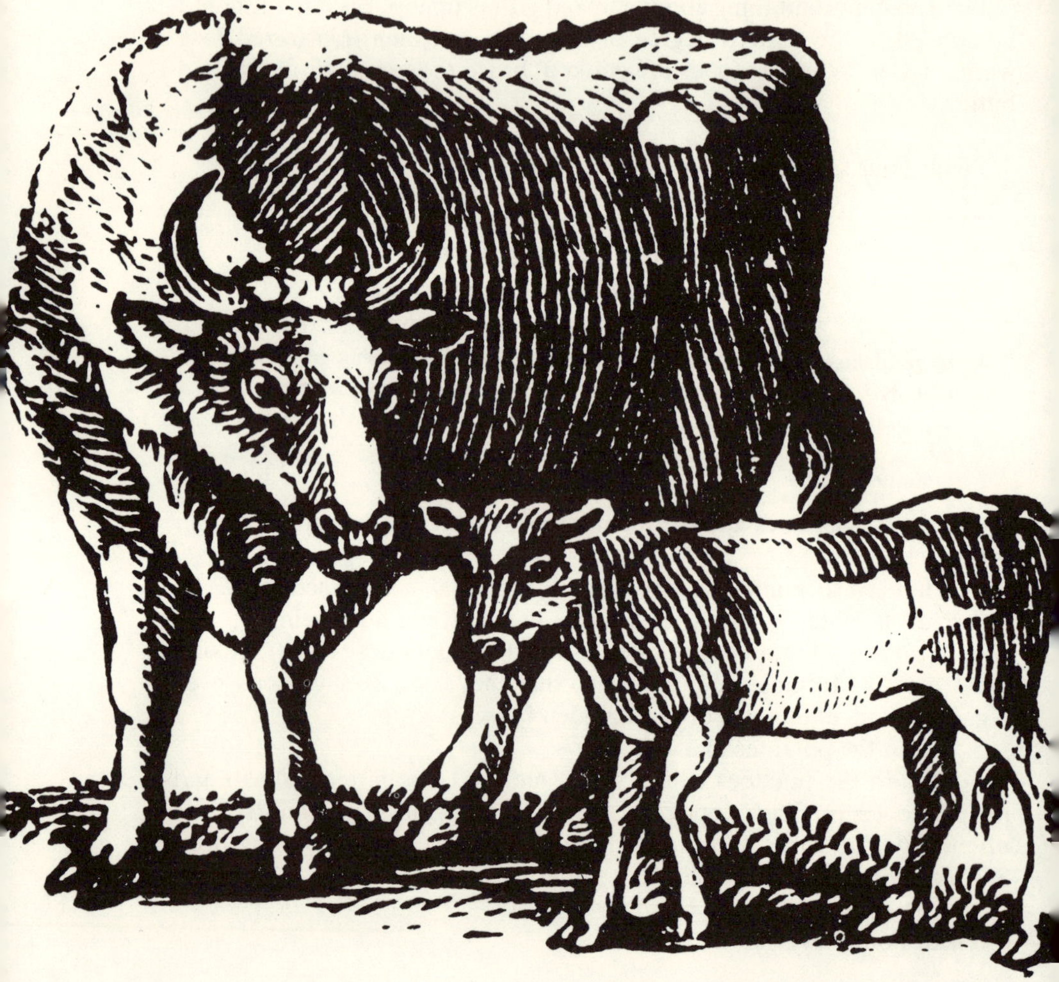

Veal and Calves' Liver

FOR VARIOUS REASONS, AN ENTIRE VOLUME on hasty cooking or cooking within the span of an hour could be devoted to recipes using veal scaloppine alone.

In the first place scaloppine must, as I have often mentioned, be cooked in a hurry and, preferably, over high heat, lest the meat dry out and become tasteless. Because of the "neutral" flavor of veal (which is to say it does not have an obvious taste like pork or beef or game), it marries well with an endless assortment of flavors such as herbs, spices, and vegetables that have a more or less assertive nature.

Green peppers cut into strips and stuffed green olives blend well with veal scaloppine and give to it what might be called a Mediterranean or perhaps Italian aspect.

In that the dish printed here is of my own creation, I have chosen to call it escalope de veau italienne, containing as it does in addition to peppers and olives, tomatoes and a touch of oregano.

The vegetable that accompanies it is more or less in the same vein, broccoli that is blanched and cooked briefly in olive oil with garlic and hot red pepper flakes.

The preferred way to proceed with this meal, if it is to be cooked in less than an hour, is to make all the food preparations necessary in advance. That is to say, remove the ingredients from the refrigerator or vegetable bin; chop what needs to be chopped and measure the ingredients as indicated.

You may prepare the broccoli, including the cooking, several minutes in advance of the time it is to be served. This will leave you time to dip the scaloppine in egg and to sauté it before adding the tomato, green pepper, and olive mixture.

Escalopes de Veau Italienne
(Veal scaloppine with tomatoes and olives)

8	slices veal scaloppine, about 1¼ pounds	24	small stuffed green olives
	Salt and freshly ground pepper	2	teaspoons finely minced garlic
1	egg, lightly beaten	½	cup chopped onion
1	tablespoon water	½	cup drained, canned tomatoes
¼	cup flour	1	teaspoon dried oregano
2	tablespoons peanut, vegetable, or corn oil	2	tablespoons red wine vinegar
7	tablespoons butter	3	tablespoons finely chopped parsley
1	cup sweet red or green pepper cut into thin julienne strips		

1. Pound each piece of meat lightly between two sheets of plastic wrap with a flat mallet or the bottom of a heavy skillet. Sprinkle the meat on both sides with salt and pepper to taste.

2. Beat the egg with the water in a shallow dish.

3. Coat the scaloppine on both sides with flour. Dip them into the egg mixture until well coated on both sides.

4. Heat the 2 tablespoons of oil and 1 tablespoon of the butter in one or two large skillets. If necessary, increase the oil and butter slightly.

5. Add the pieces of veal and cook over high heat about 1 minute. Turn and cook on the other side for 1 minute. As the pieces are cooked transfer them to a warm platter.

6. Rinse out and dry the skillet. To the clean skillet add the remaining 6 tablespoons butter.

7. Add the red or green pepper strips, olives, garlic, and onion. Add salt and pepper to taste. Cook, tossing and stirring, until the peppers are crisp tender. Add the tomatoes and cook about 1 minute. Add the oregano and vinegar and cook over high heat about 30 seconds. Pour the mixture over the veal and sprinkle with parsley. Serve.

Yield: Four to six servings.

Broccoli Sauté

1 bunch broccoli, about 1½ pounds	Salt and freshly ground pepper
3 tablespoons olive oil	¼ teaspoon dried hot red pepper flakes
2 teaspoons finely minced garlic	

1. Cut the broccoli into large flowerets. Peel the large remaining stems and cut them into one-and-one-half-inch lengths. Set all the pieces aside.

2. Bring enough water to the boil to cover the broccoli when added. Add the broccoli pieces. When the water returns to the boil, let simmer about 3 minutes. Drain well.

3. Heat the oil in a skillet and add the broccoli. Cook, stirring and tossing, about 40 seconds. Add the garlic, salt and pepper to taste, and hot red pepper flakes. Cook about 15 seconds and serve.

Yield: Four servings.

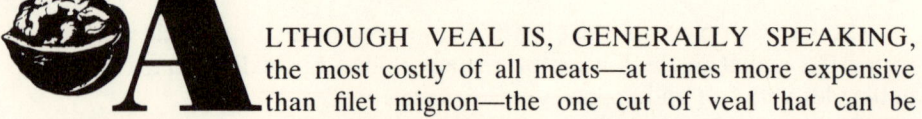

ALTHOUGH VEAL IS, GENERALLY SPEAKING, the most costly of all meats—at times more expensive than filet mignon—the one cut of veal that can be "stretched" to best advantage is the thin cut known as scaloppine. There are many ways to make a small amount of veal scallops go a long way, and that has to do with garnishes. You may bread them, you may garnish them in countless ways—with anchovies, capers, chopped egg, and so on. And veal scaloppine lend themselves to thousands of interesting stuffings. When stuffed, the scallops are often called veal birds, rollatine, veal ripieno, and so on.

The advantages of scaloppine of veal are obvious. As I have noted a few hundred times, veal scaloppine must be cooked fairly quickly, or else they tend to be dry and tough.

One of the best and tastiest fillings is a blend of Gorgonzola cheese and walnuts. The Gorgonzola gives the meat a special, inimitable tang. The walnuts provide a nutty, meaty quality.

There are two ways in which scaloppine are normally filled. They may be stuffed, with the sides folded over each other to enclose the filling, envelope fashion. Or the filling may be placed in the center of one scaloppine and covered with a second thin slice. When this is done, it is best to seal the edges of the two slices by brushing between them with a little beaten egg or egg yolk.

When the Gorgonzola filling is used, it tends to melt inside and become somewhat liquid. I have found that, for this particular stuffing, it is best to use the flat scaloppine covered with a second scaloppine to prevent the Gorgonzola from running out.

I have recommended in this recipe that the meat be pounded lightly before using. This will hasten the cooking. Care must be taken, however, that the meat does not tear when it is pounded, for the cheese may ooze out. An ideal accompaniment for the dish is a purée of vegetables, in this particular case a purée of green beans.

Veal Scaloppine with Gorgonzola and Walnuts

8	veal scaloppine, about 1¼ pounds total weight	1	egg, lightly beaten
	Salt and freshly ground pepper	2	tablespoons flour
¼	pound soft Gorgonzola cheese	1½	cups fine fresh bread crumbs
½	cup coarsely chopped walnuts		Oil for shallow frying, about 3 cups
2	tablespoons heavy cream		
1	tablespoon Marsala or Madeira wine		

1. Place each scaloppine between sheets of plastic wrap and pound lightly with a flat mallet. Do not break the flesh. If the flesh is broken, the cheese will ooze out. Sprinkle with salt and pepper to taste.

2. Combine the cheese, walnuts, heavy cream, and wine in a mixing bowl. Blend well.

3. Spoon equal portions of the mixture into the center of each of four pieces of veal. Brush around each filling with beaten egg. Top with a second piece of veal and press around the edges to seal. Carefully dip each package of veal on both sides in flour. Then dip in egg and finally in bread crumbs. Press lightly to make the crumbs adhere.

4. Heat the oil in a skillet. When it is quite hot, add the veal packages.

5. Cook until golden on one side, about 3 minutes. Turn carefully and cook until golden brown on the second side. Drain on absorbent paper toweling.

Yield: Four servings.

Purée de Haricots Verts
(Purée of green beans)

1¼	pounds fresh green beans	⅛	teaspoon freshly grated nutmeg
	Salt		Freshly ground pepper
3	tablespoons butter		

1. Cut or break off the ends of the green beans.

2. Bring enough water to the boil to cover the beans when they are added. Add salt to taste and the beans. Simmer 10 minutes or until beans are tender. Drain the beans.

3. Put the beans into the container of a food processor or through a food mill. Process the beans to a fine purée. There should be about 1½ cups or slightly less.

4. Combine the beans, butter, nutmeg, and salt and pepper to taste in a saucepan and cook, stirring, until the beans are just piping hot.

Yield: Four servings.

ALTHOUGH I HAVE ALWAYS TAKEN A GREAT deal of pleasure in foraging for food—hunting wild deer and pheasant and quail in season, fishing for trout and bass and tending my own garden—I have never had a great interest in hunting for wild mushrooms.

It probably has something to do with my childhood. In the small town in Burgundy where I was raised, we were always treated to the delights of freshly harvested morels brought in from the mountains miles away, and my mother made great use of them in the kitchen. She would sauté them in hot oil until they were crisp-tender and drain them well. She would cook them a second time in butter and with garlic or shallots and parsley added for flavor.

I don't think I really realized what a luxury those brown-capped, honeycombed delicacies were until I came to this country—and a luxury they are, whether fresh or dried. It is almost impossible to obtain fresh morels during the winter, but the markets in Manhattan where luxury foods are sold generally have great quantities of dried morels on hand.

Recently, during the holidays, I was given a small quantity of dried morels, and at about the same time I dined with friends at Le Cirque restaurant in Manhattan. One of the dishes we dined on was côte de veau belle des bois—veal chops with morels in cream sauce.

The dish is relatively simple. It takes, from start to finish, less than half an hour. After soaking the dried mushrooms, you simply cook them in butter with white wine, shallots, and cream. The chops are cooked on both sides until nicely browned and done. They are deglazed with Madeira and the sauce is added. This is, admittedly, an expensive dish, one for special occasions. But it is well worth it. Buttered, fine noodles and a salad are ideal accompaniments for the veal.

Côtes de Veau Belle des Bois
(Veal chops with morels in cream sauce)

- 1 cup dried morels, about 50 or 60
- 4 veal chops, about ¾ pound each
- Salt and freshly ground pepper
- ¼ cup flour
- 4 tablespoons butter
- 2 tablespoons finely chopped shallots
- ½ cup dry white wine
- ½ cup heavy cream
- ½ cup dry Madeira

1. Soak the morels in warm water to cover for at least 30 minutes.

2. Sprinkle the chops with salt and pepper to taste. Dredge the chops on both sides in flour and shake off any excess.

3. Melt 3 tablespoons of butter in a heavy skillet and add the chops. Cook about 4 or 5 minutes or until the chops are nicely browned on one

side. Turn and cook on the second side 8 to 10 minutes. Transfer the chops to a warm platter.

4. Squeeze the morels to extract most of the liquid.

5. Melt the remaining tablespoon of butter in a saucepan and add the shallots and cook briefly. Add the morels and the dry white wine. Cook down by half and add the cream. Cook about 1 minute. Add salt and pepper to taste.

6. Meanwhile, pour off the fat from the skillet in which the chops cooked. Add the Madeira and cook down until almost totally reduced. Add the morels in cream sauce and blend. Serve the sauce spooned over the chops.

Yield: Four servings.

Nouilles Fines au Beurre
(Buttered fine noodles)

½ pound thin noodles
Salt
2 tablespoons butter at room temperature

Freshly ground pepper

1. Drop the noodles into a large quantity of boiling salted water. Cook about 2 or 3 minutes or until tender. Do not overcook.

2. Drain the noodles and return them to the pot. Toss them with the butter and add salt and pepper to taste. Serve hot.

Yield: Four servings.

Salade de Laitue
(Lettuce salad)

2 heads Boston lettuce
2 tablespoons tarragon vinegar
1 clove garlic, finely minced
1 tablespoon imported mustard such as Dijon or Düsseldorf

6 tablespoons olive oil
Salt and freshly ground pepper

1. Core the lettuce and separate the leaves. Rinse the leaves and shake off any excess moisture.

2. Blend the vinegar, minced garlic, and mustard in a mixing bowl. Stir with a whisk, gradually adding the oil. Add salt and pepper to taste.

3. Toss the lettuce with the dressing.

Yield: Four servings.

A FEW WEEKS AGO WE WERE PLAYING AROUND with foods that we chose to call "once-in-a-lifetime dishes." These were dishes which, for one reason or another, were too tedious, costly or time-consuming to duplicate with any enthusiasm more than once ever.

We spoke of duck à la presse, which requires a special and costly utensil for squeezing the roast duck pieces to extract their juices; coulibiac of salmon, which requires a combination of sauces and pastries to prepare, and veal Orloff, which, in its classic form, demands an entire saddle of veal that must be roasted, carved and reassembled with an assortment of sauces including one made of cheese and another of mushrooms and onions.

One recent evening in my home, a weekend guest expressed a desire to sample veal Orloff, but, she protested, she would never ask me to spend that much time in mid-summer in a hot kitchen.

I mulled that over in the afternoon in my boat while fishing for flounder in Gardiner's Bay.

In late afternoon I went to my local butcher and ordered four veal chops that have, admittedly in this day and age, a special price tag. But this was a special guest. I shopped for eggs, cheese, and mushrooms and other staples that are needed for veal Orloff.

On my return home, I proceeded to make a 60-minute version of veal chops Orloff. And I must say that the dish, in all its expediency, turned out to be just as good as the saddle of veal version and without all the theatrics that are needed for the original. This is Orloff reduced to its absolute minimum where time is concerned. It is best served with new peas flavored with fresh mint.

Côtes de Veau Orloff
(Veal chops Orloff)

4 veal chops, about ¾ pound each	1 cup milk
Salt and freshly ground pepper	½ cup heavy cream
½ pound fresh mushrooms	2 tablespoons grated Gruyère or Swiss cheese
6 tablespoons butter	
¼ cup finely chopped onion	⅓ cup dry white wine
Juice of half a lemon	⅓ cup water
3 tablespoons flour	1 egg yolk, lightly beaten

1. Preheat the oven to 400 degrees.
2. Sprinkle the chops with salt and pepper to taste and set aside.
3. Chop the mushrooms finely on a flat surface. There should be about 1¾ cups.
4. Melt 2 tablespoons of the butter in a small skillet. Add the onion and cook, stirring, until wilted. Add the mushrooms and sprinkle with lemon

juice. Cook, stirring, until the mushrooms become fairly dry. Add salt and pepper to taste. Stir and set aside.

5. Melt 2 tablespoons of butter in a saucepan and add the flour. Cook, stirring briefly, without browning. Add the milk, stirring rapidly with a whisk. When blended and smooth, add the cream, stirring. Add salt and pepper to taste.

6. Remove from the heat and add the cheese. Stir to blend and set aside.

7. Melt the remaining 2 tablespoons of butter in a large, heavy skillet. Add the chops and cook 6 minutes on one side or until nicely browned. Turn and cook about 6 minutes on the other side until well browned.

8. Transfer the chops to a baking dish. Spoon equal portions of the mushroom mixture over each chop. Smooth it over.

9. Pour off the fat from the skillet in which the chops cooked. Add the wine and water, stirring to dissolve the brown particles that cling to the bottom and sides of the skillet. Pour the pan sauce into a small saucepan and set aside.

10. Add the beaten egg yolk to the cheese sauce and stir to blend. Spoon equal portions of the sauce over each chop.

11. Place the chops in the oven and bake 15 minutes. Run the dish briefly under the broiler until it is nicely browned. Reheat the pan sauce and serve it spooned around each serving.

Yield: Four servings.

Petits Pois à la Menthe
(Green peas with mint)

1½ to 2 cups shelled peas	1 tablespoon finely chopped mint
2 tablespoons butter	½ teaspoon sugar
Salt and freshly ground pepper	

1. If the peas are extremely fresh and new, they do not have to be parboiled in water. If they are a bit old, it is best to parboil them by dropping them into boiling water and letting them cook from 2 to 5 minutes, depending on age. If cooked, drain.

2. Melt the butter in a skillet and add the peas, salt and pepper to taste, mint, and sugar. Stir. Cook, covered, about 1 minute or until the peas are cooked and heated through.

Yield: Four servings.

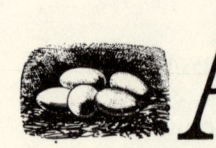

A FRIEND AND NEIGHBOR RECENTLY OBserved that I have often offered recipes in my column that are basically Italian or variations on basically Italian dishes.

While it is true that I have not spent a great deal of time in Italy—perhaps a month in all over a period of years—I have many good friends who are Italian and with whom I've spent numerous hours in the kitchen.

It is also true that, perhaps more than in most cuisines, excellent Italian dishes lend themselves to the premise that good food can be prepared in less than an hour. And one reason for this is that veal scaloppine is a basic ingredient for many Italian dishes.

One of the most interesting things about scaloppine is that it blends well with so many other ingredients, be they vegetables, herbs, spices, or other meats like ham or prosciutto.

One of my favorite scaloppine dishes bears the odd name of saltimbocca. I say odd because the word literally translates as "jump in the mouth." I am not at all certain why it is called that, but I have had many versions of this dish. The most basic is simply a combination of thinly sliced scaloppine attached (with a toothpick) to a thin slice of prosciutto with a sage leaf sandwiched in between. The "package" is cooked quickly in butter or butter and oil and served.

One of the best and most elaborate versions of the dish is that of Eduardo Giurici, the owner-chef of Casa Albona, an excellent restaurant in Amagansett, L.I. His saltimbocca consists not only of scaloppine and prosciutto but a fine Marsala sauce plus a garnish for each serving of half a hard-cooked egg.

Mr. Giurici's version is also served on a bed of escarole sautéed quickly in olive oil and flavored with a touch of garlic. Two saltimboccas should be served per person. This is a very easy dish to cook within 60 minutes.

Saltimbocca

8	thin veal scallopine, about 1 pound	½	cup Marsala wine Italian-style Escarole (see recipe)
	Salt and freshly ground pepper		
2	tablespoons flour	4	thin slices ham, preferably prosciutto
3	tablespoons olive oil		
6	tablespoons butter	2	tablespoons finely chopped parsley
2	hard-cooked eggs, peeled and cut in half lengthwise		

1. Put each piece of veal between plastic wrap and pound lightly with a flat mallet. Flatten lightly without breaking the meat.

2. Sprinkle the veal with salt and pepper to taste. Dredge lightly on both sides in flour.

3. Heat the oil in one or two large skillets (if two skillets are used, you may have to add a little more oil). When the oil is piping hot, add the veal. Cook quickly until golden brown on one side. Turn and cook on the other side until golden brown.

4. Meanwhile, melt the butter in a separate skillet. As the meat is cooked transfer it to the skillet with the butter.

5. Arrange the hard-cooked egg halves over the veal. Sprinkle the Marsala over the meat. Cover the skillet and cook about 4 minutes. Uncover and cook about 2 minutes longer or until the sauce is slightly thickened.

6. Arrange equal portions of hot escarole on each of four plates. Cover each serving of escarole with two slices of veal, slightly overlapping. Cover each serving with a slice of prosciutto. Top each serving with half a hard-cooked egg. Spoon the pan sauce over each serving. Sprinkle with chopped parsley and serve.

Yield: Four servings.

Italian-style Escarole

1	head of escarole, about 1 pound	Salt and freshly ground pepper
2	tablespoons olive oil	
4	cloves garlic, each cut lengthwise into three pieces	

1. Pull the leaves from the center core of the escarole. Discard the core. Rinse the leaves in cold running water and drain.

2. Bring enough water to boil to cover the leaves when they are added. Add the escarole leaves and stir down so that they cook evenly. Let simmer about 5 minutes. Drain well. Squeeze to extract excess liquid.

3. Heat the oil in skillet and add the garlic. Cook until it starts to brown. Add the escarole and salt and pepper to taste. Cook, stirring, until heated. Discard the garlic pieces and serve.

Yield: Four servings.

SOMEONE ONCE REMARKED THAT A REALLY talented cook could make a thistle palatable, and it is a sentiment with which I am in total accord. I have yet to find a food—freshly purchased or left over—that could not be turned into a highly edible dish with a little imagination.

Perhaps it is my predilection for pâtés and terrines, but I find ground meats among the most interesting kinds of ingredients with which to experiment. Ground beef, lamb, chicken, game, fish, veal, or liver are, where flavors are concerned, the most flexible of foods.

I have heard chefs expound at length on the best combination of meats for the perfect meat loaf. Some say beef for flavor, veal for texture and pork for richness. I find the combination of veal and pork to be just about ideal. The veal lends itself to a smooth texture and the pork adds an admirable rich quality.

You can, of course, reduce your meat-loaf making almost to a formula. For a pound and a half of meat you need about half a cup of bread crumbs, which "loosen" the texture of the meats. You need one large egg and then seasonings to taste.

One of the finest additions to a meat loaf may be chopped or sliced mushrooms, and the critical thing, to my mind, are the seasonings. Many meat loaves are, I find, overpowering in their flavors because of too heavy a hand in the spice cabinet.

Some of the best meat loaves are seasoned with a touch of rosemary and parsley: say, two tablespoons of parsley and a teaspoon of chopped fresh rosemary. Or half the amount dried. The meat loaf may be served, if desired, with a simply made tomato sauce.

To prepare this meal, you will need to exercise a bit of rapidity in preparing the meat before baking. That is in order to work it into a 60-minute framework. It can be done, however. The baking time on the meat loaf is from 40 to 45 minutes. The tomato sauce and a salad can be prepared as the loaf bakes.

Pain de Viande Champignons
(Meat loaf with mushrooms)

- ¾ pound ground lean veal
- ¾ pound ground lean pork
- 1 tablespoon butter
- ½ cup finely chopped onions
- ¼ pound mushrooms, thinly sliced or chopped, about 2 cups
- ¼ cup heavy cream
- 1 large egg, lightly beaten
- ½ cup fine, fresh bread crumbs
- 2 tablespoons finely chopped parsley
- 1 teaspoon finely chopped rosemary
- Salt and freshly ground pepper
- 1 sprig fresh rosemary, optional
- Tomato sauce (see recipe)

1. Preheat the oven to 425 degrees.
2. Ideally, you should use a loaf pan smaller than the standard size. This recipe was tested in a loaf pan that measures approximately 2½ by 4½ by 8½ inches.
3. Put the veal and pork in a mixing bowl.
4. Melt the butter in a small skillet and add the onions. Cook, stirring, until wilted. Add the mushrooms and cook until wilted. When the mushrooms give up their liquid, continue cooking until the liquid evaporates. Let cool briefly and add the onion and mushroom mixture to the meat.
5. Add the cream, egg, bread crumbs, parsley, chopped rosemary, and salt and pepper to taste.
6. Pack the mixture into the loaf pan and smooth it over. Press the rosemary sprig down the center of the meat loaf.
7. Place the meat loaf in the oven and bake 40 to 45 minutes. Serve with tomato sauce.

Yield: Four to six servings.

Sauce Tomate
(Tomato sauce)

1¼ pounds red, ripe tomatoes, peeled and seeded, or use an equal amount of drained canned tomatoes	3 tablespoons butter ⅓ cup finely diced onion 1 teaspoon finely minced garlic Salt and freshly ground pepper

1. Cut the tomatoes into cubes. There should be about 2 cups.
2. Melt 1 tablespoon of butter in a saucepan and add the onion and garlic. Cook, stirring until wilted. Add the tomatoes and salt and pepper to taste and bring to the boil. Let simmer 10 to 15 minutes. Swirl in the remaining butter and serve.

Yield: About 2 cups.

I SERIOUSLY DOUBT THAT THERE IS A SINGLE food on earth that would meet with universal praise. One of the finest chefs I know has a positive loathing for cheese in all of its forms, grated, served as a separate course or used as an ingredient. I have even known those who hate caviar and consider chocolate pedestrian.

An aversion to chocolate, cheese, or caviar is, admittedly, a rare exception. It is more understandable that variety meats—the odd parts of the animal such as liver, brains and sweetbreads—do not have a universal appeal.

This occurred to me recently when I had guests in my home, a couple whom I had not seen in recent years. As I prepared dinner, the husband came into the kitchen and noted that I had slices of liver on hand, making it ready to be floured before cooking in a skillet.

I noticed that he winced slightly when he noted the ingredients at hand and then he confided that his wife ranks liver high on her list of nonpreferences.

Because of the circumstances, however, I had little choice. It was serve that liver or take them all out to dinner. I then decided to try a diversionary tactic. I thought if I added a few sautéed white seedless grapes to my liver dish, it would, in part at least, make the food more palatable to her. And I must say it worked. My friend's wife ate every bite and seemed sorry when the platter was finished.

The combination of liver with seedless grapes may be commonplace, but on that evening it was original and spontaneous. What I did basically was to prepare the liver meunière-style, lightly coated in flour and sautéed quickly in butter. The liver must be cooked quickly lest it become dry and tough. I added a touch of red wine vinegar to the pan to deglaze it, and the tartness of the vinegar also helped, no doubt, to make the dish more palatable to my friend's wife.

Leeks are an excellent accompaniment for this dish. I serve them in a quickly made and delicate cream sauce.

Foie de Veau aux Raisins Blancs
(Calf's liver with white grapes)

4 slices calf's liver, about 1½ pounds
Salt and freshly ground pepper
⅓ cup flour
6 tablespoons butter
3 tablespoons chopped shallots
2 cups white seedless grapes
¼ cup red wine vinegar

1. Sprinkle the liver with salt and pepper to taste. Dredge the liver on all sides in flour and shake off excess.

2. Melt 3 tablespoons of the butter in a large, heavy skillet and add the liver slices. Cook about 2 minutes on one side over relatively high heat

until nicely browned. Turn and cook about 2 minutes on the second side.

3. Remove the liver to a warm serving platter.

4. To the skillet add one tablespoon of butter and add the shallots. Cook briefly and add the grapes. Swirl the grapes around and add the vinegar. Cook over high heat while swirling in the remaining 2 tablespoons butter. The total cooking time for the sauce with grapes after the liver is removed is about 3 minutes.

5. Pour the sauce over the liver and serve.

Yield: Four servings.

Poireaux à la Creme
(Leeks in cream)

4	large leeks, about 1½ pounds	Freshly grated nutmeg to taste
2	tablespoons butter	½ cup heavy cream
	Salt and freshly ground pepper	¼ cup water

1. Trim off the ends of the leeks. Cut the leeks crosswise into one-and-one-half-inch lengths. Rinse and drain thoroughly.

2. Melt the butter in a heavy saucepan and add the leeks. Cook briefly, stirring. Add salt and pepper to taste and the nutmeg. Add the cream and stir. Add the water and cover with a tight-fitting lid. Cook 15 minutes.

Yield: Four servings.

AT TIMES THERE IS NO ACCOUNTING FOR THE place names that are attached to various dishes. The name Argenteuil is on asparagus dishes because the town is associated with asparagus culture. For the same reason, dishes made with carrots are called Crecy. Who knows why quickly-sautéed liver with onions came to be so closely associated with two European cities, Lyons and Venice? And who knows which dish was created first, foie de veau lyonnaise or fegato alla veneziano, as the dishes are known respectively?

According to Waverley Root, in his book, *The Food of Italy* (Atheneum, 1971), the Venetians say they invented the dish. But then again, my Italian friends constantly try to promote that old canard that all of classic French cooking derives from Catherine de Médicis, who brought Italian cooks with her when she became queen of France in the sixteenth century.

Actually, the combination of liver and onions is as natural as ham and eggs, and it is eaten throughout the Western world. But I must say that, for no accountable reason, the finest dish of liver and onions I ever ate was in Venice about two years ago.

Basically, the Lyonnaise and Venetian preparations are the same. The Venetians may have cut the liver into finer julienne strips than the Lyonnaise. And the Italian version has a touch of sage, which is not characteristically French. In each case, both dishes depend on rapid cooking for their success. If you don't cook the liver hastily, it tends to "bleed" and lose its tender texture. The dish must be cooked in two or three minutes.

Either rice or potatoes goes well with liver and onions. I offer here, to accompany the liver and onions Venetian-style (there *is* a touch of sage), an easily made mashed potato dish baked with cheese.

Venetian-Style Liver with Onions

1½   pounds calf's liver
7   tablespoons peanut or corn oil
2   cups onions, cut into the thinnest possible slices
2   tablespoons unsalted butter
1   tablespoon red wine vinegar
½   teaspoon finely chopped sage
2   tablespoons finely chopped parsley

1. Trim off and discard any tough veins and fibers from the liver. Cut the liver into very thin (julienne) strips. Set aside.

2. Heat 1 tablespoon of the oil in a heavy skillet and, when it is quite hot, add the onions. Cook, stirring often, about 10 minutes or until the onions are golden brown and starting to caramelize. Set aside.

3. Heat 3 tablespoons oil in a heavy skillet, and, when it is almost smoking, add half the liver. Cook, shaking the skillet and stirring often over very high heat, about 1½ minutes. Drain the liver in a colander.

4. Wipe out the skillet and add the remaining oil. When it is very hot, add the remaining liver and cook in the same quick manner. Drain.

5. Melt the butter in a skillet and add the onions. Cook, shaking the skillet, until the onions are frying briskly. Add the vinegar, liver, and sage. Stir to blend, about 10 seconds. Sprinkle with chopped parsley. Serve immediately.

Yield: Four to six servings.

Pommes Purées au Gratin
(Mashed potatoes baked with cheese)

4 large potatoes, about 1½ pounds	2 tablespoons butter
Salt	2 tablespoons finely grated Parmesan cheese
1 cup milk	

1. Preheat the broiler.
2. Peel the potatoes and rinse well. Cut the potatoes lengthwise in half. Cut each half into four pieces. There should be about 4 cups.
3. Put the potatoes in a saucepan with water to cover. Add salt to taste and bring to boil. Cook 12 to 15 minutes or until the potatoes are tender. Drain. Put through a food mill or food ricer into a saucepan.
4. Meanwhile, heat the milk in a saucepan.
5. Add the butter to the potatoes and stir with a wooden spoon until the butter has melted. Add the hot milk gradually, stirring with the spoon. Add salt to taste.
6. Spoon the potatoes into an ovenproof serving dish. (An oval dish measuring 1½ by 6½ by 9½ inches is suitable.) Smooth the top of the potatoes with a spatula.
7. Sprinkle with Parmesan cheese and place under broiler until nicely browned.

Yield: Four servings.

WHEN I WROTE RECENTLY THAT A READER had asked why there were so few duck recipes in my column, I stated that it was impossible to prepare roast duck in less than one and a half hours. I, therefore, offered a less-than-60-minute version of a duck dish, one in which the bird was cut into serving pieces and broiled, then roasted.

This brought an inquiry from another reader, asking if that great delicacy known in French as ris de veau and in English as calf's sweetbreads could be prepared and cooked in less than an hour. The answer is that it can be done if you are willing to forgo some of the refinements in sweetbread preparation. That is to say, the long soaking that whitens the flesh of the sweetbreads, and the extended period of "weighting" the sweetbreads once they are blanched.

My own attitude is that if I have sweetbreads and limited time to prepare them, by all means, use the shorter preparation. When I tested this recipe, I dispensed entirely with the soaking (which generally involves soaking a considerable time under cold running water or in several changes of cold water). I cooked the sweetbreads directly from the butcher wrap in water flavored with onion, bay leaf, and so on. When done, I split them in half and made a gesture in the direction of weighting them. I placed them between racks with a weight on top (a flat mallet) and let them stand until I was ready to cook.

I used the traditional method for breading the sweetbreads—no short cuts there. This involves, of course, dipping the sweetbread pieces first in flour, then in beaten egg, and then in fine fresh bread crumbs.

Incidentally, I heartily recommend using fresh bread crumbs made from bread slices that have had the crusts cut away. The meal of sweetbreads was consumed with great satisfaction by guests who did not know of my short cuts, and they dined with praise.

Riz de Veau Panées à l'Anglaise
(Breaded sweetbreads)

2 to 4 pairs sweetbreads, about 1½ pounds total weight	1 egg
Salt	3 tablespoons water
4 peppercorns	Freshly ground pepper
¼ cup coarsely chopped onion	1 tablespoon plus ⅓ cup vegetable, corn, or peanut oil
1 bay leaf	⅓ cup flour
½ teaspoon dried thyme	2 cups fine fresh bread crumbs
2 sprigs fresh parsley	6 tablespoons butter

1. Put sweetbreads in a saucepan and add cold water to cover. Add salt to taste, peppercorns, onion, bay leaf, thyme, and parsley sprigs. Bring to the boil and let simmer 10 minutes. Drain thoroughly. Run under cold water to chill.

2. Split the sweetbreads in half lengthwise. Put the halves on a rack and cover with another rack. Place a weight on top and let stand until ready to cook, 15 minutes or longer.

3. Put the egg in a flat dish and add the water, salt and pepper to taste, and 1 tablespoon of oil. Beat to blend.

4. Put the flour and bread crumbs in separate flat dishes.

5. Dip the sweetbread pieces first in flour, then in egg, then in bread crumbs. The sweetbreads should be thoroughly coated, but shake off any excess. Pat the pieces all over to make the crumbs adhere.

6. Heat the remaining oil in a skillet large enough to hold the pieces in one layer. Cook on one side until golden. Turn and cook until golden on the other side. Cook, turning occasionally, about 10 minutes.

7. Melt the butter in a large, heavy skillet and cook, swirling it around, until foamy and starting to turn hazelnut brown. Add the sweetbreads and heat. Serve the sweetbreads with the butter poured over.

Yield: Four servings.

Haricots Verts à la Crème
(Green beans in cream)

1 pound fresh, unblemished green beans	½ cup heavy cream
Salt and freshly ground pepper	⅛ teaspoon freshly grated nutmeg
2 tablespoons butter	½ teaspoon dried tarragon

1. Trim off the ends of each green bean. Put them in a saucepan with water to cover and salt to taste. Bring to the boil and let simmer until tender, 5 minutes or longer. Cooking time will depend on the size and age of the beans. Do not overcook.

2. Drain the beans and put in a saucepan. Add salt and pepper to taste, butter, cream, nutmeg, and tarragon. Bring to the boil, stirring. Cook briefly until the cream is slightly reduced and thickened.

Yield: Four servings.

THERE ARE SOME FOODS, OF WHICH I AM ESpecially fond, that I feel have a definite place in any compilation of 60-minute dishes that require a minimum of preparation the night before.

One of these is sweetbreads. These should be put in cold water to soak overnight before they are made ready for a final preparation. And thus, if you wish to eat sweetbreads while cooking them à la minute, as we say in French, you are advised to purchase them the day before.

Sweetbreads, as any connoisseur can tell you, are among the most sophisticated and elegant of dishes, lending themselves to scores of superb preparations. They can be studded with truffles and braised and as such they are known as Regence. They can be studded with truffles and slices of calf's tongue and braised and as such they are known as financière. These are dishes that require considerable technique and are not within the scope of my column.

Some of the finest and most comprehensible sweetbread preparations start off meunière style. That is to say that the blanched sweetbreads (sweetbreads are usually almost always cooked briefly in water or blanched before given a final cooking) are sliced, dipped in flour and sautéed in butter. With that as a base there are many delectable variations.

One of my personal favorites is grenobloise. That implies sweetbread slices that have been cooked meunière style and then garnished with capers after adding a little lemon or vinegar. Most grenobloise recipes call for lemon, but vinegar seems especially suited to the flavor of sweetbreads.

An excellent accompaniment for sweetbreads grenobloise are potatoes and peas cooked briefly in a light cream sauce and sprinkled with chives. The bland nature of this dish makes an excellent foil for the slightly tart nature of the sweetbreads with capers.

Riz de Veau Grenobloise
(Sweetbreads with capers and vinegar)

1¼ pounds sweetbreads	2 teaspoons red wine vinegar
Salt and freshly ground pepper	2 tablespoons well-drained packed capers
Flour for dredging	
¼ cup peanut, vegetable, or corn oil	1 tablespoon finely chopped parsley
6 tablespoons butter	

1. Put the sweetbreads in a mixing bowl and add cold water to cover. Refrigerate overnight.

2. Drain the sweetbreads. Put them in a saucepan with cold water to

cover and salt to taste. Bring to the boil and let simmer gently about 5 minutes.

3. Drain the sweetbreads again. Run them under cold running water until thoroughly chilled. Trim the sweetbreads neatly to remove any outer membranes and tough portions. Cut the sweetbreads horizontally through the center to make flat slices.

4. Sprinkle the sweetbreads with salt and pepper to taste. Dip each slice into flour on both sides. Shake off any excess.

5. Heat the oil in a heavy skillet and add the slices. Cook about 2 minutes or until golden brown on one side. Turn and cook about 2 minutes on the second side. As the slices cook, transfer them to a warm serving dish.

6. Melt the butter in a small skillet and cook, swirling the butter around, until it foams up. Continue cooking and swirling it around until it becomes hazelnut brown. Do not burn.

7. Add the vinegar and capers and give the butter one final swirl. Pour the butter mixture over the sweetbreads. Serve sprinkled with chopped parsley.

Yield: Four servings.

Pommes de Terres et Pois à la Crème
(Potatoes with peas in cream)

4 potatoes, about 1¼ pounds	Freshly ground pepper
Salt	⅛ teaspoon freshly grated nutmeg
1 cup milk	2 cups fresh or frozen green peas
½ cup heavy cream	¼ cup chopped chives

1. Put the potatoes in a saucepan with water to cover and salt to taste. Bring to the boil and simmer 20 minutes or until tender without being mushy.

2. When cool enough to handle, peel the potatoes and cut them into quarter-inch rounds. There should be about 4 cups.

3. Put the slices in a saucepan and add the milk and cream.

4. Place on the heat and add salt and pepper to taste and nutmeg. Bring to the boil and simmer over high heat about 5 minutes.

5. Meanwhile, if fresh peas are to be used, cook them in boiling salted water until tender. Drain and add them to the potatoes in cream. If frozen peas are used, simply defrost, add and cook with the potatoes. Add the chives and stir. Cook about 1 minute.

Yield: Four servings.

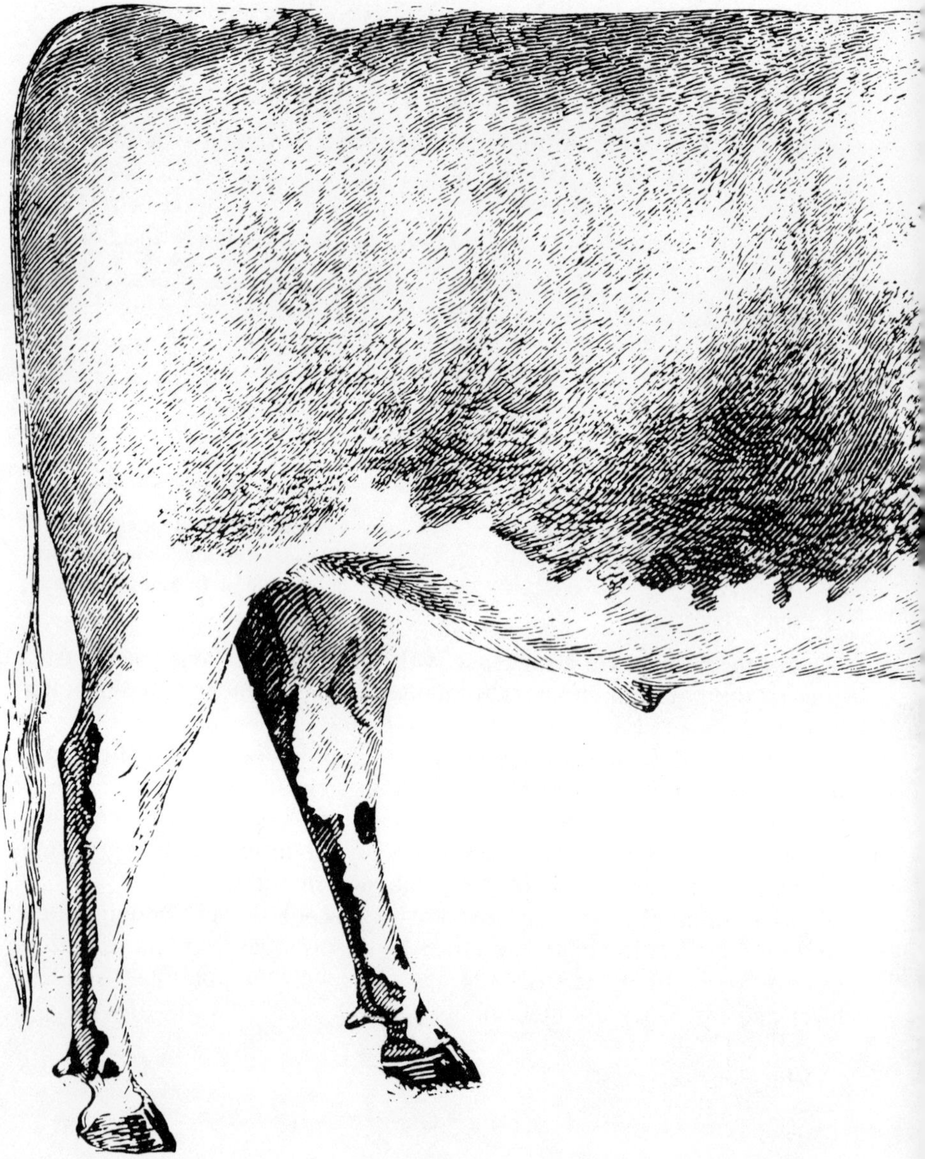

Beef

TASTE HAS ALWAYS BEEN BASED ON CUSTOM. I know people who did not like the taste of their first olive as well as people who actually hated the flavor of white truffles on first sampling.

Hams and sausages were first smoked and/or salted down, not for the sake of flavor but as a means of preserving them during the winter. Gradually, the flavor of the smoking and/or salting became an end in itself.

The same is true of game marinades. Centuries ago, one cook or another devised the notion that freshly killed game would be tenderized or would perhaps keep better without refrigeration if it were put in a bowl and covered with wine and vinegar and spices, all of which would act as preservatives. When the game was cooked, the natural flavor of the bird or beast had been altered and desirably so.

That is why it is not uncommon, in French kitchens at least, to take a meat that is not "gamey" and to "cure" it overnight in a marinade that will give it the flavor of game. These dishes go by numerous names. Sometimes they are called "à l'ivrogne," which means drunkards' style, and sometimes "en chevreuil," which means treated as though it were venison or roebuck.

In my own kitchen, the steak is marinated overnight in a marinade that includes red wine, vinegar, chopped vegetables, and spices such as rosemary, sage, and coriander seeds.

Strictly speaking, this is not a "60-minute dish," but it can be prepared an evening before cooking. When you are ready to cook the meat, the total preparation and cooking time will be less than half an hour. An ideal accompaniment for the steak is potatoes in cream. Put the potatoes on to cook before you start cooking the meat and sauce.

Steak en Chevreuil
(Marinated steak)

- 1 top round steak, 4 pounds, about 1½ inches thick
- Salt and freshly ground pepper
- 2 cups red wine
- ¼ cup red wine vinegar
- ½ teaspoon dried rosemary leaves
- ½ teaspoon powdered dried sage
- ½ teaspoon dried coriander seeds
- 2 bay leaves
- ½ teaspoon dried thyme
- 10 peppercorns, crushed
- 2 whole cloves
- ⅓ cup thinly sliced onion
- ¼ cup thinly sliced carrot
- ¼ cup finely chopped celery
- 2 tablespoons thinly sliced shallots
- 1 clove garlic, unpeeled and crushed
- 6 sprigs fresh parsley
- 2 tablespoons peanut oil
- ½ teaspoon arrowroot or cornstarch
- 1 teaspoon water
- 1 tablespoon currant jelly
- 2 tablespoons cognac

1. Sprinkle the steak on both sides with salt and pepper to taste. Put the steak in a dish in which it fits compactly but not too snugly.

2. Combine 1 cup of wine, the vinegar, rosemary, sage, coriander seeds, bay leaves, thyme, peppercorns, and cloves in a small saucepan and bring to the boil. Remove from heat. Let cool.

3. Add the onion, carrot, celery, shallots, garlic, and parsley to the steak. Pour the wine and spice mixture and remaining wine over the steak. Cover and refrigerate overnight.

4. Remove the steak from the marinating liquid and set aside. Strain the marinade into a saucepan. Discard the solids. Bring the marinade to the boil and cook down until it is reduced to about ¾ of a cup.

5. Heat the oil in a large, heavy skillet in which the steak will fit comfortably. When the pan is very hot and starting to smoke, add the steak. Cook over high heat about 3 minutes until nicely seared on one side. Sprinkle with salt and pepper and turn. Continue cooking over moderately high heat about 3 minutes. Turn the steak. Continue cooking, turning the meat occasionally so that it cooks evenly. The total cooking time is 15 minutes for rare meat.

6. Blend the arrowroot or cornstarch with the water and stir it into the cooked-down sauce. Stir in the jelly until melted.

7. Transfer the steak from the skillet to a hot serving plate.

8. Pour off the fat from the skillet. Add the cognac and ignite it. Add the sauce and cook, stirring with a wooden spoon to dissolve the brown particles that cling to the skillet.

9. Pour the sauce over the meat. Slice the meat on the diagonal and serve hot.

Yield: Six or more servings.

Pommes à la Crème
(Potatoes in cream)

1¾ pounds small, new, red-skinned potatoes	½ cup heavy cream
Salt	Freshly ground pepper
1 cup milk	⅛ teaspoon freshly grated nutmeg
	⅛ teaspoon cayenne pepper

1. Put the unpeeled potatoes into a saucepan and add water to cover and salt to taste. Bring to the boil and simmer until potatoes are tender, about 20 minutes. Drain.

2. When the potatoes are cool enough to handle, peel and cut them into slices slightly thicker than one-quarter inch. Put the slices in a small saucepan and add the milk, cream, salt and pepper to taste, nutmeg, and cayenne. Bring to the boil and simmer about 5 minutes. Serve.

Yield: Four servings.

LESS WELL KNOWN OR FAR LESS USED IN SOME professional kitchens is a red counterpart of beurre blanc called beurre rouge. This is made in an identical fashion but it is made with red wine rather than white. The preparation of a beurre rouge requires a minimum of time. In fact, it must be made hurriedly or else it might curdle or separate. This particular sauce is excellent served with red meats such as broiled or grilled steak.

Here is a hastily made main course—steak with beurre rouge. The steak would go well with skillet potatoes and a salad.

Steak Grillé au Beurre Rouge
(Grilled beef)

1 2-pound boneless sirloin steak, about 1½ inches thick
2 tablespoons peanut, vegetable, or corn oil
Salt and freshly ground pepper
3 tablespoons finely chopped parsley
Beurre rouge (see recipe)

1. Preheat the broiler to high.
2. Rub the steak on both sides with oil.
3. Sprinkle the steak with salt and pepper to taste. Use a generous amount of pepper.
4. Place the meat on a broiler rack and let it cook about 4 or 5 inches from the source of heat. Broil about 3 to 5 minutes and turn the meat. Broil on the other side from 3 to 5 minutes. Cooking time will depend on the desired degree of doneness.
5. Transfer the steak to a hot platter and cover loosely with aluminum foil. Let the steak stand in a warm place about 5 minutes to redistribute the internal juices of the meat.
6. Slice the steak on the diagonal (across the grain of the meat) and serve with beurre rouge.

Yield: Four servings.

Beurre Rouge
(Red butter sauce)

6 tablespoons finely chopped shallots
1½ cups red Burgundy wine
12 tablespoons butter
Salt and freshly ground pepper

1. Combine the shallots and wine in a saucepan and bring to a vigorous boil.

2. Let the wine cook down to about ⅓ cup. Continue cooking over high heat, stirring rapidly with a wire whisk. Add the butter about 2 tablespoons at a time. Add salt and pepper to taste.

Yield: About 1¼ cups.

Pommes de Terre Sautées
(Skillet potatoes)

4 medium-size potatoes, about 1¼ pounds	1 tablespoon butter
Salt	Freshly ground pepper
3 tablespoons peanut, vegetable, or corn oil	

1. Place the unpeeled potatoes in a saucepan and add cold water to cover. Add salt to taste and bring to the boil. Simmer 15 to 20 minutes until tender. Do not overcook. The potatoes must remain firm. This may be done a day in advance.

2. Peel the potatoes and cut them into slices ¼ inch thick or slightly thicker.

3. Heat the oil and butter in a heavy skillet and add the potato slices. Add salt and pepper to taste. Cook, shaking and tossing the skillet to redistribute the potatoes. Cook until the potatoes form a crisp outside crust and are nicely browned. Serve hot.

Yield: Four servings.

ONE OF MY EARLIEST OBSERVATIONS ABOUT nouvelle cuisine, when it first came into being in the late 1970s, was that salads which blend freshly cooked meats and seafood with salad greens—watercress, Boston lettuce, chicory, field salad, endive, and so on—is one of the hallmarks of that "new" type of cooking. There are many such hallmarks, of course, including vegetables that are slightly undercooked, occasional uses of raw fish such as scallops, many dishes with the sauce known as beurre blanc, and so on.

I had never really pondered the origin of that "hot meat and cold salad greens" combination until several years ago when I dined in the home of a friend from Thailand. I was then served a fairly exotic salad composed of sliced, freshly cooked steak on a bed of assorted salad ingredients including tomato wedges, onion rings, fresh coriander leaves, and different types of lettuce.

That is not to propose that the nouvelle cuisine idea is wholly based on Thai cooking, but that the idea probably derives from some Oriental inspiration. I know that the Vietnamese also prepare a similar salad and that they, like the Thai, use a very salty fish sauce in their salad dressing and almost invariably lemon or lime juice rather than vinegar.

Over the years I have made many such salads and one of the best to my taste was recently prepared in my home a short while ago. This one was made with steak and, because it was mid-summer, grilled over charcoal. Although the recipe looks somewhat lengthy, it can easily be prepared within the space of an hour. The steak can just as easily be cooked under the home broiler and for about the same length of time.

Steak Salad

- 3 shell steaks, about ¾ pound each
- Salt and freshly ground pepper
- 6 tablespoons plus 2 teaspoons peanut, vegetable, or corn oil
- 1 or 2 yellow squash, about ½ pound
- 1 or 2 zucchini, about ½ pound
- 1 sweet red or green pepper, cored and seeded
- 3 ears fresh corn on the cob, or 1 cup cooked corn kernels
- 1 tablespoon imported mustard such as Dijon or Düsseldorf
- 2 tablespoons raspberry or red wine vinegar
- 1 tablespoon chopped fresh tarragon
- 1 cup thinly sliced onion rings
- 1½ cups shredded Boston lettuce or, preferably, arugula

1. Preheat a charcoal grill.

2. Sprinkle the steaks with salt and pepper to taste. Brush on all sides with 2 teaspoons of oil and set aside.

3. Trim the yellow squash and zucchini. Cut each squash and zucchini

into 1½-inch lengths. Cut each piece crosswise into ½-inch slices. Stack the slices and cut them into ½-inch "sticks." There should be about 2 cups of each or a total of 4 cups. Set aside.

4. Cut the sweet pepper lengthwise into thin strips. There should be about 1 cup. Set aside.

5. Bring enough water to the boil to cover the squash, zucchini, and sweet pepper when added. Add the vegetables. When the water returns to the boil, drain quickly. Run the vegetables under cold running water to chill briefly. Drain well.

6. Drop the ears of corn into boiling water. When the water returns to the boil, let simmer about 30 seconds. Drain. Cut the corn from the cob. There should be about 1 cup. Set aside.

7. Put the steaks on the grill, about 3 inches from the source of heat. Broil about 3 to 4 minutes on one side. Turn and broil about 2 to 3 minutes on the other side. Remove the steaks from the grill.

8. Trim off the fat from the steaks. Cut the steak on the diagonal (across the grain of the meat) into very thin slices. Set aside. Reserve any steak juices that flow from the meat.

9. Put the mustard in a mixing bowl and add the vinegar, stirring with a wire whisk. Beat in the remaining oil gradually. Add salt and pepper to taste and the tarragon.

10. Add the onion rings, corn, squash, zucchini, red or green pepper, steak, and any steak juices. Stir to blend. Add a generous grinding of black pepper. Spoon the salad onto the center of a serving dish. Garnish with shredded lettuce arranged around the salad. Serve at room temperature.

Yield: Eight or more servings.

Nouilles Persillées au Fromage
(Noodles with parsley and cheese)

½	pound wide or medium noodles	1	tablespoon chopped fresh parsley
	Salt		
2	tablespoons butter	1	tablespoon grated Parmesan cheese
	Freshly ground pepper		

1. Cook the noodles in boiling salted water to cover.

2. Drain well and return to the pot. Add the butter and salt and pepper to taste, and toss. Add the parsley and cheese, toss, and serve hot.

Yield: Four servings.

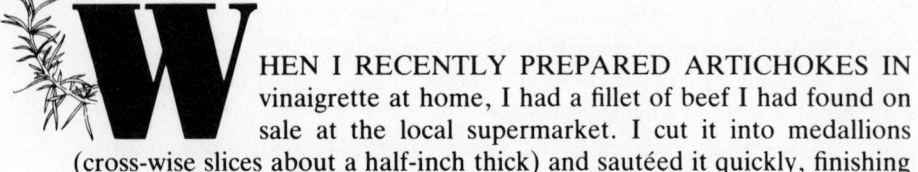

WHEN I RECENTLY PREPARED ARTICHOKES IN vinaigrette at home, I had a fillet of beef I had found on sale at the local supermarket. I cut it into medallions (cross-wise slices about a half-inch thick) and sautéed it quickly, finishing the dish off at the stove with a few fresh mushrooms, sliced and cooked, plus sour cream that had been given an additional tang with a touch of vinegar and capers.

When I was a young chef in Paris, we rarely, if ever, used fresh dill in the kitchen. Since coming to this country I have decided it is one of the best-tasting of fresh herbs. I sprinkled a tablespoon of chopped dill on the beef before serving, and it is a fine addition. As a side dish I recommend cooked brown rice.

Médaillons de Boeuf à la Scandinave
(Fillet of beef with sour cream)

2 pounds well-trimmed fillet of beef	2 tablespoons red wine vinegar
Salt and freshly ground pepper	2 tablespoons capers
3 tablespoons butter	1 cup sour cream
¼ pound mushrooms, thinly sliced, about 2 cups	1 tablespoon finely chopped fresh dill or parsley
1 tablespoon finely chopped shallots	

1. Cut the fillet into 12 crosswise pieces of equal size, about half an inch thick. Sprinkle the slices with salt and pepper to taste.

2. Melt 2 tablespoons of the butter in a skillet large enough to hold the pieces comfortably without crowding. Add the pieces of meat and cook over moderately high heat about 30 to 45 seconds. They should be nicely browned on one side. Turn the pieces and cook about 30 to 45 seconds on the second side.

3. Immediately transfer the pieces to a warm serving platter. Add the mushrooms to the skillet and stir. Add the shallots and cook about 15 seconds. Add the vinegar and capers and stir.

4. Add the sour cream and stir. Let the sauce come to the simmer. Add any juices that have accumulated around the steak. Remove from the heat. Swirl in the remaining butter.

5. Return the meat to the sauce and sprinkle the dill on top. Serve with brown rice.

Yield: Four servings.

Brown Rice

1	cup brown rice		Salt and freshly ground pepper
2	tablespoons butter	1	bay leaf
4	teaspoons chopped onion	1	sprig fresh parsley
¼	teaspoon finely minced garlic	1	sprig fresh thyme or ¼
1¾	cups water or chicken broth		teaspoon dried thyme

1. Rinse and drain the rice and set aside.

2. Melt 1 tablespoon of the butter in a saucepan and add the onion and garlic. Cook, stirring, until the onion is wilted.

3. Add the rice, water, salt and pepper to taste, bay leaf, parsley, and thyme. Bring to the boil and cover closely. Let simmer for 40 minutes.

4. Remove from the heat. Discard the bay leaf, parsley, and thyme. Fluff the rice with a two-pronged fork and stir in the remaining butter.

Yield: Four servings.

IT IS FASCINATING THE NUMBER OF TIMES I have been asked by readers and friends to explain to them what a chateaubriand is. (The word, I know, is also sometimes spelled chateaubriant.)

It is a preparation and cut of meat that is widely admired both in this country and in France and for very good reasons; it is extremely lean, flavorsome, and as tender as butter. What, people ask, is the difference between a chateaubriand and a fillet mignon?

They do, of course, come from the same cut of beef, notably the whole fillet. The chateaubriand is the thickest portion of the fillet. To my mind it is the choicest part of the fillet and, heaven knows, the cooking of a chateaubriand is simplicity itself. The total broiling time is about 15 minutes (or slightly longer if you like well done meat, which I don't). After broiling, the meat is left to stand about 15 minutes to redistribute the internal juices. The seasonings are simply salt and pepper. And the ultimate sauce to be served with a chateaubriand is a béarnaise sauce. As the meat cooks, there is ample time to make that sauce, using as it does butter, shallots, peppercorns, vinegar, and tarragon.

The only involved thing about a properly made chateaubriand is the advance preparation. When the meat is cut it should be stood on end. You cover the top with a clean cloth and pound it with a flat mallet (the bottom of a clean skillet might be used). You turn it to the other end and pound once more. When ready to cook, the meat will have been flattened until it is about 5 inches in diameter and about 2 inches thick or slightly less.

It almost goes without saying that a chateaubriand is an expensive cut of meat. But it is generally served on special occasions, and to very special guests.

Chateaubriand Grillé
(Broiled chateaubriand)

1 trimmed, ready-to-cook chateaubriand, about 1¼ pounds
1 tablespoon peanut, vegetable, or corn oil

Salt and freshly ground pepper
Béarnaise sauce (see recipe)

1. Preheat the broiler to high.
2. Place the chateaubriand cut side down on a flat surface. Cover with a clean cloth towel and pound with a flat mallet. Turn the chateaubriand, cover with the cloth and pound on the second side. The meat at this point should measure about 5 inches in diameter and about 1½ to 2 inches thick.
3. Sprinkle the meat on both sides with salt and papper to taste. Brush all over with oil.
4. Place the chateaubriand on a broiler rack. Place it under the broiler

so that the top of the meat is only about 2 inches or slightly less from the source of heat. Broil about 5 minutes.

5. Turn the meat and continue broiling 5 minutes.

6. Shift the broiler rack to the bottom of the oven or to a point where the meat will be about 14 inches from the source of heat. Continue broiling about 5 minutes.

7. Transfer the meat to a carving board and cover with foil to keep warm. Let stand 15 minutes before carving.

8. Carve the chateaubriand and serve with sauce béarnaise.

Yield: Two to four servings.

Sauce Béarnaise
(A shallot and peppercorn butter sauce)

12	tablespoons butter	1	teaspoon dried tarragon
2	tablespoons finely chopped shallots	2	egg yolks
		2	tablespoons cold water
½	teaspoon crushed peppercorns		Salt
⅓	cup red wine vinegar		Pinch of cayenne pepper

1. Let the butter melt over very low heat. Take care that it does not brown or take on color. Pour the butter into a glass measuring cup. Skim off and discard the white foam from the surface. Set aside briefly.

2. Combine the shallots, peppercorns, vinegar, and tarragon in a saucepan. Bring to the boil and cook until the wine is totally evaporated. Let the mixture cool slightly.

3. Add the yolks and water to the shallot and peppercorn mixture. Set the pan in a basin of boiling water. Stir briskly and constantly with a wire whisk until the yolk mixture becomes slightly thickened and foamy. Take care that the yolks do not become overheated or they will scramble.

4. Remove the saucepan from the heat and gradually add the melted butter, stirring rapidly. Do not add the milky sediment that rests in the bottom of the cup. Add salt to taste and the cayenne. This sauce may be strained through a fine sieve if desired.

Yield: About ¾ cup.

IF YOU ARE A PROFESSIONAL CHEF FOR A good many years it takes a certain amount of time to get into "modern" cooking techniques. And I put that word modern in quotation marks because I am referring to pressure cookers which have been around, in this country at least, for several decades. There are many reasons why it took me a spell to get into attempting to cook with a pressure cooker.

In the first place, I spent a large part of my life working in a professional kitchen and there are not, as far as I know, any vast pressure cookers manufactured for turning out the greatest French dishes on a monumental scale. In the second place, when I retired to cooking in my own home, I found and find a great pleasure in a leisured, unhurried form of cookery.

I enjoy cooking, find it relaxing, and often in the evening find myself with ample time to spare, whether I am preparing a six-course dinner for ten or twelve or a small, intimate buffet for four or six.

When I first experimented with pressure cookers a year or so ago, I was amazed by the incredible speed with which foods can be cooked. Since then, I have experimented often with "classic" and traditional regional dishes from my years at the stove. I have made beef ragoûts, pork chop casseroles, chicken stews, and so on with great—and hurried—success. The utensils are, needless to say, a great boon to the cook-in-a-hurry.

One of the most basic dishes that I have made, and which my family and friends have enjoyed, is a fine beef stew in the style of Provence. It is, with the aid of a pressure cooker, one of the easiest dishes to prepare in a hurry. You simply brown a lean cut cubed steak in a small amount of fat and add the remaining ingredients. When they have cooked briefly on top of the stove you fasten the lid of the cooker and let it puff away for about 20 to 25 minutes—and that is it. Sprinkle with parsley and serve with buttered noodles or steamed potatoes and a simple salad on the side. It is an excellent main course for an evening meal in any season of the year.

Daube de Boeuf Provençale
(Braised beef with tomatoes and herbs)

- 3 pounds lean chuck steak, cut into 1½-inch cubes
- Salt and freshly ground pepper
- ½ pound whole mushrooms, quartered or left whole, depending on size
- 2 tablespoons finely chopped garlic
- ½ pound onions, cut into 1-inch cubes or left whole if quite small
- ¼ cup flour
- 1 cup dry red wine
- 2 cups canned imported tomatoes, left whole if small or cut in half if large
- 3 tablespoons olive oil
- 24 pitted, stuffed green olives
- 1 bay leaf
- ½ teaspoon dried thyme
- Pinch of cayenne pepper
- ½ teaspoon stem saffron, optional
- ¼ cup finely chopped parsley

1. Trim the meat of all fat, and sprinkle the cubes with salt and pepper to taste.
2. Heat the oil in a pressure cooker until quite hot and almost smoking. Add the beef cubes and cook, stirring often, over high heat until the meat is lightly brown all over.
3. Add the garlic and stir. Add the onions and mushrooms and stir. Sprinkle with flour and stir to coat the pieces evenly. Add the wine, tomatoes, thyme, bay leaf, salt and pepper to taste, cayenne, and saffron. Stir while bringing to the boil. Add the cover of the pressure cooker and the pressure regulator.
4. Reduce the heat and cook according to manufacturer's instructions, 20 to 25 minutes. Uncover as directed. Pour the beef into a serving dish and sprinkle with chopped parsley.

Yield: Six servings.

Pommes Vapeur
(Steamed potatoes)

---

1 pound new, red potatoes	2 tablespoons butter, optional
Salt	Freshly ground black pepper

1. Rinse and drain the potatoes and put them in a small kettle or deep saucepan.
2. Cover with water and salt to taste. Bring to the boil and simmer 20 minutes or until tender. Drain and, when cool enough to handle, peel.
3. Melt the butter in a heavy saucepan and add the potatoes. Sprinkle with salt and pepper to taste. Cover and heat thoroughly.

Yield: Four servings.

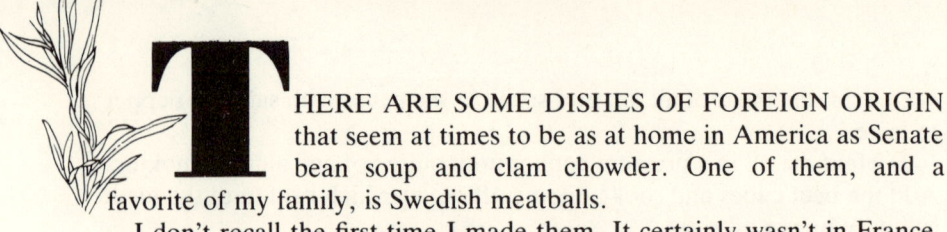

THERE ARE SOME DISHES OF FOREIGN ORIGIN that seem at times to be as at home in America as Senate bean soup and clam chowder. One of them, and a favorite of my family, is Swedish meatballs.

I don't recall the first time I made them. It certainly wasn't in France, where I had never heard of them. I probably first sampled them when I worked for a brief stint many years ago at the Waldorf Astoria.

Until quite recently I had never questioned the authenticity of the meatballs that I was preparing and alluding to as Swedish. It came about when I was challenged at table by a friend from Stockholm.

At his request I resorted to several books written by Swedish cooks, and I was amused to think that on several points I was wide of the mark. What surprised me was that the basic meat was not ground veal as I had always presumed it to be but generally a combination of beef and pork and occasionally with veal added. Dill was not the common herb I had believed it to be and the only spice called for in any of the recipes was a touch of allspice.

Traditional Swedish meatballs are easy to prepare and can be made in far less than an hour. The last time I served them was with brown rice. On many occasions I have printed a recipe for "perfect" white rice, which is baked or cooked on top of the stove in exactly 17 minutes. Readers have desired a rice recipe precisely timed for brown rice. The cooking time was longer: I found it to be 40 minutes. There are those who say, of course, that brown rice is more nutritious than the white.

In preparing a meal of Swedish meatballs and brown rice I would propose that you get the rice on the stove before preparing the meatballs in the interest of conserving time.

Swedish Meatballs

- ½ pound ground beef (may be part veal)
- ½ pound ground pork (may be part veal)
- 2 tablespoons plus 1 teaspoon butter
- ½ cup finely chopped onion
- ½ cup bread crumbs
- ½ cup milk
- 1 egg
- Salt and freshly ground pepper
- ⅛ teaspoon ground allspice
- 1½ tablespoons flour
- 1 cup chicken broth
- 1 cup heavy cream
- 2 tablespoons aquavit, optional

1. Combine the beef and pork in a mixing bowl.

2. Melt 1 teaspoon butter in a small skillet. Add the onion. Cook, stirring, until onion is wilted. Combine bread crumbs and milk in a bowl.

3. Add the onion, bread crumb mixture, egg, salt and pepper to taste, and allspice to the meat. Blend well.

4. Shape the meat into 28 or more meatballs, each about one to one-and-a-half inches thick.

5. Melt the remaining two tablespoons of butter in a large skillet and add the meatballs. Or use two skillets and twice the amount of butter. Cook the meatballs over gentle heat, turning them carefully with a spatula so that they brown evenly. Cooking time is about 10 minutes.

6. When the meatballs are done, transfer them to a saucepan.

7. To the small amount of fat left in the skillet, add the flour and stir to distribute it over the bottom of the skillet. Add the broth, stirring. Cook about 1 minute. Add the cream and cook about 2 minutes longer. Strain the sauce over the meatballs. Add freshly ground pepper to taste. Bring to the boil. If desired, stir in the aquavit. Serve with brown rice.

Yield: Four servings.

Brown Rice

1	cup brown rice		Salt and freshly ground pepper
2	tablespoons butter	1	bay leaf
4	teaspoons chopped onion	1	sprig fresh parsley
¼	teaspoon finely minced garlic	1	sprig fresh thyme or ¼ teaspoon dried thyme
1¾	cups water or chicken broth		

1. Rinse the rice and set aside.

2. Melt 1 tablespoon of the butter in a saucepan and add the onion and garlic. Cook, stirring, until the onion is wilted.

3. Add the rice, water, salt and pepper to taste, bay leaf, parsley, and thyme. Bring to the boil and cover closely. Let simmer 40 minutes.

4. Remove from the heat. Discard the bay leaf, parsley, and thyme sprigs. Fluff the rice with a two-pronged fork and stir in the remaining butter.

Yield: Four servings.

IN ALL MY YEARS AS A PROFESSIONAL CHEF, I have never met a colleague who was weaned on what is called haute or classic cuisine. Most chefs, including myself, were born in modest circumstances in which eating was a major diversion. The food in my own home was definitely cuisine bourgeoise or family-style cooking, and as such was marked by a simplicity both in ingredients and cooking techniques. It was also marked by economy.

One of the favorite dishes of my childhood is called hachis Parmentier. The word "hachis" is derived from the French "hacher," meaning to chop. It refers to a dish made with chopped or ground meat. Incidentally, that is where the American dish called hash came from. Parmentier pertains to the potatoes used in the dish. Antoine-Auguste Parmentier was a French economist who is credited with making potatoes popular in France during the late eighteenth century.

A fine hachis Parmentier is the French equivalent of the English shepherd's pie, though I believe the English version is almost always made with lamb. The French creation can be made with almost any kind of meat or poultry, cooked or not, that is made into a stew, covered with mashed potatoes and baked. The recipe here is simple and economical. The "hash" here consists of ground beef cooked in a light tomato sauce with seasonings. It is quickly made, too. While the potatoes for the topping are cooked before mashing, there is ample time to prepare the ground meat base. The mushroom sauce to accompany it can be made in a very few minutes before it is allowed to simmer on its own.

Hachis Parmentier
(A meat and potato pie)

4 potatoes, about 1¼ pounds	¼ cup tomato paste
3 tablespoons butter	½ cup milk
1 cup finely chopped onions	⅛ teaspoon freshly grated nutmeg
1 small clove garlic, finely minced	3 tablespoons finely chopped parsley
1½ pounds ground beef	¼ cup grated Parmesan cheese
Salt and freshly ground pepper	
1 bay leaf	
2 sprigs fresh thyme or ½ teaspoon dried	

1. Peel the potatoes, cutting each into six pieces of equal size. Put the potatoes in a saucepan and add water to cover. Bring to the boil and simmer about 20 minutes or until tender.

2. Melt 1 tablespoon butter in a saucepan and add the onion and garlic. Cook, stirring, until onions wilt.

3. Add the beef and cook, chopping down with the side of a heavy metal spoon to break up the lumps. When the meat has lost its raw color,

add salt and pepper to taste, the bay leaf, thyme, and tomato paste. Cover and cook about 20 minutes. Discard the bay leaf.

4. Preheat the broiler to high.

5. Meanwhile, drain the potatoes and put them through a food mill or potato ricer. Return the potatoes to the saucepan and add the remaining 2 tablespoons butter, stirring until the butter melts.

6. Heat the milk and add it gradually to the potatoes, beating with a wooden spoon. Add salt to taste, the nutmeg, and half the parsley.

7. Add the remaining parsley to the beef mixture.

8. Spoon the beef into a flame-proof baking dish. A dish that measures about 8 by 11½ by 2 inches is ideal for this. Spoon the potatoes over the meat and smooth the top with a spatula. Sprinkle with the cheese.

9. Place the dish under the broiler and broil about 5 minutes or less, until the potatoes are nicely browned. Serve with mushroom sauce.

Yield: Four servings.

Sauce aux Champignons
(Mushroom sauce)

¼ pound fresh mushrooms	Salt and freshly ground pepper
2 tablespoons butter	¼ cup dry white wine
¾ cup finely chopped onion	1½ cups chopped canned tomatoes
½ teaspoon finely minced garlic	¼ cup heavy cream

1. Slice the mushrooms thinly. There should be about 2 cups. Set aside.

2. Melt 1 tablespoon of butter in a saucepan and add the onion and garlic. Cook until the onion wilts.

3. Add the mushrooms and salt and pepper to taste. Cook, stirring often, until the mushrooms give up their liquid. Cook until this liquid evaporates.

4. Add the wine. Cook until wine almost evaporates. Add tomatoes and stir. Cover and cook about 15 minutes.

5. Stir the remaining butter into the sauce and add the cream. Bring to the boil and serve hot.

Yield: Four servings.

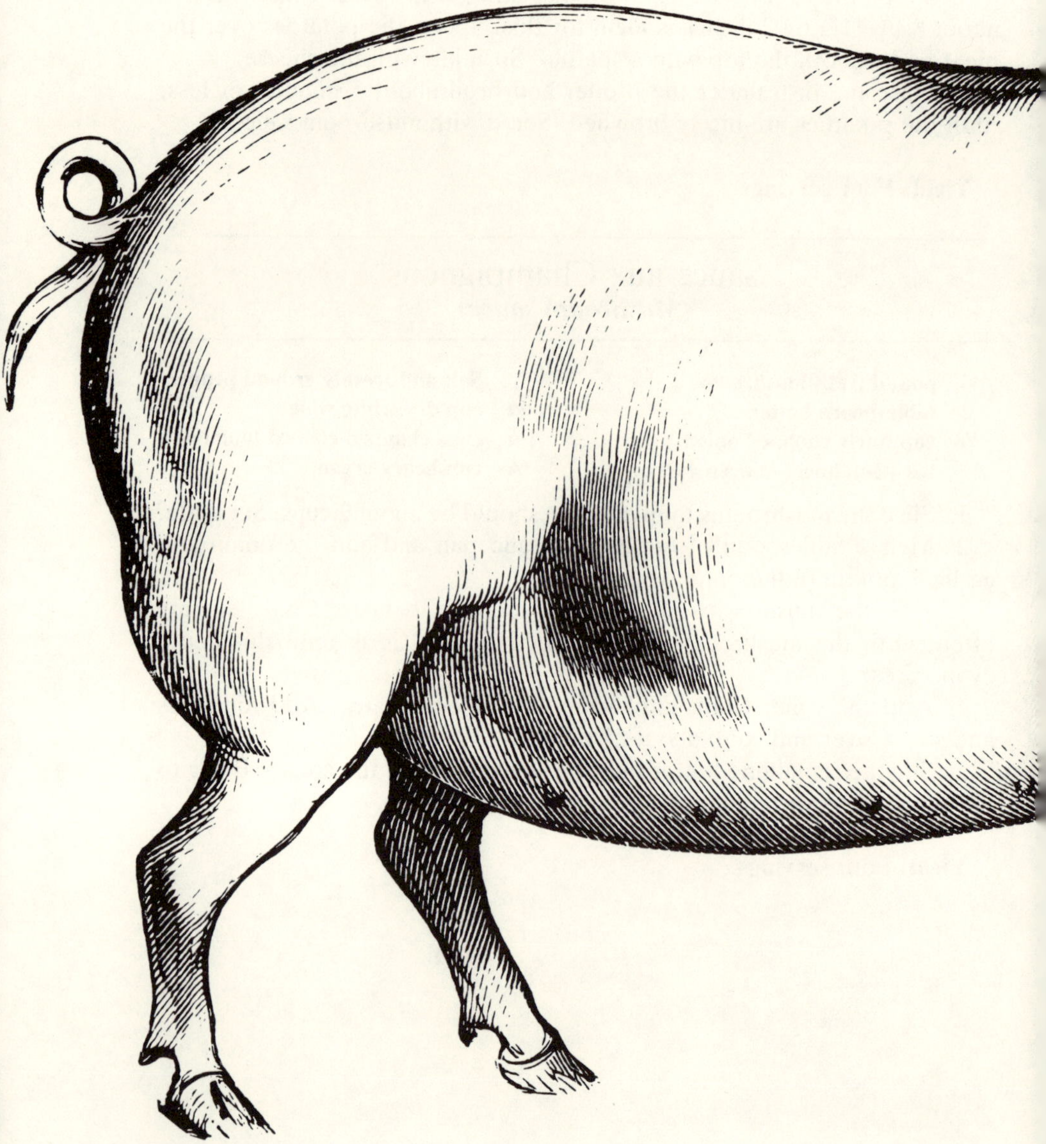

Pork and Ham

IN FRENCH MENU PLANNING, SEVERAL GENeral, all-purpose names signify foods that are unpretentious and family-style. These are not classic names like Du Barry (which always means cauliflower in a dish) or Argenteuil (which indicates asparagus) or Crécy (which indicates carrots). These are names like ménagère and paysanne and bonne femme. They stand for rustic simplicity.

On a recent occasion in my home I prepared for my family and neighbors a simple but good dish of pork chops that had been braised and cooked with potatoes and onions. It was an impromptu meal, assembled and put together on the spur of the moment. One of the guests asked me the name of the dish, and I answered almost reflexively "bonne maman," for that is another of those vague terms that stand for the feel of a dish rather than one to indicate a traditional or classic composition. Bonne maman, of course, means good mother, and I have eaten dishes that bore that name since I was an infant.

As I said, that meal came about using foods that were readily available in my home at that time. Cauliflower was just coming into the roadside markets in Long Island. This became the accompanying vegetable, an improvised and incredibly easy dish to make. You simply parboil the cauliflower to get rid of the raw taste, drain and chop it in the saucepan with the side of a heavy metal kitchen spoon, add a dash of curry powder and chopped shallots and cream and it is ready to serve.

The pork chops bonne maman demand a total cooking time of about half an hour. It is best to get them started on the stove before getting on to the cauliflower. Once the pork chops have started to brown on one side, you should break the cauliflower into "flowerets" and proceed from there. The two dishes can easily be timed to be ready for the table at more or less the same moment.

Côtes de Porc Bonne Maman
(Braised pork chops with potatoes and onions)

4 center-cut loin pork chops, each about ½ pound	8 very small white onions, peeled (see note)
Salt and freshly ground pepper	2 tablespoons red wine vinegar
4 potatoes, about 1 pound	½ cup water
1 tablespoon oil	

1. Sprinkle the chops with salt and pepper to taste and set aside.

2. Peel the potatoes and cut them lengthwise into quarters. Put them in a saucepan with cold water to cover. Bring to the boil, add salt to taste, and simmer about 30 seconds. Drain and set aside.

3. Heat the oil in a heavy skillet large enough to hold the chops in one

layer. Add the chops and cook on both sides until golden brown all over, about 5 minutes.

4. Scatter the onions and potatoes around the chops. Cook, turning the potatoes, onions, and chops, until the potatoes and onions start to take on color, about 5 minutes. Cover closely and cook about 10 minutes.

5. Pour off all the fat from the skillet. Add the vinegar and water. Cover and cook 15 minutes until chops are tender.

Yield: Four servings.
Note: If very small onions are not available, use two larger onions cut into quarters.

Chou-fleur au Cari
(Curried cauliflower)

1 **head of cauliflower, about 2 pounds, with leaves**	1 teaspoon curry powder
¼ **cup milk**	½ cup heavy cream
Salt	Freshly ground pepper
1 **tablespoon finely chopped shallots**	1 tablespoon butter

1. Cut away and discard the leaves from the cauliflower. Cut away and discard the core of the cauliflower.

2. Break the cauliflower into large flowerets. Put the pieces into a saucepan and add cold water to cover. Add the milk and salt to taste.

3. Bring to the boil and cook 15 to 20 minutes or until the cauliflower is tender but not soft. Drain. Return the cauliflower to the saucepan. Using the side of a heavy spoon, chop the pieces of cauliflower until they are coarse. Add the shallots, curry powder, and cream. Add salt and pepper to taste. Cook, stirring, until piping hot. Stir in the butter.

Yield: Four servings.

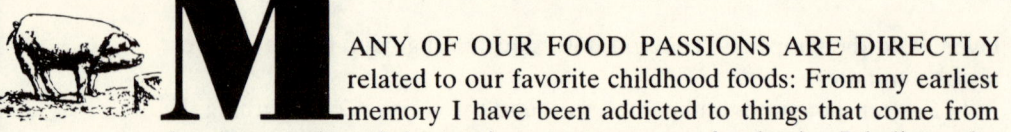

MANY OF OUR FOOD PASSIONS ARE DIRECTLY related to our favorite childhood foods: From my earliest memory I have been addicted to things that come from the charcuterie: pâtés, terrines, sausages, and salamis. I believe the reason my region, Burgundy, was well-known for such things is because pork was traditionally plentiful and cheap. Therefore, it was put to as many good uses as chicken.

One of the foods that I hunger for is pork chops. And pork is, in a relative sense, at least, a very good buy. It may not be as inexpensive as chicken, but it is almost always less costly than lamb or veal or beef. One of the choicest ways of cooking pork chops is charcutière, which is to say in the style of the pork butcher, who is, of course, the charcutier, or the man who produced all those pâtés and terrines of my early youth.

A sauce charcutière involves cooking the chops until nicely browned and cooked throughout. When the chops are removed from the skillet, the pan is deglazed with white wine or vinegar. A bit of broth is added and then a final fillip is applied in the form of a dash of mustard and chopped cornichons, those sour tarragon-flavored gherkins that have in recent years become almost as well known in this country as in France.

Incidentally, if you can't find imported cornichons, chopped sour pickles (and, in a pinch, even dill pickles) will do. Pork is, of course, a naturally fatty meat, and tart and acid ingredients, such as mustard and pickles, complement and flatter the richness of the food.

Broccoli complements pork chops charcutière. When getting ready to cook, assemble and prepare the basic ingredients for both dishes. Begin by cooking the chops. Put the broccoli on to simmer. By the time the chops are ready the broccoli will be ready for draining and putting into the food processor. It can be finished in seconds.

Côtes de Porc Charcutière
(Pork chops with mustard sauce)

- 4 center-cut loin pork chops, about 1 inch thick
- Salt and freshly ground pepper
- 1 teaspoon peanut, vegetable, or corn oil
- ⅓ cup finely chopped onion
- ½ teaspoon finely minced garlic
- ½ cup dry white wine
- ½ cup plus 2 tablespoons fresh or canned chicken broth
- ¼ teaspoon arrowroot or cornstarch
- 1 teaspoon mustard such as Dijon or Düsseldorf
- 2 tablespoons thinly sliced imported cornichons (gherkins)
- 2 tablespoons finely chopped parsley

1. Sprinkle the chops on both sides with salt and pepper to taste.
2. Heat the oil in a skillet large enough to hold the chops comfortably

without crowding. When the oil is very hot, add the chops and cook over moderately high heat about 5 minutes.

3. Turn the chops and cook on the second side about 5 minutes. Reduce the heat and continue cooking about 5 minutes. Cook 10 minutes longer, turning the chops occasionally.

4. Transfer the chops to a warm serving dish.

5. Pour off most of the fat from the skillet. Add the onion and garlic and cook, stirring, until the onion is wilted. Add the wine and stir to dissolve the brown particles that cling to the bottom and sides of the pan. Cook until the wine is reduced to about 2 tablespoons. Add half a cup of broth and bring to the boil.

6. Blend the arrowroot and remaining two tablespoons of chicken broth and stir it into the sauce. Add the mustard and cornichons and any juices that have accumulated around the chops.

7. Spoon the sauce over the chops and sprinkle with chopped parsley.

Yield: Four servings.

Purée de Broccoli
(Purée of broccoli)

---

1 bunch broccoli
2 tablespoons butter
1 clove garlic, peeled and left whole
Salt and freshly ground pepper
¼ cup heavy cream

1. Break the broccoli into flowerets. Trim off the outer coating of the stems. Cut the stems in half. There should be about 1 pound of ready-to-cook broccoli.

2. Bring enough water to the boil to cover the broccoli when added. Add the broccoli and cook about 10 minutes until the broccoli is tender but still a bit resilient.

3. Drain the broccoli and put it into the container of a food processor. Process to a fine purée.

4. Melt the butter with the whole garlic clove in a skillet or saucepan. Add the broccoli and salt and pepper to taste. Add the cream and stir to blend. Heat thoroughly. Remove the garlic clove and serve hot.

Yield: Four servings.

LIKE MOST PEOPLE, I LIKE STUFFED FOODS. They lend themselves to a good deal of versatility and offer a nice contrast in flavors.

Now, it is apparent that most bread stuffings in this world are made of white bread for the simple reason that there is more white bread than bread of other colors and flavors.

One recent evening in my home, however, I was surprised to discover that there wasn't a crumb of bread left over from a French loaf anywhere to be found. There was, however, a partly used loaf of a very good rye bread with caraway seeds.

The dish that evening was to be pork chops. They were about one inch thick at the bone. I decided to stuff them, cut the rye bread into small cubes and prepared a stuffing. The flavor of caraway has always been well suited to almost any dish made with pork.

The chops were cooked after browning well on both sides over very low heat to insure their tenderness when done. To accompany them, I used another batch of leftovers, zucchini and carrots sautéed together and sprinkled with chopped basil leaves.

Côtes de Porc Farcis au Karvi
(Pork chops stuffed with caraway rye)

4 loin pork chops, each about one inch thick	½ cup finely minced parsley
	1 teaspoon caraway seeds
1 cup rye bread with caraway seeds cut into quarter-inch dice	1 egg, lightly beaten
	Salt and freshly ground pepper
¼ cup butter	2 tablespoons peanut, vegetable, or corn oil
1½ cups finely chopped onions	
½ teaspoon finely minced garlic	2 tablespoons red wine vinegar
¼ pound mushrooms, cut into quarter-inch dice, about one cup	¾ cup fresh or canned chicken broth

1. Preheat the oven to 300 degrees.

2. Cut each pork chop lengthwise from the outside to the bone. Holding the knife parallel to the surface of the meat, split each chop in half to the bone, top to bottom, but do not cut entirely through. Set aside.

3. Put the bread cubes into a baking dish and place in the oven. Bake about 5 minutes or until lightly browned.

4. Melt ¼ cup of butter in a saucepan and add 1 cup of the chopped onion, the garlic, and mushrooms. Cook, stirring, until wilted. Spoon the mixture into a mixing bowl and add the parsley, caraway seeds, and egg and stir. Add salt and pepper to taste. Place the flaps of each chop on a flat surface and pound with a flat mallet. Do not break the flesh or the stuffing will ooze out.

5. Stuff each pork chop with equal portions of stuffing. Fold the flaps together to enclose the stuffing. Secure the openings with two or more toothpicks for each chop. Sprinkle the chops on both sides with salt and pepper to taste.

6. Heat the oil in a heavy skillet large enough to hold the chops in one layer without crowding.

7. Add the chops and cook over moderately high heat until well browned on one side, about 4 minutes. Turn and brown on the other side, about 4 to 5 minutes.

8. Continue cooking, turning the chops occasionally, about 15 minutes.

9. Transfer the chops to a serving dish. Put the chops briefly in the oven to keep warm.

10. Meanwhile, pour off the fat from the skillet and add the remaining onion. Cook, stirring, about 1 minute and add the vinegar. Stir to dissolve the brown particles that cling to the bottom and sides of the skillet.

11. Add the chicken broth and bring to the boil, stirring.

12. Remove the chops from the oven. Remove and discard the toothpicks.

13. Strain the sauce over the chops, pushing through as much of the solids as possible. Serve hot.

Yield: Four servings.

Zucchini et Carottes Sautés
(Sautéed zucchini with carrots)

5 or 6 carrots, about ¾ pound, trimmed and scraped	¼ cup thinly sliced small white onions or the white part of scallions
2 zucchini, about ¾ pound, trimmed at each end	Salt and freshly ground pepper
2 tablespoons butter	3 tablespoons chopped fresh basil

1. Put the carrots on a flat surface and cut them into very thin rounds. Or use a food processor outfitted with a slicing disk to do this. There should be about 1½ cups.

2. Cut the zucchini into very thin rounds. There should be about 3 cups.

3. Melt the butter in a small but wide saucepan and add the carrots. Cook, stirring occasionally, about 4 minutes. Add the onion and stir. Cook about 1 minute. Add the zucchini and cook, stirring and shaking the skillet, about 1 minute. Add salt and pepper to taste. Cover and continue cooking about 4 minutes or until the vegetables are crisp tender. Sprinkle with basil and serve hot.

Yield: Four servings.

NEXT TO FISHING, THE THING I LIKE MOST about summer is cooking out-of-doors. I have great recollections of my days over an open fire, one of the greatest of them being at an outdoor camp beside a stream in Wyoming, where we hauled trout directly from those cold running waters, fired up a bunch of twigs and cleaned and cooked the still-quivering fish in a bit of fat and butter and practically no other seasoning. It was one of the great feasts of that year.

Although I have a variety of outdoor cooking gadgets and utensils, I find it isn't necessary to have the most expensive grill to achieve satisfactory results. You simply need a good fire that is left burning until it is not too hot, a suitable grill or surface to fit over it, and fresh ingredients.

I have never known why some people look on outdoor grilling (and outdoor cooking in general) as a complicated process and marinades as something mysterious. In my own kitchen, the vast majority of marinades used for outdoor grillings consist of nothing more complicated than a vinaigrette sauce plus herbs and spices. And a vinaigrette sauce is nothing more than a judicious blend of oil and vinegar, or for more delicate results, oil and lemon juice.

There is no absolute rule as to when you use vinegar and when you use lemon juice, but as a very broad rule of thumb I would say that lemon juice is suitable for the most delicate kinds of meat and fish, such as shellfish, chicken, or veal; and vinegar is best for the more robust meats like pork, beef, game, and the rest.

As far as flavors are concerned, that is a question of taste. My only caution is not to use them excessively. Boneless medallions of pork are highly recommended if hasty cooking is what you have in mind.

Médaillons de Porc Grillé aux Herbes
(Pork medallions grilled with herb marinade)

1½ pounds boneless loin of pork	1 teaspoon chopped fresh or dried rosemary
¼ cup olive oil	
2 tablespoons red wine vinegar	1 teaspoon dried cumin
Salt and freshly ground pepper	¼ cup hot melted butter

1. Preheat a charcoal or gas grill to the desired degree of heat for grilling.

2. Cut the pork into 8 slices of approximately the same thickness. Put each slice on a flat surface and pound slightly with a flat mallet.

3. Put the oil, vinegar, and salt and pepper to taste in a flat dish and stir to blend. Add the rosemary and cumin and stir again.

4. Add the pork slices and turn them in the marinade. Cover with foil and set aside until ready to cook.

5. Add the medallions to the grill and cook 3 or 4 minutes on one side. Turn and cook 2 or 3 minutes on the second side. Continue cooking turning often, for a total of about 10 minutes. Transfer to a warm serving dish and brush with melted butter.

Yield: Four servings.

Riz au Four
(Baked rice)

3 tablespoons butter	Salt and freshly ground pepper
⅓ cup minced onion	2 sprigs thyme or ½ teaspoon dried thyme
1½ cups uncooked rice	
2¼ cups water	½ bay leaf
2 sprigs parsley	Tabasco sauce to taste

1. Preheat the oven to 400 degrees.
2. Melt half the butter in a saucepan and add the onion. Cook, stirring, until wilted. Add the rice and stir to blend.
3. Add the water, stirring to make certain there are no lumps in the rice. Add the remaining ingredients. Cover with a close-fitting lid and when the water boils, place the pan in the oven.
4. Bake exactly 17 minutes. Remove the cover and discard the parsley, bay leaf, and thyme sprigs. Using a two-pronged fork, stir in the remaining butter. If the rice is not to be served immediately, keep covered in a warm place.

Yield: Four servings.

THERE IS SOMETHING ABOUT THE CASUAL NAture of cooking in summer that has a special appeal to me. It probably has to do with the fact that I'm out in my boat a lot and I garden with enthusiasm. The combination of these whets the appetite. My handiest and one of the most used cooking apparatuses for those months of the year is my outdoor charcoal grill which is kept fired for numerous hours in the course of a week. I keep it directly outside the kitchen door for ready access at noon or in the evening. The foods that I cook on that grill are, generally speaking, of the quick-cooking variety— a split chicken half, a steak, a slice of veal, even hamburgers and hot dogs.

One of my favorite meats for summer cooking is medallions of pork which are lean and boneless. Generally speaking, I select a boneless loin of pork for this, but I may also cut away the bone from thinly sliced pork chops to serve as well. You can facilitate and minimize cooking times if you put the pieces of pork on a flat surface and pound them lightly with a flat mallet or the bottom of a small heavy, clean saucepan. You should not pound heavily, however, or you will break the meat fibers. When ready to cook, I marinate the slices briefly in a mixture of oil, lemon juice, and cumin. Or I might change the nature of the spice, adding, at times, chopped rosemary or fresh tarragon.

There is in the French kitchen, one sauce that is ideally suited to many pork dishes and it is called charcutiere, which is to say a sauce in the style of the charcutier. It is interesting to note, by the way, that the word charcutier derives from chair cuit, or the cooked meat of the pig. The charcutier prepares an endless variety of pork products including pâtés and terrines, salamis and sausages.

A sauce charcutiere is like a deviled sauce and is made with sliced cornichons, mustard, and vinegar. It is the perfect flavor foil for medallions of pork or pork chops that have been simply cooked. Serve the pork with a quickly cooked vegetable dish, such as grilled zucchini and/or mushrooms.

Médaillons de Porc Charcutière
(Grilled pork with mustard sauce)

- 12 thin boneless pork slices, about 3 ounces each, preferably from the loin of pork
- 2 tablespoons peanut, vegetable, or corn oil
- 2 tablespoons lemon juice
- Salt and freshly ground pepper
- 2 teaspoons ground cumin
- Sauce charcutière (see recipe)

1. Preheat a charcoal grill.
2. Pound the pork slices on a flat surface but do not break the fibers of the meat. Put the slices in a flat dish and add the oil, lemon juice, salt and pepper to taste, and cumin. Blend with the hands to combine well.

3. Put the pork medallions on the grill and cook, turning often, for about 10 minutes or until throughly cooked. Do not overcook or the medallions will be dry. Serve with charcutiere sauce.

Yield: Four servings.

Sauce Charcutière
(Mustard and cornichon sauce)

16	drained cornichons, available in specialty shops, or use ½ cup chopped sour pickles		Salt and freshly ground pepper
		1	tablespoon tomato paste
		1	bay leaf
3	tablespoons butter	1	sprig fresh thyme or ½ teaspoon dried thyme
⅔	cup finely chopped onion		
½	teaspoon finely minced garlic	1	tablespoon imported mustard, preferably Dijon
2	tablespoons red wine vinegar		
½	cup fresh or canned chicken broth		

1. Cut the cornichons into very thin slices, an eighth of an inch thick or less. There should be about ½ cup. Set aside.
2. Melt 1 tablespoon butter in a saucepan and add the onions. Cook, stirring often, until lightly browned.
3. Add the vinegar and cook briefly.
4. Add the chicken broth, salt and pepper to taste, and tomato paste. Bring to the boil, stirring. Add the bay leaf and thyme. Let simmer about 5 minutes and remove from the heat.
5. Stir in the mustard. Swirl in the remaining butter and serve.

Yield: About ¾ cup.

I HAVE STATED BEFORE AND OFTEN, PERHAPS, that I have a passion for pork. I like it in all of its forms, other than raw, of course. I dote on sausages and salamis, prefer a fine roast loin of pork to the finest beef with truffles, and find a ham, either fresh or cured, one of the most sublime of meats.

Some of my favorite pork preparations are those made with ground meat. There are thousands of preparations of ground pork dishes, not the least of which are boulettes of pork seasoned with caraway and cooked with sauerkraut for an interesting addition to choucroute garnie.

One of my greatest pleasures for breakfast is ground pork wrapped in caul fat and cooked with simple seasonings in the same way you cook hamburgers.

A favorite way of cooking ground pork and one that pleases the members of my family consists of seasoning the pork lightly with onion and cumin seeds (one of the most versatile of spices) plus bread crumbs to lighten the texture. When the pork "burger" is cooked, I deglaze the pan with heavy cream and finally stir in sour cream.

Any chef worth his salt knows that one of the finest accompaniments for pork dishes is cabbage in one form or another (including sauerkraut, of course).

This particular dish is excellent served on a bed of shredded cabbage cooked simply in butter. It should be cooked over fairly low heat for about 20 minutes.

This particular dish calls for only half a head of cabbage, the remainder of which may be used in salads at a later meal. Cabbage has the best keeping quality of almost any vegetable.

If you are to make this pork dish, it is best if you start the cabbage before preparing the pork.

Bitoks de Porc au Chou
(Pork burgers with sautéed cabbage)

1½ pounds ground lean pork	Salt and freshly ground pepper
1 teaspoon butter	3 tablespoons peanut, vegetable, or corn oil
½ cup finely chopped onion	
½ cup fine fresh bread crumbs	Sautéed cabbage (see recipe)
1 teaspoon crushed cumin seeds	1 teaspoon paprika
¼ cup finely chopped parsley	⅓ cup heavy cream
1 egg	½ cup sour cream

1. Put the pork in a mixing bowl.
2. Melt the butter in a saucepan and add the onion. Cook, stirring, until wilted.
3. Add the onion to the pork. Add the bread crumbs, cumin, parsley, egg, and salt and pepper to taste. Blend well.

4. Divide the mixture into 8 equal portions, forming them into hamburger-shaped patties.

5. Heat the oil in a heavy skillet large enough to hold the patties. Add the patties and cook about 10 minutes. Turn and cook 10 minutes longer.

6. Arrange the cabbage on a heat-proof platter. Arrange the patties over it.

7. Add the paprika to the pan drippings and stir over high heat. Cook briefly and add the heavy cream. Bring to the boil. Turn off the heat and stir in the sour cream. Reheat gently without boiling or the sauce will curdle.

8. Spoon the sauce over the pork patties and serve.

Yield: Four servings.

Chou Sauté au Beurre
(Sautéed cabbage)

½ small head cabbage, about 1 pound	2 whole cloves
4 tablespoons butter	Salt and freshly ground pepper

1. Cut away the core of the cabbage. Cut the cabbage into quarters. Cut each quarter crosswise into very thin slices. There should be about 6 cups.

2. Melt the butter in a saucepan and add the cabbage. Add the cloves and salt and pepper to taste. Cook, stirring often, without browning, about 15 minutes.

Yield: Four servings.

THERE IS NO DOUBT THAT TASTES AND APpetites change over the years and mostly, I would presume, by association. Until I came to New York many years ago, my diet and gastronomic persuasions were almost wholly dictated by my childhood, apprenticeship, and chefhood. I had never been exposed to highly spiced foods and the only really assertive spice that passed through my hands and into a casserole was a touch of cayenne pepper that went primarily and in the most limited amounts into cheese dishes, fish stews, and so on.

The first time I tasted chile con carne I certainly didn't relish it. In fact, I would have tended to classify it as a "barbaric" Americanism. As time has passed, however, I guess you might say that I have become an "aficionado," through my association with various home cooks who are dedicated chili makers. As someone has pointed out earlier, chili is one of the simplest, easiest of all dishes to concoct and it certainly seems to have a universal appeal. Not long ago I had the occasion to prepare a chili for a fairly large gathering and subsequently had numerous requests for the recipe.

I doubt that my version is all that different from the next home cook's, although I am firmly convinced that the best meat to use is a combination of coarsely ground beef and coarsely ground pork. Otherwise, to my taste, the chili turns out to be more like a soup than something you want to bite into. Although I am told by "purists" that sour cream and lime wedges are a citified conceit, I think they both add a good deal to the flavor. The sour cream, in particular, goes a long way in ameliorating the spicy nature of the dish.

The smooth texture of an avocado makes a natural foil for chili, of course, and I consider an avocado, onion, and tomato salad the best of accompaniments for the dish. My version of chile con carne requires only half an hour of cooking and, like most chilies, it is even better on reheating. As it cooks, there is plenty of time to prepare the avocado salad.

Chili à la Franey

- 1 pound very lean coarsely ground pork
- 1 pound very lean coarsely ground beef
- 1 tablespoon olive oil
- 2 cups finely chopped onions
- 1 cup finely chopped green pepper
- 1 cup finely chopped celery
- 1 tablespoon finely minced garlic
- 1 tablespoon crumbled dried oregano
- 2 bay leaves
- 2 teaspoons ground cumin
- 3 tablespoons chili powder
- 3 cups tomatoes with tomato paste
- 1 cup beef broth
- 1 cup water
- Salt and freshly ground pepper

½ teaspoon dried hot red pepper flakes	Sour cream as garnish, optional
2 cups drained kidney beans	Lime wedges as garnish, optional

1. If possible, have the pork and beef ground together.
2. Heat the oil in a large heavy kettle and add the meat. Cook, chopping down and stirring with the side of a heavy metal kitchen spoon to break up the lumps.
3. Add the onions, green pepper, celery, garlic, oregano, bay leaves, chili powder, and cumin. Stir to blend well.
4. Add the tomatoes, broth, water, and salt and pepper to taste. Add the red pepper flakes. Bring to the boil and cook, stirring often, about 20 minutes. Add the beans and cook 10 minutes longer. Serve in hot bowls with a dollop of sour cream and lime wedges, if desired.

Yield: Eight or more servings.

Avocado and Tomato with Lime Sauce

1 large unblemished, ripe but firm avocado	½ teaspoon freshly ground coriander seeds
1 red, ripe tomato	Salt and freshly ground pepper
1 red onion	1 small, fresh, hot green chili, seeded and chopped, optional
2 teaspoons finely chopped garlic	Lettuce leaves
3 tablespoons fresh lime juice	
¼ cup olive oil	

1. Cut the avocado in half. Discard the pit. Peel the avocado and cut it into one-inch cubes. Put the cubes in a mixing bowl.
2. Core the tomato and cut it into one-inch cubes. Add it to the bowl.
3. Peel the onion and cut it into half-inch cubes. Add it to the bowl. Add the garlic, lime juice, olive oil, coriander, and salt and pepper to taste. Add the hot chili. Toss and chill.
4. Serve on lettuce leaves.

Yield: Six servings.

WHEN I RECENTLY WROTE A FEW WORDS IN praise of and offered a recipe to be cooked in a pressure cooker, a neighbor of mine expressed keen delight in the thought that I was finally "coming around" to the twentieth century. I reminded him that although I am heartily in favor of the pressure cooker's use and will use my version often in the years to come, I still prefer the old-fashioned methods of cookery, which is to say slow cooking either on top of the stove or in the oven.

I repeat my feeling that while a pressure cooker—in France a pressure cooker is know as a *cocotte minute* or a *marmite a la vapeur*—can be extremely serviceable, it is a bit difficult to determine in advance the precise moment that a meat or poultry will be *a point* without having it overcooked.

It occurred to me recently that pork, in particular, should be an excellent meat for pressure-cooking for the simple reason that many cuts of pork tend to be quite dry no matter how long you braise them. When a friend of mine offered me a recipe for a Mexican-style dish—a sort of green chile con carne—I perused the recipe and noted that it was to be cooked in two hours.

I decided to put this recipe to the test, using the pressure cooker in which the meat would cook for thirty minutes. At the end of the half hour of cooking, I removed the lid and discovered that while the meat was quite tender and very tasty, it was still surrounded by what I considered an excess of liquid. Thus, I reduced the cooking time to twenty minutes, uncovered the cooker and let the sauce cook down to what I considered the proper consistency.

This is an interesting recipe that is best made, for the sake of authenticity, with those green "tomatoes" known in Spanish as tomatillos, which are available in specialty food shops that specialize in Mexican products (including Casa Moneo in New York). Red, ripe tomatoes can easily be substituted, however.

The seasonings for the preparation include green chiles, garlic, and, if available, fresh coriander leaves otherwise known as cilantro or culantro. Serve with a cumin-flavored rice.

Chile Verde
(Green chile con carne)

2½ pounds boneless pork loin
3 tablespoons corn or safflower oil
2½ cups cored, seeded green peppers cut into 1 inch cubes
1 tablespoon finely minced garlic
3 cups drained, canned Mexican green tomatoes (tomatillos enteros), or use 3 cups chopped, peeled, seeded, red ripe tomatoes, or use canned imported tomatoes

1 6-ounce can chopped green chiles (you may use part chopped fresh or canned jalapeño peppers)	¼ teaspoon ground cloves 2 tablespoons chopped fresh coriander 1 cup dry white wine
2 tablespoons ground cumin	Salt and freshly ground pepper

1. Cut the meat into 1½-inch cubes.
2. Heat the oil in a pressure cooker. When it is quite hot add about one third of the meat cubes. Cook, stirring, until nicely browned.
3. Using a slotted spoon, transfer the cubes to a platter. Add another third of the meat cubes and brown them. Transfer them to the platter. Cook the remaining cubes and transfer them to the platter.
4. Add the green peppers to the fat remaining in the cooker and cook until wilted. Add the garlic and cook about 5 seconds, stirring.
5. Return the cubed meat to the cooker. Add the remaining ingredients. Cover the cooker with the lid and pressure regulator. Cook 20 minutes. Remove the lid from the cooker following the manufacturer's instructions. Cook down uncovered about 10 minutes or until the sauce is reduced slightly.

Yield: Four to six servings.

Riz au Cumin
(Cumin rice)

2 tablespoons butter	2 teaspoons ground cumin
2 tablespoons finely minced onion	1½ cups chicken broth
1 small clove garlic, finely minced	1 bay leaf
1 cup rice	

1. Melt half the butter in a saucepan and add the onion and garlic. Cook until the onion is wilted. Add the rice and cumin and stir to coat the rice.
2. Add the broth and bay leaf. Cover and bring to the boil. Cook exactly 17 minutes. Uncover, remove the bay leaf, and stir in the remaining tablespoon of butter.

Yield: Four servings.

IHAVE NOTED BEFORE THAT THERE ARE NUmerous prepared foods in supermarkets and grocery stores that can greatly facilitate cooking when you are mindful of the time. For a hasty lunch I am by no means above dining on a tin of sardines, a sandwich made of tuna, chopped celery, onion, and green pepper and freshly made mayonnaise (which must be the quickest and most easily made sauce on earth).

One of the greatest boons to a quick meal is ham steak, which comes in a variety of sizes and styles. I find American ham steaks quite tasty, and the only cooking that they need basically is a heating-through. There is a recipe here for ham steaks served in a cream sauce with white seedless grapes, which are to my mind one of the greatest innovations of the past generation. These grapes, called Thompson seedless, are, to my taste, sui generis where both taste and texture are concerned.

There are many so-called sophisticates in this world who cannot abide combining a savory food (such as ham) with a sweet fruit (such as grapes). They detest anything Veronique (which means with grapes) or à l'orange or peaches or apples or whatever. This has nothing to do with ultimate taste. If anyone needs an argument, you could turn to numerous dishes in the Chinese culture or the culture of the Middle East where sweet fruits and savory meats combine with the greatest harmony and have for a few thousand years.

Jambon aux raisins (raisins is, of course, the French word for fresh grapes and does not mean the dried fruit as it does in this country) is made with a hastily prepared cream sauce, Madeira wine, and the grapes. If you plan to make this dish, and seedless grapes are no longer available, you can substitute drained, canned white seedless grapes. A good accompaniment to this dish would be spätzle (the Swiss noodle dish that is now available in cartons throughout America) with a touch of cheese and mushrooms.

Jambon aux Raisins
(Ham steaks with grapes)

- 1 tablespoon butter
- 1 tablespoon finely chopped shallots
- 2 ham steaks, 1 pound each
- 2 tablespoons plus 1 teaspoon Madeira wine
- 2 cups fresh seedless white grapes (or use 2 cups drained, canned seedless white grapes)
- 1 cup heavy cream
- 1 teaspoon arrowroot or cornstarch

1. Rub the bottom of a large shallow skillet with a little of the butter.
2. Sprinkle the shallots over the butter.
3. Arrange the steaks in the skillet (they may be slightly overlapping).

4. Dot the steaks with the remaining butter and pour 2 tablespoons of the Madeira wine around the steaks.

5. Place the skillet on the stove and cover loosely. Cook 5 minutes.

6. Pour the cooking liquid from the steaks into a small skillet. Keep the ham steaks covered.

7. Bring the liquid to the boil in the other skillet and add the grapes. Cook about 3 minutes and add the cream. Cook about 5 minutes over high heat.

8. Blend the arrowroot with the remaining teaspoon of Madeira wine and stir it into the sauce. When thickened, pour the grapes and sauce over the ham and serve.

Yield: Four servings.

Spätzle au Fromage
(Swiss-style dumplings with cheese)

1 package spätzle, 10 ounces, Swiss-style dumplings, available in cartons in grocery stores and supermarkets	1 cup thinly sliced mushrooms
	2 tablespoons heavy cream
	½ cup freshly grated Parmesan cheese
3 tablespoons butter	

1. Cook the spätzle according to package directions.

2. As the spätzle cooks, melt one tablespoon of the butter in a small skillet and add the mushrooms. Cook, shaking the skillet and stirring, until mushrooms give up their liquid. Cook until liquid evaporates.

3. Drain the spätzle and add the remaining 2 tablespoons of butter, the mushrooms, and cream. At the last minute, add the Parmesan cheese. Toss to blend.

Yield: Four servings.

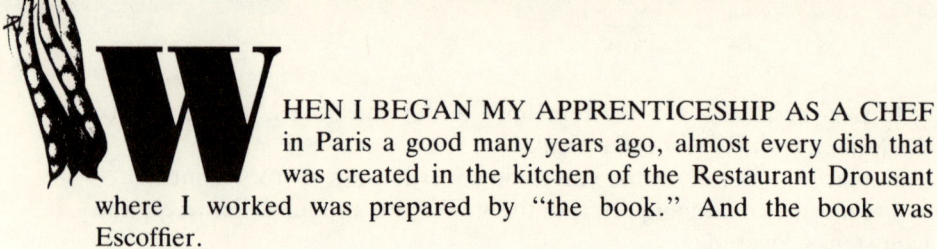

WHEN I BEGAN MY APPRENTICESHIP AS A CHEF in Paris a good many years ago, almost every dish that was created in the kitchen of the Restaurant Drousant where I worked was prepared by "the book." And the book was Escoffier.

Unlike today, it wasn't often that chefs varied from the rules as laid down in that volume. Even if I were to prepare a "classic" menu today, it would still be according to Escoffier, who was to food what Hoyle was to games-playing.

For the most part, however, my time is spent in creating new dishes. If I prepare something that has not been devised or improvised in my kitchen, I frequently wonder as to its origin and how I first came to know it.

One such dish is a tasty, easily made casserole of cooked ham slices wrapped around asparagus spears, topped with a Mornay sauce, and baked or broiled until bubbling and golden brown on top. For the life of me I can't recall where I first sampled it. I know that it isn't French and I seriously doubt that it is a regional American dish of long standing.

For one reason or another I find this an especially good dish to be used as a luncheon or supper entrée, particularly when fresh asparagus is in season in abundance.

Asparagus and ham Mornay, while excellent to the taste both from the standpoint of flavor and texture, is the kind of dish that I would probably teach in a beginning class in cookery because of the simplicity of its preparation. The only complicated or time-consuming element in its preparation is the making of a basic white sauce (butter, flour, and milk) that is turned into a Mornay by the addition of cheese and an egg yolk.

This sauce can be made with store-bought Swiss cheese, but I find it infinitely more tasty if genuine imported Gruyère cheese can be obtained. If served as a simple luncheon dish, a vegetable accompaniment may not be necessary. A good one, however, is a dish of green peas cooked quickly in butter with freshly sliced mushrooms.

Asperges et Jambon Mornay
(Asparagus and ham Mornay)

24	asparagus spears, about 2 pounds
	Salt
3	tablespoons butter
4	tablespoons flour
1½	cups milk
1	cup grated cheese, preferably Gruyère or Swiss
1	egg yolk
	Freshly ground pepper
⅛	teaspoon freshly grated nutmeg
	Pinch of cayenne pepper
24	thin slices cooked ham or prosciutto

1. Place the spears on a flat surface. Cut off the bottoms so that all the asparagus spears are of the same length, about seven inches long.

2. Bring enough water to the boil in a skillet to cover the asparagus. Add salt to taste. Add the asparagus spears and cook about 1 minute or longer. The cooking time will depend on the individual's taste. After 1 minute they will still be al dente. If you like them softer, cook 3 to 4 minutes. Drain well.

3. Meanwhile, melt the butter in a saucepan and add the flour, stirring with a wire whisk. Add the milk, stirring rapidly with the whisk. Cook, stirring, about 5 minutes until thickened and smooth. Remove from the heat.

4. Add ¾ cup of the grated cheese, stirring rapidly with the whisk. Add the egg yolk, pepper to taste, nutmeg, and cayenne and beat to blend.

5. Preheat the broiler to high.

6. Select a baking dish large enough to hold the asparagus spears in one layer slightly overlapping. Wrap one slice of ham compactly around each asparagus spear. Arrange the asparagus spears slightly overlapping in the dish.

7. Spoon the sauce over all and sprinkle with the remaining ¼ cup cheese.

8. Run the dish under the broiler about five inches from the source of heat. Broil until bubbling and golden brown on top. Serve immediately.

Yield: Four servings.

Petits Pois Forestière
(Buttered green peas with mushrooms)

2 tablespoons butter	2 cups freshly shelled small peas or use one 10-ounce package frozen peas
¼ pound thinly sliced mushrooms, about 2 cups	
Salt and freshly ground pepper	½ cup finely chopped scallions

1. Melt the butter in a saucepan and add the mushrooms. Cook, stirring, about 30 seconds. Add salt and pepper to taste.

2. Add the peas and scallions and cook, shaking the skillet and stirring, about 1½ to 2 minutes or just until the peas are piping hot.

Yield: Four servings.

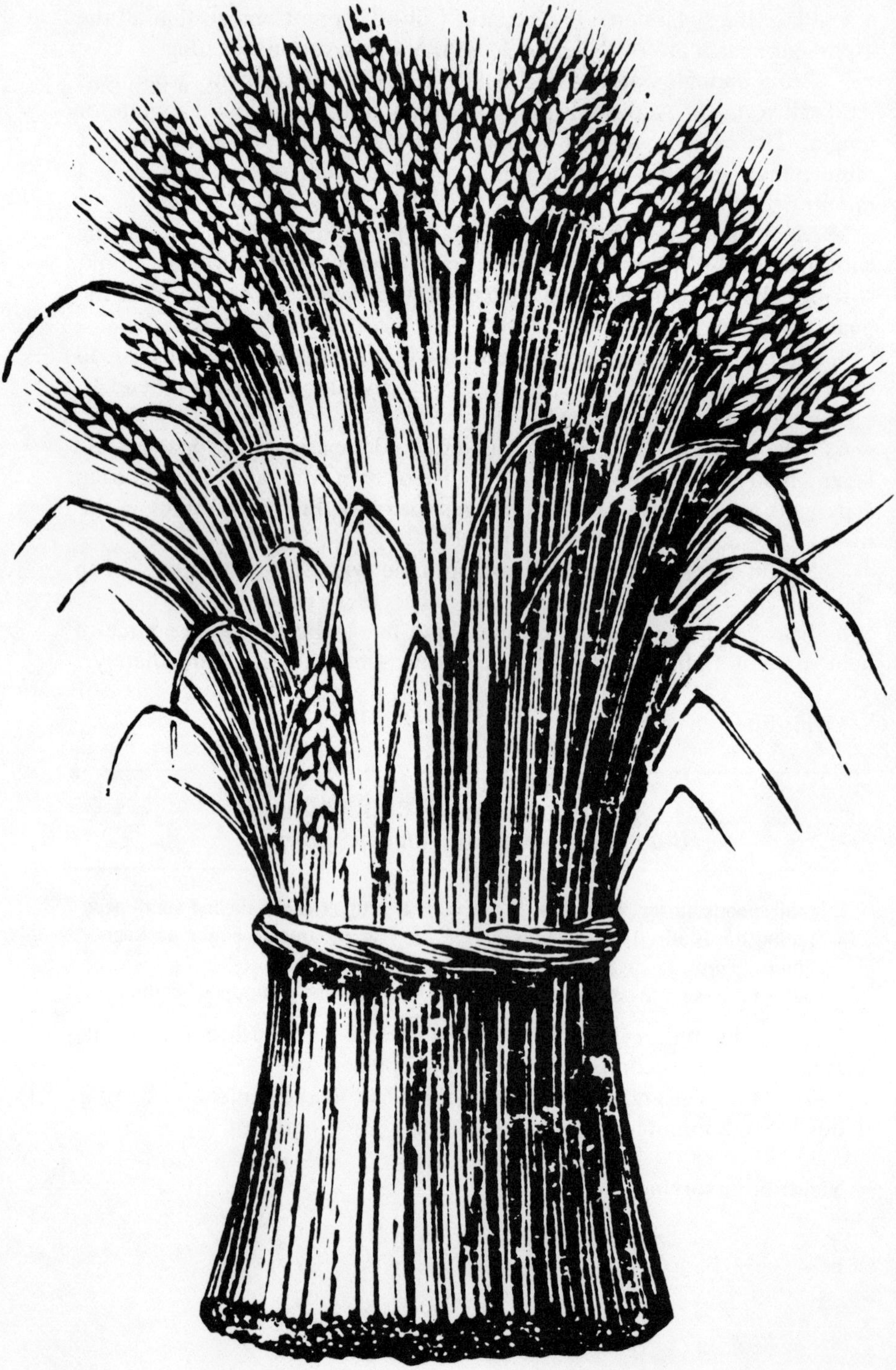

Pasta

ONE OF THE GREAT PLEASURES THAT I HAVE found in cooking over the years is the adventure involved in "playing around" with ideas. I have noted before that until I came to America, we rarely used any special kind of pasta. We did serve noodles with many, many foods principally ragouts and stews, but they were simply a side dish such as rice or steamed potatoes would be. On rare occasions if a guest wanted a Milanese-style dish, I would prepare spaghetti with a tomato sauce and grated cheese and that was about it.

When they were young, my children had a great fondness for spaghetti and then it was served in my own home. But I never seriously studied pasta cooking until I became associated in friendship with numerous good Italian cooks who introduced me to the thought that there are almost limitless kinds of pasta and sauces that go with them.

Some of the most interesting (and most easily prepared, by the way) are blends of pasta with vegetables, which had certainly never occurred to me in my youth.

Over a long period of time I have experimented with many pasta and vegetable dishes and they are outlined here. Any of these—fettuccine with peas, pasta with marinara sauce, linguine with roast pepper, or rigatoni with broccoli—would be excellent as a simple luncheon dish with a mixed green salad and cheese. Or they might serve as a first course before a simple and quickly grilled chop.

Fettuccine con Piselli
(Fettuccine with peas)

- 1 cup freshly shelled peas, or 1 10-ounce package frozen peas
- ½ cup heavy cream
- 1 pound fettuccine
- 8 tablespoons butter, cut into small pieces
- ¾ cup freshly grated Parmesan cheese
- ⅛ teaspoon freshly grated nutmeg
- Salt and freshly ground pepper

1. Drop the peas into boiling water. If fresh, they should cook 1 or 2 minutes. If frozen, they should cook 10 seconds or just until the peas no longer stick together. Drain and run briefly under cold water. Drain again and return to a saucepan. Add the cream and set aside.

2. Cook the pasta according to package directions and drain quickly.

3. Put the butter in a hot serving dish for tossing the pasta. Add the hot pasta.

4. Heat the peas in the cream briefly. Add the peas in the cream to the pasta. Add the cheese, nutmeg, and salt and pepper to taste. Toss well and serve hot.

Yield: Four servings.

Rigatoni con Broccoli
(Tubular pasta with broccoli)

- 1 bunch broccoli, about 1¼ pounds
- 6 tablespoons olive oil
- 2 teaspoons finely chopped garlic
- ¼ teaspoon dried hot red pepper flakes
- ⅓ cup fresh or canned chicken broth
- Salt and freshly ground pepper
- 1 pound rigatoni, cooked according to package directions

1. Cut the broccoli flowerets off the stems. Cut the stems into ample, bite-size pieces. (You can use the large stems, too.) Cut away the outer skin. Cut the stems into 1¼-inch lengths. Cut the pieces into ½-inch slices. Cut the slices into quarter-inch strips. There should be about 6 cups of stem pieces and flowerets.
2. Bring a large quantity of water to the boil and add the broccoli. Cook about 1 to 3 minutes and drain. Do not overcook. The broccoli must remain slightly crisp. Run cold water over the broccoli to chill quickly.
3. Heat the oil in a skillet and add the garlic. Cook briefly, without browning. Add the broccoli and toss to heat through. Add the pepper flakes, the broth, and salt and pepper to taste and bring to the boil.
4. Toss with the hot cooked rigatoni and serve immediately.

Yield: Four to six servings.

Pasta con Salsa Marinara
(Pasta with tomato and garlic sauce)

- 6 tablespoons olive oil
- 2 teaspoons finely chopped garlic
- 2 cups fresh tomato sauce (see recipe)
- 1 teaspoon crumbled dried oregano
- ¼ teaspoon dried hot red pepper flakes
- 2 tablespoons chopped fresh basil leaves or 1 teaspoon dried
- 2 tablespoons finely chopped parsley
- Salt and freshly ground pepper
- 1 pound spaghetti or spaghettini, cooked
- Freshly grated Parmesan cheese

1. Heat 4 tablespoons oil in a saucepan and add the garlic. Cook briefly, without browning, and add all the ingredients except the pasta and Parmesan cheese. Bring to the boil and simmer briefly.

2. Toss the cooked pasta with the remaining 2 tablespoons oil. Serve with the hot sauce. Serve sprinkled with the Parmesan cheese.

Yield: Four servings.

Salsa di Pomodoro Fresca
(Fresh tomato sauce)

- 2½ pounds tomatoes, cored and peeled
- Salt and freshly ground pepper

1. Cut the tomatoes in half. Cut the halves into 2-inch cubes. There should be about 4 cups.

2. Put the tomatoes into a skillet or saucepan and cook about 20 minutes. This should reduce to about 2 cups.

3. Add salt and pepper to taste.

Yield: About 2 cups.

Linguine con Peperoni Freschi
(Linguine with roast peppers)

4	sweet red or green peppers or, preferably, a combination of both	2	cups fresh tomato sauce (see previous recipe)
1	small onion		Salt and freshly ground pepper
¼	cup olive oil	¼	cup finely chopped parsley
1½	teaspoons finely chopped garlic	1	pound linguine, cooked according to package directions
¼	teaspoon dried hot red pepper flakes		

1. Preheat the broiler to high. Place the peppers on a sheet of heavy-duty aluminum foil and broil, turning often, until the skins are burnt all over.
2. Hold the peppers under cold running water and pull off the skin with the fingers. Cut the peppers into strips (julienne). There should be 1⅓ cups.
3. Cut the onion in half. Slice it thinly. There should be about 1 cup.
4. Heat the oil in a skillet and add the onion. Cook, stirring, until the onion starts to brown. Add the garlic and cook quickly.
5. Add the cooked pepper strips, pepper flakes, tomato sauce, and salt and pepper to taste. Cook, stirring gently, until the tomato sauce is piping hot. Stir in the parsley. Serve with linguine.

Yield: Four to six servings.

UNTIL I CAME TO THE UNITED STATES I HAD scant knowledge of Italian cooking. And my first samplings of it in America were, for the most part, Neapolitan, a robust form of cookery based largely on tomatoes and garlic. Over the years I have discovered, in kitchens both professional and private (and in the course of visits to Italy), that Italian cooking is as varied as the French and in some areas equally as subtle and sophisticated.

The first dish I can recall that impressed me was linguine with clam sauce served in two versions—white with olive oil, garlic, parsley and clam broth and red with tomato sauce added. I have made both many times for my family and friends.

It recently occurred to me that I had never eaten nor heard of linguine with oyster sauce. If the dish is good with clams, why not with oysters? Italian friends explained to me that although oysters exist in certain Italian waters—in Italy the name for oysters is ostriche—they were considered a rarity.

At that point I set about experimenting with my own version of linguine with oysters. I tried them with oil and garlic and with tomato sauces. The version that I preferred in these efforts was, perhaps, more French than Italian. It turned out to be linguine with oysters in a cream sauce made with butter, parsley, garlic and a few hot red pepper flakes. It is an incredibly simple dish to prepare and serves quite well as a main course. If you plan to make it, by all means ascertain that your oysters have sufficient liquor; you will need about half a cup.

The only accompaniment you will need for this dish is a well-flavored salad, and I propose a salad of cooked cauliflower dressed with sieved hard-cooked egg and parsley vinaigrette. This salad may be served warm or at room temperature. Prepare and start to cook the cauliflower before you prepare the quickly made linguine with oyster sauce.

Linguine with Oyster Sauce

1 quart shucked oysters
2 tablespoons butter
¼ cup finely chopped shallots
1 teaspoon finely chopped garlic
1 cup heavy cream
 Salt and freshly ground pepper
⅛ teaspoon dried hot red pepper flakes
¼ cup finely chopped parsley
¾ pound linguine, cooked according to package directions or to taste

1. Place a sieve inside a mixing bowl. Add the oysters to drain. There should be about ½ cup of oyster liquor. Reserve the liquor.

2. Melt the butter in a shallow skillet and add the shallots and garlic. Cook briefly, stirring. Add the oyster liquor and bring to the boil. Add the

cream and salt and pepper to taste. Simmer, stirring often, about 5 minutes.

3. Add the oysters and pepper flakes. Cook about 3 minutes or until the oysters become plump and are heated through. Do not overcook or the oysters will toughen. Add the parsley.

4. Pour the cooked linguine into the sauce. Toss and serve.

Yield: Four servings.

Chou-fleur Mimosa
(Cauliflower with egg and parsley)

1 cauliflower, about 1 pound	2 tablespoons wine vinegar
¼ cup milk	6 tablespoons olive oil
Salt	Freshly ground pepper
1 egg, at room temperature	2 tablespoons chopped parsley
1 teaspoon imported mustard such as Dijon or Düsseldorf	

1. Trim off the leaves of the cauliflower. Using a sharp knife, cut away the core of the cauliflower.

2. Put the cauliflower in a saucepan with water to barely cover. Add milk and salt to taste. Bring to the boil and simmer 15 minutes or until cauliflower is tender but not mushy. Do not overcook.

3. Drain and let cool until ready to serve. Do not chill.

4. Meanwhile, as the cauliflower cooks, cook the egg in boiling water for 12 minutes. Drain. Peel.

5. Put the egg through a fine sieve into a mixing bowl. Add the mustard and vinegar. Gradually add the oil, beating briskly with a wire whisk. Add salt and pepper to taste. Add the parsley.

6. Spoon the sauce over cauliflower. Serve.

Yield: Four servings.

IF I HAD TO NAME THE GREATEST REVOLUtion in my own taste since I came to America more than 40 years ago, it would probably be my enthusiasm for pasta. At almost every meal when I was a child, we dined on either rice or potatoes or, one of the most basic forms of pasta, noodles. The noodles (which were never referred to as pasta) were always served with any of several kinds of stews or ragouts: veal marengo, which is with tomatoes and mushrooms; chicken in Burgundy wine sauces; rabbit, hunter's-style, and so on. But I don't recall ever having spaghetti, which is basic on American menus, and certainly not the more unusual forms of pasta like fettuccine and linguine.

My initiation into the many kinds and uses of pasta came during a trip with friends some years ago through Rome, Milan, Genoa, and Florence. I was introduced to scores of sauces, including those made with many kinds of fish and shellfish, a fine ragout of rabbit or hare with broad noodles known as pappardelle, and a marvelous walnut sauce known as salsi di noce served with stuffed dumplings known as pansoti.

Some of my favorite ways of preparing pasta are with vegetables in season, and one of these was borrowed from a friend, Vivian Collyer, an expert cook who caters from her home in Mountainside, New Jersey. At a recent birthday party she prepared a sauce of Gorgonzola cheese with pieces of asparagus that had been cooked al dente. The incredible thing about most of the sauces that I prepare is that they all can be made in minutes and, if the ingredients are ready to cook, in about the time it takes to cook the pasta.

A nice appetizer for pasta dishes—a main course in itself—is roasted sweet peppers with anchovies. For a less-than-an-hour meal, prepare the peppers and anchovies before you make the pasta dish.

Pasta with Chicken and Asparagus

- 1 skinless, boneless chicken breast, about 1 pound
- 1 pound fresh asparagus spears
- 2 tablespoons butter
- ¾ pound linguine or fettucine
- Salt and freshly ground pepper
- 3 tablespoons finely chopped shallots
- 1 cup heavy cream
- 1 dried hot red pepper
- ⅛ teaspoon freshly grated nutmeg
- ¼ pound Gorgonzola cheese
- 2 tablespoons chopped fresh tarragon or ½ teaspoon dried
- ½ cup freshly grated Parmesan cheese

1. Remove all sinews and soft cartilage from the chicken breast. Cut the breast into small strips about one and a half inches long and half an inch wide. There should be about 1½ cups.

2. Scrape and trim the asparagus. Cut off and discard any tough ends.

Cut the asparagus on the bias into 1½-inch lengths. Drop the pieces into boiling water and drain. Set aside.

3. Bring enough water to a boil to cook the pasta when added. Add the pasta and cook to the desired degree of doneness.

4. Meanwhile, melt the butter in a large saucepan. Add the chicken strips and cook, stirring to separate the pieces. Cook quickly. Add salt and pepper to taste. Cook about 30 seconds or just until the chicken changes color.

5. Add the asparagus and stir. Add salt and pepper to taste and the shallots and cook briefly, about 30 seconds. Add the cream, red hot pepper, and nutmeg and stir.

6. Break the cheese into small pieces and add it. Cook just until the cheese melts. Add a generous grinding of black pepper and the tarragon. Stir. Drain the pasta and add to the sauce. Toss well. Serve with grated cheese on the side.

Yield: Four to six servings.

Poivrons aux Anchois
(Sweet peppers with anchovy vinaigrette)

4	to 8 sweet green or red peppers		Juice of half a lemon
8	to 16 anchovy fillets	¼	cup finely chopped parsley
1	tablespoon finely minced garlic		Lemon wedges
¼	cup olive oil		

1. Preheat the broiler to high.

2. Line a baking tray with aluminum foil and arrange the peppers on it. Place about four or five inches from the source of heat and cook, turning occasionally, until the skin is slightly burnt and charred all over.

3. Hold the peppers under cold running water and pull away the skin. Drain well. Cut away and discard the cores. Cut the peppers in half and scrape away the seeds.

4. Arrange equal portions of the peppers on four chilled salad plates. Arrange two to four crossed anchovies on each serving.

5. Blend the garlic, oil, lemon juice, and parsley in a small bowl. Spoon this over the peppers and anchovies. Garnish each serving with lemon wedges.

Yield: Four servings.

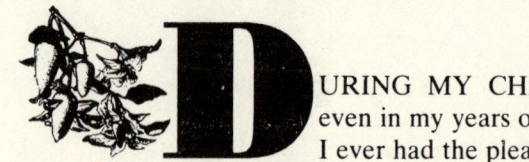

DURING MY CHILDHOOD IN BURGUNDY AND even in my years of apprenticeship in Paris, I don't think I ever had the pleasure of dining on clams, either cooked or raw. Although clams of one sort or another are found in the Midi, or the southern part of France, they never were on my family's table. And clams are rarely, if ever, found in classic French cooking.

My first encounters with clams came when I moved out to East Hampton to be chef at Henri Soule's summer restaurant, the Hedges. That was many years ago, of course, but I moved to the eastern end of Long Island and bought a small house by the side of Accabonac Bay, which abounds in fresh clams.

Over the years I have cooked clams in a multitude of ways and enjoyed many a meal starting with raw clams on the half shell. Last spring, when the first beefsteak tomatoes came to the market, I prepared chopped clams with a sauce made of cubed tomatoes, thinly sliced zucchini, and a tablespoon of chopped basil fresh from my herb garden.

This is a recipe that is, along with a mixed salad, a meal in itself. For pasta, you use either spaghetti or linguine which, for some reason that I am unable to fathom, seems to go particularly well with clams. In cooking the pasta I resort to a "trick" that I discovered some years ago. The pasta will be more tasty if you use the clam liquid to cook it in. Therefore, it is best to have the liquid saved when the clams are shucked either at home or at the fish market.

I also find that a touch of hot red pepper flakes is enormously compatible with most cooked clam dishes and only a pinch is necessary.

Once your clams are shucked, the dish may be prepared, start to finish, in about half an hour or less. Serve with a tossed green salad or the salad of mixed vegetables outlined here.

Spaghetti et Palourdes Printanière
(Spaghetti with clams and fresh vegetables)

24	cherrystone clams	2	tablespoons coarsely chopped fresh basil
1	or 2 zucchini, about ½ pound	¼	teaspoon dried hot red pepper flakes
1¼	pounds tomatoes, cored		
¼	cup olive oil		
1	tablespoon finely minced garlic	¾	pound spaghetti
	Salt and freshly ground pepper	½	cup heavy cream

1. Open the clams and reserve both the clam meat and the juice. There should be about 1½ cups of clams and 2½ cups of juice.

2. Chop the clams and set aside.

3. Trim off the ends of the zucchini. Cut the zucchini lengthwise into quarters. Cut each quarter crosswise into quarter-inch-thick pieces. There should be about 2 cups. Set aside.

4. Cut the tomatoes into half-inch cubes. There should be about 3 cups. Set aside.

5. Heat the oil in a skillet and add the zucchini. Cook about 30 seconds and add the garlic. Cook, stirring, about 10 seconds and add the tomatoes. Cook about 3 minutes. Add salt and pepper to taste and the basil and hot pepper flakes.

6. Meanwhile, put the clam juice in a large pot. Add enough water to cook the spaghetti. Bring to the boil. Add the spaghetti and cook to the desired degree of doneness. Drain. Return the spaghetti to the pot and add the heavy cream.

7. Add the chopped clams to the tomato and zucchini sauce.

8. Pour the tomato and zucchini sauce over the spaghetti and toss. Serve immediately.

Yield: Four servings.

Salade de Légumes Vinaigrette
(Assorted vegetable vinaigrette)

The vegetables:
- ½ cauliflower
- 1 carrot, trimmed and scraped
- 1 or 2 stalks broccoli
- Salt

The sauce:
- 1 teaspoon imported mustard such as Dijon or Düsseldorf
- 1 teaspoon red-wine vinegar
- ¼ cup peanut, vegetable, or corn oil
- Salt and freshly ground pepper
- ½ cup coarsely chopped red onion
- 2 tablespoons chopped parsley

1. Break the cauliflower into flowerets. There should be about 3 cups.

2. Cut the carrot into half-inch-thick rounds. There should be about 1 cup.

3. Cut the broccoli into flowerets of the same size as the cauliflower. There should be about 1 cup.

4. Cook the cauliflower, carrot, and broccoli in three separate saucepans. Bring enough water to the boil to cover each vegetable when added. Add salt to taste and the vegetables.

5. Cook cauliflower about 10 minutes. Cook carrot and broccoli about 5 minutes each. Drain well.

6. To make the sauce, put the mustard in a salad bowl and add the vinegar. Start beating with a wire whisk while adding the oil. Add salt and pepper to taste, chopped onion, and parsley.

7. Add vegetables and toss until blended. Serve at room temperature.

Yield: Four servings.

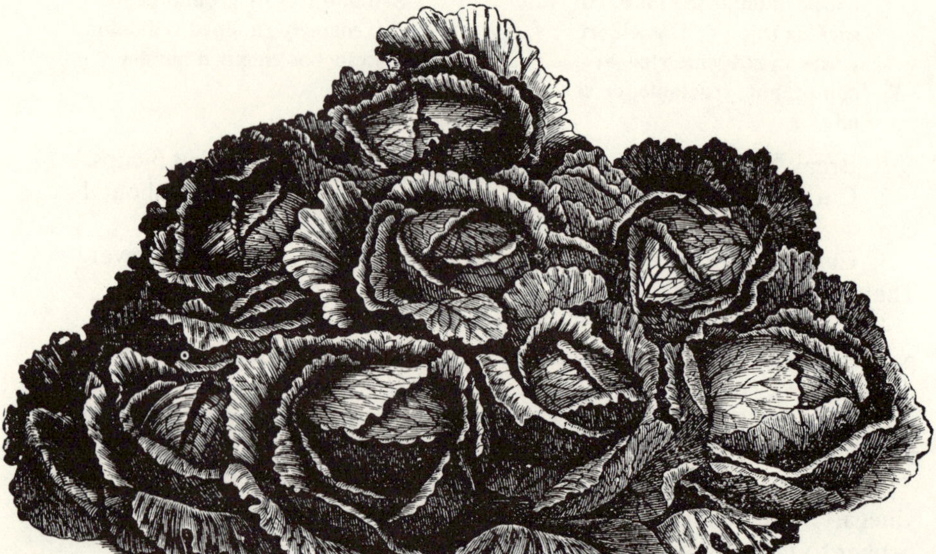

Vegetables

AS A PROFESSIONAL CHEF I AM OFTENTIMES asked whether or not I ever resort to foods that have been put up in cans. The answer is yes, but in limited quantities. It just so happens that I have a fairly keen liking for canned tuna (as well as sardines and, on occasion, salmon) and during the summer months I sometimes use it in various salads, which are eaten as such, or as fillings for sandwiches. It almost invariably goes into my salade niçoise, or into those the basis for which is the tuna itself.

I have pointed out a hundred times and more that people feast with the eyes as well as the palate. And if you are going to serve a dish as "humble" as tuna salad you should present it in style. The summer is the ideal season for that, for the simple reason that nothing blends as neatly with tuna salad, where flavor is concerned, as freshly picked, red ripe tomatoes. This is also the time when you have access to other flavors that complement tuna, notably such fresh herbs as basil.

A fine presentation for tuna salad is an opened up tomato, made by putting the tomato cored side down on a flat surface. Slice four to six times, cutting part way to but not through the core. Open up the tomato and add a scoop of salad, garnish with quartered egg wedges, slices of avocado, and basil leaves.

In my own garden I had a particularly fine year for fresh arugula which, I have become convinced, is one of the most palatable and interesting salad greens. It is pungent in flavor and, at times, a bit biting in its strength, a pungency that seems not unrelated to hot mustard or horseradish. There are those who propose that arugula should always be blended with other greens such as Boston lettuce or red leaf lettuce. I, personally, prefer it pure and unadulterated except with a salad dressing, in a salad bowl. It goes remarkably well with tomatoes stuffed with tuna salad.

Tomates Surprise
(Summer stuffed tomatoes)

4	red, ripe tomatoes, about 1½ pounds
2	7-ounce cans solid white tuna
½	cup finely chopped scallions
¼	cup chopped fresh basil
½	cup homemade mayonnaise
	Dash of Tabasco
½	teaspoon Worcestershire sauce
	Freshly ground pepper
4	hard-cooked eggs
1	ripe but firm unblemished avocado
8	basil leaves

1. Cut the cores from the tomatoes. Place the tomatoes, one at a time, on a flat surface, cored side down. Make five equally spaced downward slices starting at the bottom almost but not down to the surface. As they

are cut, open up the tomatoes and arrange them on four individual large salad plates.

2. Combine the tuna, scallions, basil, mayonnaise, Tabasco, Worcestershire sauce, and pepper in a mixing bowl. Blend well. Spoon equal portions of the tuna salad into each opened-up tomato.

3. Cut the eggs into quarters. Arrange one quartered egg equally spaced around the base of each filled tomato.

4. Peel the avocado and remove and discard the seed. Cut in half and cut the halved avocado into lengthwise strips. Arrange the strips between the egg wedges. Garnish each serving with basil.

Yield: Four servings.

Arugula and Red Onion Salad

½ pound arugula leaves, approximately
1 cup chopped red onion
½ cup finely chopped parsley, preferably flat-leaf Italian parsley

1½ tablespoons red wine vinegar
Salt and freshly ground pepper
¼ cup olive oil

1. Pick over the leaves and remove and discard any tough stems. Rinse and drain the leaves well. Pat dry. There should be about 6 cups loosely packed. Put the leaves in a salad bowl and add the onion and parsley.

2. Put the vinegar in a bowl and add salt and pepper to taste. Start beating while gradually adding the oil.

3. Pour the sauce over the salad and toss to blend.

Yield: Four servings.

IF I WERE TO OUTLINE MY SPECIAL FAVORITES among vegetables, it is quite certain that eggplants would be high on the list. That particular vegetable has a special character, a flavor, and texture that is not like any other. It has a sort of meatiness about it and it is certainly one of the most versatile of all vegetables.

I can practically make a meal of deep-fried eggplant strips, enjoy it in scores of Italian preparations from Parmigiana to rollatine, and for a really hurried vegetable accompaniment, I simply brush slices with melted butter or olive oil and cook under the broiler on both sides until tender.

Eggplant also has one of the most appealing names in all of French cookery. Aubergines (they are also called that in England) are as much a part of southern French cooking as thyme, tomatoes, and bay leaf, and I am particularly keen on one specialty of Nice, a simple casserole made with eggplant, onion, and garlic.

And there is another quickly made casserole dish of which my family is particularly fond, a casserole of lamb with eggplant. Lamb is one of those meats that seem particularly compatible to eggplant, as Greek and Turkish cooks have known for years in the preparation of their moussakas. The casserole here is reminiscent of a moussaka, but it is much less elaborate both in preparation and in cooking. My version does not have the custard sauce on top, but there is a sprinkling of crumbs and grated cheese.

Either of these dishes may be made in much less than an hour. The eggplant casserole can also be served as a vegetable (or it could be served cold as a leftover for an appetizer).

Aubergine Niçoise
(Eggplant casserole)

1 large eggplant, about 1½ pounds
½ cup olive oil
½ cup coarsely chopped onion
1 tablespoon finely minced garlic
⅓ cup red wine vinegar
¾ cup water
1 bay leaf
1 tablespoon ground coriander seeds
1 teaspoon dried thyme
Salt and freshly ground pepper

1. If the eggplant is not young and tender, peel it; otherwise, leave the skin intact and just trim the ends.

2. Cut the eggplant into 1-inch-thick slices lengthwise. Cut the slices into strips 1 inch wide. Cut the strips into 1-inch cubes. There should be about 6 cups.

3. Heat the oil in a heavy casserole and add the eggplant. Cook, stirring, about 2 minutes.

4. Add the remaining ingredients and cover. Cook 15 minutes. Scrape the mixture into a serving bowl and let stand until cool before serving.

Yield: Four or more servings.

Casserole of Lamb and Eggplant

1 large eggplant, about 1½ pounds	1 bay leaf
¼ cup olive oil	1 dried hot red pepper
1 teaspoon finely minced garlic	4 cups (1 1-pound, 12-ounce can) tomatoes with tomato paste
1½ pounds ground lamb or beef	1 cup bread crumbs
Salt and freshly ground pepper	½ cup grated Parmesan or Gruyère cheese
½ teaspoon ground cinnamon	

1. Preheat the oven to 425 degrees.
2. If the eggplant is not young and tender, peel it. Otherwise, leave the skin intact and just trim the ends.
3. Cut the eggplant lengthwise into 1-inch-thick slices. Cut the slices into strips 1 inch wide. Cut the strips into 1-inch cubes. There should be about 6 cups.
4. Heat the oil in a casserole and add the onion and garlic. Cook, stirring, until the onion is wilted. Add the lamb, chopping down with the side of a heavy metal spoon to break up any lumps. Add the eggplant and cook, stirring often, about 5 minutes.
5. Add the pepper, cinnamon, bay leaf, hot pepper, and tomatoes. Cook, stirring, about 5 minutes.
6. Spoon and scrape the mixture into a casserole or baking dish. Sprinkle with a mixture of crumbs and cheese. Place in the oven and bake 15 minutes.

Yield: Four to six servings.

I HAVE NOT THE LEAST RECOLLECTION OF when I first sampled that Provençale dish called ratatouille, but I suspect that it must have been in my childhood. Or at least it was a dish that resembled ratatouille.

In our Burgundy home, my mother often concocted a vegetable stew that was made with tomatoes, garlic, eggplant, and onions, which she made in a large batch. Like most ratatouilles, it was a dish that improved with age. She frequently turned this dish, or rather the leftovers of this dish, into a fine evening meal by breaking eggs onto the top and baking it in the oven until the eggs were set, the whites firm and the yolks still runny.

It was not until recently that I became curious to learn the origin of the name ratatouille, and I found from an old French dictionary that it comes from a Provençale word "ratatoulho." This same dictionary also adds that ratatouille, in some circles, is a less than flattering name for a badly made stew. If that is true, I can recall quite a few ratatouilles I have been served in my life that did not contain tomatoes, garlic, and eggplant.

I find ratatouille with eggs to be a highly agreeable dish for Sunday night supper, and guests have also enjoyed it as a midday meal. Incidentally, one guest who came from the Riviera said that she had dined on a similar dish in her childhood; it differed in that the eggs had been fried rather than baked and served on top of the ratatouille, but it is a small point.

Some people might feel that most ratatouilles should be baked much longer than one hour, but I disagree. If you follow the recipe printed here—the preparation, cooking on the stove, and baking require less than 60 minutes—I think you will be agreeably surprised at the results.

Serve the dish with a crusty loaf of French bread that has been split in half and lightly broiled on the cut surface. That plus a salad. And, if you desire, a platter of fresh fruit for dessert.

Ratatouille aux Oeufs
(Ratatouille with eggs)

- 1 eggplant, about 1 pound
- 1 or 2 zucchini, about 1 pound
- ⅓ cup olive oil
- 1 cup cored, seeded, and cubed green pepper
- 1 cup cubed onion
- 1 tablespoon finely minced garlic
- 2 cups cubed, red, ripe tomatoes, or use imported canned tomatoes
- 3 tablespoons tomato paste
- 1 bay leaf
- ½ teaspoon dried thyme
- Salt and freshly ground pepper
- 8 eggs
- ¼ cup freshly grated Parmesan cheese

1. Preheat the oven to 400 degrees.
2. Trim and peel the eggplant. Cut it into 1-inch or slightly smaller cubes. There should be about 4 cups.
3. Trim the ends of the zucchini. Do not peel it. Cut the zucchini into 1-inch or slightly smaller cubes. There should be about 4 cups.
4. In a heavy casserole, heat the oil and when it is very hot, add the eggplant and zucchini and cook, stirring often, about 2 minutes. Add the green pepper and onion and cook about 6 minutes, stirring. Add the garlic and stir.
5. Add the tomatoes, tomato paste, bay leaf, and thyme. Add salt and pepper to taste. Bring to the boil, stirring. Place the casserole in the oven and bake 20 minutes.
6. Pour and scrape the mixture into a baking dish. A dish that measures 8½ by 13½ by 2 inches is a good choice. Make eight indentations in the center of the ratatouille and break 1 egg into each indentation.
7. Sprinkle the cheese evenly over the surface of the dish. Place in the oven and bake 10 minutes. Serve immediately.

Yield: Four servings.

Salade de Cresson et Oeufs Durs
(Watercress and hard-cooked egg salad)

2 bunches firm, deep green, unblemished watercress	2 hard-cooked eggs, peeled and sliced or chopped
1 tablespoon imported mustard such as Dijon or Düsseldorf	2 tablespoons coarsely chopped red onion
2 tablespoons red wine vinegar	1 tablespoon finely chopped parsley
Salt and freshly ground pepper	
6 tablespoons peanut, vegetable, or corn oil	

1. Trim off the tough ends of the watercress and discard. Rinse the leaves and tender stems and drain well. Shake or pat dry.
2. Put the mustard, vinegar, and salt and pepper to taste into salad bowl. Blend with wire whisk. Add the oil, beating with the whisk.
3. Add the watercress, sliced or chopped egg, and chopped onion.
4. Sprinkle with parsley and toss.

Yield: Four servings.

WHEN I WAS A VERY YOUNG CHEF IN FRANCE, the world seemed like a very well ordered universe where the variety of foods was concerned. There were peas to be turned into petits pois à la Française, carrots for making dishes named Crécy, and asparagus for all those foods listed on menus as Argenteuil. The vegetables in the garden were all well catalogued and finite.

When I came to the United States, I realized that there were numerous vegetables that were totally new to me, among them bean sprouts, arugula, broccoli rape, and bitter melon. The astonishing thing, however, is that the seed companies are "inventing" vegetables unknown 20 years ago. One of the most intriguing of these is spaghetti squash. It is an interesting novelty that is becoming more and more popular in this country. I harvested my first crop this year. It is one of the simplest foods to cook. You prick the skin (it is the shape of a yellow football) with the tines of a fork, put the squash in a kettle of water and let it cook for 30 minutes. When it is done, scrape out the center seeds and fibers and, finally, the edible strands, which are, of course, the "spaghetti" in the name.

A remarkable thing about spaghetti squash is its nature as a table food. It resembles spaghetti, its texture is "al dente" and, even unbuttered, it has a taste appeal—a trifle sweet but pleasant. I have eaten spaghetti squash simply buttered with a little salt and pepper added. Growers of the squash say you can serve it with any sauce used for spaghetti and I'm inclined to agree. A family favorite is a simple tomato and meat sauce with assorted spices—marjoram, oregano, rosemary and pepper flakes—plus half a cup or so of red wine.

Since the spaghetti squash requires only half an hour to cook, there will be time to prepare the sauce and produce a meal in less than an hour. Serve the "spaghetti" and meat sauce with a tossed green salad.

Spaghetti Squash

1 medium-size spaghetti squash, about 2½ pounds	4 tablespoons butter Salt and freshly ground pepper

1. Pierce the squash in several places with the tines of a fork.

2. Place the squash in a kettle and add cold water to cover. Bring to the boil and cover. Simmer 30 minutes.

3. Hold the squash over a basin to catch all interior drippings. Cut the squash in half lengthwise.

4. Using a large, heavy metal spoon, scrape out and discard the center section of each half much as you would clean a cantaloupe half. Scoop and scrape out the remainder of the squash, leaving only the shells.

5. Put the "spaghetti" strands into a skillet and add the butter and salt

and pepper to taste. Heat, tossing gently, until the strands are hot and coated with melted butter. Serve with meat sauce (see recipe).

Yield: Four to six servings.

Meat Sauce

1 tablespoon olive oil	¼ cup tomato paste
1 pound ground chuck	1 teaspoon dried marjoram
1 tablespoon finely chopped garlic	1 teaspoon dried oregano
1½ cups finely chopped onion	1 teaspoon dried rosemary
Salt and freshly ground pepper	⅛ teaspoon dried hot red pepper flakes
½ cup dry red wine	
4 cups tomatoes	

1. Heat the oil in a heavy skillet and add the meat. Cook, chopping up the meat with the sides of a heavy metal spoon to break up any lumps.

2. When the meat loses its raw red look, add the garlic, onion, salt to taste, and a generous grinding of black pepper. Stir and cook about 1 minute.

3. Add the wine and cook until most of the liquid evaporates.

4. Add the tomatoes, tomato paste, marjoram, oregano, rosemary, and pepper flakes.

5. Cook 30 minutes. Serve with spaghetti squash or pasta.

Yield: Four to six servings.

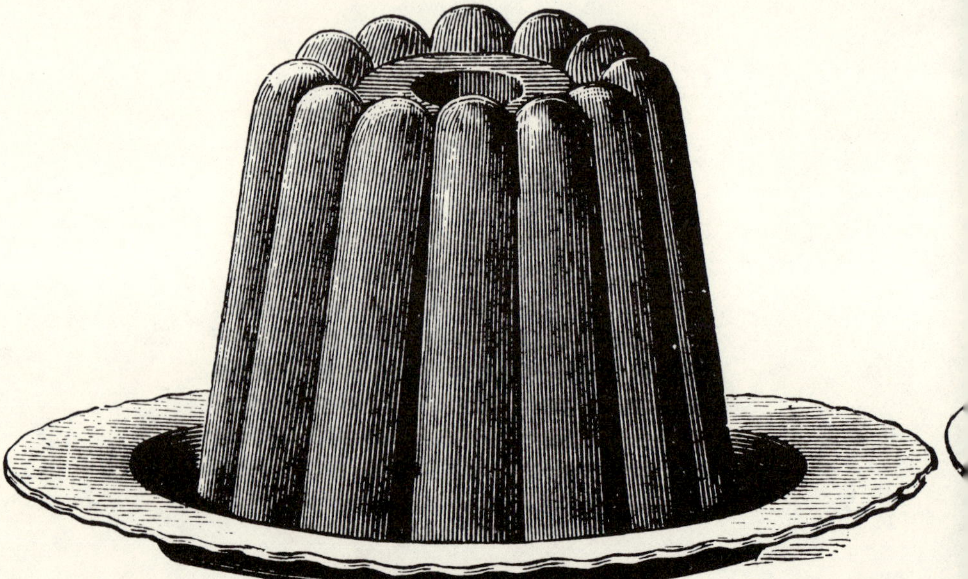

Desserts

IF I WERE TO NAME THE SINGLE MOST DIFFIcult category to incorporate in a book on cooking in less than an hour, it would most certainly be desserts. The preparation of a pastry such as a pie or a tart, even the preparation of a cookie, generally requires a good deal of blending and rolling and shaping and filling and baking, and there is simply not time to do that if you are going to serve a main course and, perhaps, a dessert as well.

The ideal solution for most menus would be, if you intend to serve a dessert, ice cream.

The serving of different and varied ice cream dishes does require some planning. Of course, there are many people for whom a cup of ice cream, day after day and meal after meal, is paradise enough. It is nothing that you, or at least I, would want to serve to guests invitation after invitation.

You should, by all means, create your ice cream or ice or sherbet dishes in accordance with the flavor. Vanilla ice cream teams well with almost all flavors and sauces and liqueurs and spirits. You can make an "instant" frozen egg nog, for example, by simply grating a little nutmeg on top of a scoop of vanilla ice cream and sprinkling it with bourbon. Almost all sherbets and ices can be given a fillip à la russe by pouring over a little vodka.

If you wish to make a classic ice cream and fruit dessert such as pears belle Hélène or peaches Melba, you will probably want to use canned pears or peaches for these are very good out of a tin.

To aid you in planning desserts for your 60-minute menus, I am including here several of my suggestions for hastily made ice cream and other desserts.

There are fruit sauces such as raspberry and strawberry; two cream sauces to be used hot or cold, one chocolate and one butterscotch. These require brief minutes to prepare. There is also a quickly cooked apple topping for ice cream.

Poires Belle Hélène
(Pears with ice cream and chocolate sauce)

4 to 8 scoops vanilla ice cream	8 tablespoons chocolate sauce (see recipe)
8 canned pear halves, drained	4 candied violets, optional

1. Put one or two scoops of vanilla ice cream in an individual serving dish.

2. Arrange 2 pear halves on each serving. Spoon 2 tablespoons of chocolate sauce over each serving and garnish, if desired, with candied violets.

Yield: Four servings.

Chocolate Sauce

4 ounces unsweetened chocolate, grated	½ cup heavy cream
1 cup water	¼ teaspoon ground cinnamon
½ cup sugar	2 tablespoons coffee liqueur such as Kahlua, optional

1. Combine the chocolate, water, and sugar in a heavy saucepan. Bring to the boil gradually, stirring constantly.

2. When the chocolate is melted, add the cream and cinnamon and stir to blend. Put the sauce through a sieve. Add the liqueur. Serve hot or cold over vanilla or chocolate ice cream.

Yield: About 1¾ cups.

Pêche Melba

4 to 8 scoops vanilla ice cream	8 tablespoons cold raspberry sauce (see recipe page 270)
8 canned peach halves, drained	¼ cup slivered almonds, optional

1. Put 1 or 2 scoops of vanilla ice cream in an individual serving dish.

2. Arrange 2 peach halves on top of each serving.

3. Spoon 2 tablespoons of raspberry sauce over each serving. Sprinkle with slivered almonds and serve.

Yield: Four servings.

Hot Strawberry Sauce

1 pint strawberries, or 1 10-ounce package frozen strawberries	2 teaspoons cornstarch
¼ to ½ cup sugar	1 tablespoon water

1. Put the strawberries into a saucepan. Add ½ cup sugar if the strawberries are fresh and ¼ cup sugar if they are frozen. Bring the mixture to the boil, stirring.

2. Blend the cornstarch and water and stir it into the sauce. Cook, stirring, about 30 seconds. Put a sieve into a mixing bowl and pour in the sauce. Push the sauce through the sieve, stirring to remove the seeds. Serve hot over vanilla, strawberry, or raspberry ice cream.

Yield: About 1 cup.

Note: Raspberries may be substituted for the strawberries.

Cold Raspberry Sauce

1 pint fresh raspberries, or 1 10-ounce package frozen raspberries Juice of half a lemon	¼ to ½ cup sugar 2 tablespoons framboise or Grand Marnier

1. If fresh raspberries are used, rinse and drain them. Put the fresh or frozen raspberries in the container of a food processor and add the lemon juice. If fresh raspberries are used, add ½ cup sugar. If frozen, add ¼ cup sugar. Blend thoroughly.

2. Add the framboise or Grand Marnier and blend. Serve with vanilla ice cream or over whole fresh fruit such as fresh strawberries or fresh raspberries.

Yield: About 1⅓ cups.

Note: Strawberries may be substituted for the raspberries.

Butterscotch-Pecan Sauce

½ cup dark corn syrup ½ cup brown sugar ¼ cup heavy cream	2 tablespoons butter ½ teaspoon vanilla extract ⅓ cup pecans

1. Preheat the broiler.
2. Combine the ingredients in a saucepan and cook, stirring, about 5 minutes.
3. Put the pecans in a small baking pan. Place them under the broiler and cook, stirring often, until lightly browned and crisp, about 30 seconds or more. Chop the nuts and add them to the sauce.
4. Serve hot or cold over vanilla or butterscotch ice cream.

Yield: About 1 cup.

Glacé "Egg Nog"
(Ice cream with nutmeg and Bourbon)

4 scoops vanilla ice cream ½ teaspoon freshly grated nutmeg	8 tablespoons Bourbon

1. Spoon one scoop of ice cream into four individual chilled small dessert bowls.

2. Sprinkle the tops of each serving with equal amounts of nutmeg. Pour the Bourbon over all and serve.

Yield: Four servings.

Glacé Hawaiien
(Ice cream with coconut and rum)

4 scoops vanilla ice cream	¼ cup shredded sweetened coconut
½ cup canned cream of coconut	
2 tablespoons dark rum	

1. Place one scoop of ice cream in each of four small, individual dessert bowls. Beat the cream of coconut with the rum. Spoon equal portions of the sauce over the ice cream.
2. Sprinkle with equal portions of coconut and serve.

Yield: Four servings.

Pommes Normande à la Glacé
(Apples with Calvados and ice cream)

4 firm, slightly tart apples such as McIntosh or Granny Smith	4 tablespoons sugar
	¼ teaspoon ground cinnamon
½ teaspoon grated lemon peel	¼ cup Calvados or applejack
3 tablespoons butter	4 scoops vanilla ice cream

1. Peel the apples. Cut them into quarters. Remove the cores and stems. Cut the quarters into thin slices. There should be about 4 cups.
2. Melt the butter in a skillet and add the apple slices and lemon peel. Sprinkle with sugar and cinnamon and cook, stirring the apples and shaking the skillet so that the apples cook evenly. Cook over very high heat. When the apples start to brown, add the Calvados and ignite it. Blend well.
3. Put 1 scoop of ice cream into each of four individual serving dishes. Put the apples on top and serve.

Yield: Four servings.

There was a time not many years ago when professional chefs in this country and abroad were reluctant to share their "secrets" or recipes with home cooks for the simple reason that most chefs considered home cooks to be incapable of understanding the proper techniques of professional cooking. That, of course, is no longer true and there is not a chef of my acquaintance who is not happy in this day and age to outline in detail even the most elaborate preparation.

When I first started preparing dishes to be turned into recipes for the average home cook I was amused to learn that the three foods that seemed most in demand were soufflés, omelets, and crêpes. These are three things which, for some reason or another, seem to intimidate most would-be cooks, particularly those who are new to the kitchen. The truth of the matter is that all three are relatively easy and, with a little practice, remarkably easy to make.

I have often been asked to include desserts in this column—sweet endings for meals that can be prepared in less than an hour. And one of the desserts most requested is that group made with crêpes.

As far as I am concerned, it is not more time consuming to prepare and serve certain crêpe desserts than to prepare and serve a fruit cup or mélange of fruits.

The first thing you will need if you have crêpes in mind, is a good crêpe pan. This is as easy to find as your nearest hardware store, provided it deals in basic kitchen equipment. Teflon pans are first rate (in fact, in my opinion, preferable for crêpe-making unless you are a professional). The best of these for making crêpes measures about six inches across the bottom (turn pan upside down to measure) and about eight inches across the top of the rim.

To make a crêpe, you work quickly and deftly. You add 2 tablespoons of batter to a pan that has been very lightly buttered, swirl it quickly around so that the bottom is completely covered and cook the crêpe less than a minute. You turn the crêpe and cook it for seconds and it is done. Serve as indicated with scoops of ice cream (these are known as crêpes Alaska) and, if desired, a garnish such as a quickly made chocolate sauce, or melted preserves or bottled marrons (chestnuts) in a brandied syrup found in specialty food shops.

Basic crêpes

1	egg	1	teaspoon sugar
½	cup flour	¼	teaspoon pure vanilla extract
½	cup plus two tablespoons milk	2	tablespoons butter

1. Put the egg and flour into a mixing bowl and start beating and blending with a wire whisk. Add the milk, stirring. Add the sugar and vanilla extract.

2. Melt 1 tablespoon of butter in a seven or eight-inch teflon pan. When it is melted, pour the butter into the crêpe batter.

3. Line a mixing bowl with a sieve and pour the batter into the sieve. Strain the batter, pushing any solids through with a rubber spatula.

4. Melt the second tablespoon of butter and use this to brush the pan each time or as necessary before making a crêpe.

5. Brush the pan lightly and place it on the stove. When the pan is hot but not burning, add 2 tablespoons of batter (it is preferable if you use a small ladle with a 2-tablespoon capacity), and swirl it around neatly to completely cover the bottom of the pan. Let cook over moderately high heat about 30 to 40 seconds or until lightly browned on the bottom. Turn the crêpe and cook the second side only about 15 seconds longer. Turn the crêpe out onto a sheet of wax paper.

6. Continue making crêpes, brushing the pan lightly as necessary to prevent sticking, until all the crêpes are made. As the crêpes are made turn them out, edges slightly overlapping onto the wax paper.

Yield: Eight to nine crêpes.

Crêpes Alaska with Peach Sauce

4	crêpes, see recipe	2	tablespoons water
4	scoops vanilla ice cream	8	teaspoons toasted pine nuts, optional
½	cup peach preserves or orange marmalade		

1. Prepare the crêpes and set them aside.

2. Put the preserves and water in a small saucepan and heat, stirring, until liquid.

3. Place one crêpe on a dessert dish. Put one scoop of ice cream in the center. Fold it over to enclose the ice cream.

4. Spoon the hot peach sauce over all. Spoon the toasted pine nuts on each end and serve.

Yield: Four servings.

Crêpes Alaska with Brandied Chestnuts

- 4 crêpes, see recipe
- 4 scoops vanilla ice cream
- 12 bottled, drained, imported brandied marrons
- 8 teaspoon sweetened whipped cream

1. Place one crêpe on each of four individual dessert plates.
2. Place one scoop of vanilla ice cream in the center of each crêpe. Fold the crêpe to enclose the ice cream.
3. Place one marron on top of each serving in the center. Spoon 1 teaspoon of sweetened whipped cream at each end of each crêpe. Place one marron on top of each teaspoon of whipped cream.

Yield: Four servings.

Crêpes Alaska with Chocolate Sauce

- 4 crêpes, see recipe
- 4 scoops vanilla ice cream
- ½ cup chocolate sauce, see recipe

1. Place one crêpe on each of four dessert plates. Place one scoop of ice cream in the center of each. Fold the crêpes over to enclose the ice cream.
2. Spoon 2 tablespoons of chocolate sauce over each serving.

Yield: Four servings.

Crêpes Normande
(Crêpes with apples)

- 8 crêpes, see recipe
- 2 large, firm, unblemished apples
- 5 tablespoons butter plus butter for buttering a baking dish
- Juice of half a lemon
- 1 teaspoon grated lemon peel
- 2 tablespoons sugar
- 1 tablespoon confectioners' sugar
- ¼ cup heavy cream
- 2 tablespoons Calvados or applejack

1. Prepare the crêpes and have them ready.
2. Preheat the oven to 450 degrees.
3. Peel the apples and cut them into quarters. Cut away the stem and core portions. Cut each quarter crosswise into thin slices.
4. Melt 3 tablespoons of the butter in a skillet and add the apple slices. Sprinkle with the lemon juice, lemon peel, and sugar. Cook, shaking the skillet and stirring gently so as not to break up the apple slices. Cook about 1 minute or until the apples are barely tender.

5. Open up the crêpes and spoon equal portions of the apple mixture into each.

6. Butter the inside of a shallow ovenproof baking dish or a pan large enough to hold the crêpes when rolled. Roll the crêpes and arrange them neatly over the bottom of the pan. Brush the top of the crêpes with 2 tablespoons of melted butter. Hold a small sieve over the crêpes. Add the confectioners' sugar and sprinkle it over the crêpes.

7. Place the pan in the oven and bake 5 minutes.

8. Remove from the oven and pour the cream and Calvados over the crêpes. Ignite the Calvados and serve immediately.

Yield: Four servings.

Zabaglione with Pecans

| 8 egg yolks, about ½ cup | ¾ cup dry Marsala wine |
| ½ cup sugar | 16 toasted pecans (see note) |

1. Select a metal mixing bowl with a round bottom, preferably copper. Bring enough water to the simmer in a skillet or casserole into which the bottom of the mixing bowl will fit comfortably.

2. Put the yolks into the round-bottom bowl. Add the sugar and Marsala wine. Beat briskly with a wire whisk.

3. Sit the round-bottom bowl in the simmering water and cook gently, beating briskly and constantly about 5 minutes until quite thickened and custard-like. Remove the bowl from the water and continue beating off the heat about 1 minute. Pour the custard into four stem glasses. Sprinkle with chopped pecans and serve. Serve hot or cold.

Yield: Four servings.

Note: To toast pecans, scatter them over a baking pan and place briefly under the broiler, stirring occasionally, about 30 seconds or until nicely browned and slightly crisp.

ALTHOUGH I DO NOT INEVITABLY SERVE DESserts at the end of every meal in my home, there are many readers who feel that a meal is horribly neglected if they do not serve or are not served a sweet of one sort or another when a meal is ended. That is why I have often been asked to please offer recipes for desserts that can be prepared and served after a main course and salad, all within the space of an hour.

If you are to serve a dessert, one that is especially made for a sixty-minute or less dinner, it should be closely tailored to the remainder of the meal. If the main course you have in mind, for example, does not demand a great deal of preparation and yet requires a comfortable amount of time in the stove or under the broiler, you will obviously be left with ample time to prepare dessert.

On a recent occasion in my home, the main dish was broiled chicken to be served with easily made and quickly cooked seasonal vegetables plus a salad and cheese. Once I placed that chicken on the grill (which I use in summertime and keep within a few steps of my kitchen door), I prepared one of the finest dessert sauces that I know, a personal favorite. This is a Grand Marnier sauce made something like a sabayon. You cook egg yolks and sugar over low heat, beating vigorously with a whisk until thick and lemon-colored. You add a touch of Grand Marnier (you could use another liqueur) and let it cool (in the freezer to save time). At the end you simply fold in a little whipped cream and it is ready to serve.

This is a most useful and highly versatile sauce and it is particularly appealing when fresh berries are on the market. It is especially good over blueberries or strawberries. It is also first rate when served over poached fruit of any kind, such as pears and apples.

If you have a source for an apple tart, preferably a one-layer tart made French-style, you will find that a Grand Marnier sauce will make an exceptional addition to the tart.

Grand Marnier Sauce

| 2 egg yolks | 2 tablespoons Grand Marnier |
| ¼ cup sugar | ½ cup heavy cream |

1. Select a 1-quart mixing bowl that will rest snugly on top of a slightly larger saucepan. Add about 2 inches of water to the saucepan and bring it to the boil.

2. Put the yolks and sugar into the mixing bowl. Start beating vigorously with a wire whisk making certain that you scrape all around the inside bottom of the bowl to cover the entire rounded surface.

3. Sit the mixing bowl inside the saucepan (over but not in the water). Continue beating constantly and vigorously up to 10 minutes or until the yolks are quite thick and pale yellow.

4. Remove the bowl from the saucepan and stir in the Grand Marnier. Scrape the mixture into a cold mixing bowl and put the bowl in the freezer temporarily. Do not allow it to freeze.

5. Whip the cream until stiff and fold it into the chilled sauce. Serve over fresh berries such as raspberries, strawberries, or blueberries or sliced fruit such as peaches or nectarines. This sauce is excellent over wedges of apple pie, purchased or homemade.

Yield: Four servings.

Poached Pears with Grand Marnier Sauce

4 firm, unblemished ripe pears, or use 8 drained canned pear halves Juice of half a lemon	1 cup sugar Grand Marnier sauce, see recipe

1. If fresh pears are used, peel them. leaving the stems on. As each pear is peeled drop it into water with lemon juice to prevent discoloration.

2. Measure 3 cups of water in a saucepan and add the sugar. Bring to the boil and add the pears. Cook the pears in the liquid, occasionally turning them gently, until they are tender but firm, about 20 minutes.

3. Serve in individual dessert bowls with the sauce spooned over.

Yield: Four servings.

Fraises Romanoff

2 pints red, ripe strawberries ⅓ cup plus 2 tablespoons sugar ⅓ cup Grand Marnier or cointreau	Peel of one orange ¾ cup heavy cream

1. Remove the stems from the strawberries. Rinse well and drain. Drain further on paper towels.

2. Place the strawberries in a bowl and add ⅓ cup sugar and the Grand Marnier. Use a swivel-bladed potato peeler and cut around the orange to produce a very thin spiral of peel. Do not cut into the white pulp. Add the wafer-thin pieces of peel. Stir gently and refrigerate.

3. Whip the cream and flavor it with remaining 2 tablespoons sugar. Serve it separately.

Yield: Eight or more servings.

Blueberries with Grand Marnier Sauce

1 pint fresh blueberries (or use other berries such as strawberries or raspberries)	8 or more tablespoons Grand Marnier sauce, see recipe

1. Pick over and rinse the berries well. Drain thoroughly.
2. Put equal portions of the berries in four serving dishes. Spoon 2 or more tablespoons of Grand Marnier sauce on top of each serving.

Yield: Four servings.

Poires au Vin Rouge
(Pears in spiced red wine)

4 pears, preferably Bartlett, about 1¾ pounds	1 bay leaf
2 cups dry red wine	¼ teaspoon peppercorns
1 cup water	6 whole allspice
½ cup sugar	6 whole cloves
	1 2-inch length cinnamon stick

1. Peel the pears, but leave the stem on. Use a melon ball cutter or an apple corer and cut out the center of each pear from the bottom, but do not ream the pears all the way to the stem end.
2. Combine the remaining ingredients in a saucepan and add the pears. Bring to the boil and let simmer about 10 minutes, turning the pears occasionally in the syrup so that they cook evenly. If desired, remove the pears and cook down the syrup by half. Return the pears to the sauce. Turn off the heat and let stand until ready to serve. These pears are also delicious when served cold, but they would not become cold enough within the space of 1 hour.

Yield: Four servings.

Poires au Gingembre
(Poached pears with ginger sauce)

4 pears, preferably Anjou, about 1½ pounds	1 tablespoon syrup from preserved stem ginger
1½ cups water	8 thin slices preserved stem ginger
⅓ cup plus ½ cup sugar	
2 tablespoons chopped preserved stem ginger, available in bottles in specialty food shops	

[278]

1. Split each pear in half lengthwise. Using a melon ball scoop, remove the seedy center of each pear. Trim away and discard the tough woody line that runs from the stem to the bottom of each pear.

2. Combine the water, ⅓ cup sugar, chopped ginger, and syrup in a saucepan. Bring to the boil and simmer 5 minutes. Add the pear halves and cover. Bring to the boil and simmer 10 minutes.

3. Remove the pears and arrange them cut side down on a serving dish. Cook the syrup down to ¾ cup. Pour it over the pears. Garnish each pear with 1 thin slice of preserved stem ginger.

4. Meanwhile, put the remaining ½ cup sugar in a small saucepan and cook, stirring, until the sugar becomes liquid. Cook, watching carefully, until the sugar starts to turn light amber. Continue cooking until the sugar carmelizes, taking care the sugar does not burn and become bitter.

5. Pour the caramel over the pears and serve hot or cold.

Yield: Four to eight servings.

Pommes au Four
(Baked spiced apples)

4 Golden Delicious apples, about 2 pounds	8 tablespoons butter, at room temperature
¼ cup plus 2 teaspoons sugar	½ cup water
¼ teaspoon ground cinnamon	2 tablespoons Calvados or applejack

1. Preheat the oven to 400 degrees.

2. Peel the apples about one-third of the way down, starting at the stem end. Using an apple corer or a paring knife, cut away the center cores of each apple from both top and bottom. Run a small paring knife around the skin of each apple at the center beneath the peeled portion. This will prevent them from bursting as they bake.

3. Blend together ¼ cup sugar, cinnamon, and butter, beating with a wooden spoon until well creamed.

4. Stuff equal portions of the mixture inside each apple, filling the cores top and bottom.

5. Arrange the apples bottom side down on a baking dish. Sprinkle the tops of each apple with ½ teaspoon of sugar. Pour the water around the apples.

6. Place the apples in the oven and bake 30 minutes, basting occasionally. Sprinkle with Calvados and serve.

Yield: Four servings.

A READER RECENTLY TOLD ME—SOMEONE I ENcountered in an excursion to the local grocery store—that she frequently made the recipes from my column, but she was often frustrated in the preparation of her meals. She was tired, she complained, of serving her guests ice cream or fruit with cheese for dessert. She would prefer to make a special effort for the end of a meal.

I volunteered on the spot to prepare for her delectation and delight—and that of her guests—one of the dessert components which can be transformed with the addition of one ingredient or another into any number of fine desserts. What I had in mind is one of the dessert creams that I learned to make during the first weeks of my apprenticeship. It is known in the French kitchen as a crème patissière and in American households and pastry shops as a pastry cream. It is an exceedingly rapid dessert to make. You simply cook a blend of egg yolks, flour, cornstarch, sugar, and milk until it reaches a boil. Once thickened, you add a touch of vanilla extract and the custard is ready. It may be served hot or cold, and there are many variations possible. You may add chopped preserved ginger in syrup or chopped chestnuts (oftentimes packaged as marrons) in syrup or a spoonful or two of bottled Nesselrode mixture in rum syrup.

This hastily made dessert also makes an excellent base for fruits in season: strawberries, raspberries, or cubed nectarines and peaches.

If you plan to serve a dessert within the course of a 60-minute preparation, you should plan on a main course that requires a relatively short preparation, such as chicken, fish, or veal.

Crème Patissière
(Pastry cream)

3 egg yolks	2 cups hot milk
1/3 cup sugar	1/2 teaspoon vanilla extract
1 tablespoon flour	Sweetened whipped cream,
1 tablespoon cornstarch	optional

1. Combine the yolks, sugar, flour, and cornstarch in a mixing bowl. Beat well with a wire whisk.

2. Add the milk, stirring rapidly with the whisk.

3. Spoon and scrape the mixture into a saucepan and start stirring with a wooden spoon. Cook over low heat, stirring constantly, until the mixture comes barely to the boil. Take care that the sauce does not continue to boil or it might curdle. Add the vanilla and stir. To serve, spoon equal portions of the pastry cream into four small dessert bowls. If desired, serve with a small amount of sweetened whipped cream on each serving.

Yield: About 2½ cups or four servings.

Crème Patissière aux Fraises
(Pastry cream with strawberries)

1 recipe for crème patissière (see recipe)
32 red, ripe strawberries, about 1 pint
Sweetened whipped cream flavored with vanilla, optional

1. Prepare the pastry cream and spoon it into each of four small bowls.
2. Trim the strawberries to remove the stems and unripe or blemished spots. Cut each strawberry in half if desired.
3. Arrange equal portions of the berries on each serving, and spoon a little sweetened whipped cream on top of each serving.

Yield: Four servings.

Crème Patissière au Gingembre
(Pastry cream with ginger)

1 recipe for crème patissière (see recipe)
1 tablespoon chopped stem ginger in syrup
1 tablespoon liquid from stem ginger in syrup

1. Prepare the pastry cream.
2. Add the chopped ginger and the syrup. Blend. Serve hot or cold.

Yield: Four to six servings.

Crème Patissière Nesselrode

1 recipe for crème patissière (see recipe)
¼ cup commercially made Nesselrode fruits in rum syrup (see note)
Sweetened whipped cream flavored with vanilla, optional

1. Prepare the pastry cream and stir in the Nesselrode fruits in rum syrup. Spoon the custard into each of four small bowls.
2. If desired, spoon a little sweetened whipped cream on top of each serving.

Yield: Four servings.

Note: A very good brand of Nesselrode fruits in rum syrup is bottled by the firm of Raffetto. The name of the preparation is Nesselro.

LIKE MANY OTHER FRENCH CHEFS, I AM OFTEN asked if I do not become bored with food preparations. The answer is an unmistakable no. More often than not I cook for my family seven days a week, and on those rare occasions when I am alone I cook for myself.

I enjoy cooking. I can become as absorbed in the making of a simple omelet as in the making of a highly complicated and sophisticated pâté in pastry. I enjoy experimenting in the kitchen, and I am apt to try to recreate in my own home any dish that has fascinated me while dining in this country or abroad.

Several years ago when we dined at Freddy Girardet's well-known establishment in Crissier, Switzerland (outside Lausanne), I was much taken with a passion fruit soufflé that appeared at our table. It was an incredibly light dessert, which, Mr. Girardet confirmed, was made wholly without flour. I later dined on a similar no-flour soufflé at Le Français, the restaurant of Jean Banchet in Wheeling, Illinois, just outside Chicago.

Only recently did I get around to preparing this soufflé. I did not have access to passion fruit syrup, so I tried using orange juice and Grand Marnier. There were many variables while testing the recipe. I used various quantities of ingredients. I started baking the soufflé at 350 degrees. This was too low, and as a result did not "seize" the soufflé mixture quickly enough. The mixture started to spill over as it baked. When the heat was raised to 450 degrees, the soufflé slid straight up the sides of the dish perfectly, as any well-made soufflé should.

After an hour or so in the kitchen I had perfected my own no-flour soufflé, and it turned out to be as incredibly easy to make as it is tasty. In its final version it required less than half an hour to make, from the breaking of the eggs to the taking of the soufflé from the oven.

This is a dessert that would fit almost any menu that is tailored to be cooked in less than an hour. It would go well at the end of a meal that comprises a simple grilled meat dish such as beef, lamb, or chicken or a quick sauté of fish.

I have included here an orange sauce for the soufflé. It is, however, optional, and the soufflé can be served without it.

Soufflés à l'Orange
(Orange soufflé)

- 1 tablespoon butter
- ⅓ cup plus 3 tablespoons sugar
- 6 eggs, separated
- 2 teaspoons finely grated orange peel
- ¼ cup orange juice with the pulp
- 1 tablespoon Grand Marnier
- 1 tablespoon confectioners' sugar
- Orange sauce, optional (see recipe)

1. Preheat the oven to 450 degrees.
2. Use the butter to rub the bottom and sides of four individual (1¼-cup) soufflé dishes. Use 1 tablespoon of sugar to sprinkle the insides of the dishes.
3. Put the egg yolks in a bowl and add ⅓ cup of sugar, orange peel, orange juice, and Grand Marnier. Beat briskly and well with a wire whisk.
4. Beat the egg whites until stiff. Toward the end, beat in the remaining 2 tablespoons of sugar.
5. Spoon and scrape the egg yolk mixture into the whites. Fold in the yolks rapidly and well. Spoon equal portions of the mixture into the prepared soufflé dishes.
6. Place the dishes on a baking sheet and put in the oven. Bake 12 minutes. Put the confectioners' sugar in a sieve and sprinkle an equal amount over each soufflé. If the sauce is used, spoon out a small portion of the center of each soufflé. Spoon in a little of the sauce plus more sauce on the side.

Yield: Four servings.

Sauce à l'Orange
(Orange sauce)

1 cup apricot preserves or jam
½ cup water
½ cup orange sections, cut into pieces and with seeds removed
1 teaspoon freshly grated orange peel
1 tablespoon Grand Marnier

1. Combine the preserves and water in a saucepan. Cook slowly, stirring, until blended and smooth. Add orange sections and grated orange peel.
2. Stir in the Grand Marnier and serve.

Yield: About 2 cups.

Soufflé aux Fraises
(Strawberry soufflé)

1 pint strawberries	Butter for greasing the soufflé dishes
8 eggs, separated	Confectioners' sugar
½ cup plus ⅓ cup sugar	Strawberry sauce (see recipe), optional
Juice of half a lemon	
1 tablespoon framboise (strawberry eau de vie), optional	

1. Preheat oven to 450 degrees.
2. Pick over and remove the stems from the strawberries. Wash and drain the berries thoroughly. Put the strawberries into the container of a food processor and process to a fine purée.
3. Pour and scrape the strawberry purée into a bowl and add the egg yolks, ½ cup sugar, lemon juice, and framboise. Beat thoroughly to blend.
4. Generously butter the bottom and sides of six individual soufflé dishes, each with a 1½-cup capacity.
5. Beat the egg whites until stiff and beat in the remaining ⅓ cup sugar. Fold the whites into the strawberry mixture.
6. Spoon equal portions of the mixture into the prepared dishes. Place the dishes on a baking sheet and bake 7 minutes. Reduce the oven heat to 425 degrees and bake 7 minutes longer. Serve sprinkled with confectioners' sugar and, if desired, strawberry sauce.

Yield: Six servings.

Sauce aux Fraises
(Strawberry sauce)

1 pint strawberries	½ cup sugar

1. Pick over the strawberries and discard the stems. Rinse and drain the berries thoroughly. Cut the strawberries into thin slices.
2. Combine the strawberries with the sugar in a saucepan and bring to the boil, stirring occasionally. Cook about 1 minute and remove from the heat. Serve hot.

Yield: About 1 cup.

Soufflé au Chocolat sans Farine
(Chocolate soufflé without flour)

3	ounces sweet chocolate	8	eggs, separated
1	ounce unsweetened chocolate	4	teaspoons confectioners' sugar
½	cup sugar		
2	tablespoons coffee liqueur, cointreau, Grand Marnier, or other liqueur		

1. Preheat the oven to 425 degrees.
2. Shave the chocolate and combine in a mixing bowl. Sit the bowl over hot water until the chocolate melts. Add half the sugar and the liqueur and stir to blend. Let cool briefly.
3. Butter the bottom and sides of four individual 1½-cup soufflé dishes. Set aside.
4. Add the yolks to the chocolate mixture and beat until thoroughly blended.
5. Whip the whites separately. When they form soft peaks, start adding the remaining ¼ cup of sugar, beating constantly. Continue beating until stiff.
6. Add about half the whites to the chocolate mixture and fold them in quickly with the whisk until thoroughly blended. Add the remaining whites and fold them in with a rubber spatula.
7. Spoon equal portions of the mixture into the buttered soufflé dishes.
8. Arrange the dishes on a baking sheet and place in the oven. Bake 10 to 12 minutes. Sprinkle the tops of each with confectioners' sugar and serve.

Yield: Four servings.

Mousse au Mocha
(Coffee mousse)

¼ pound butter at room temperature	¾ cup sugar
2 tablespoons instant espresso coffee	5 egg whites
2 tablespoons warm water	¼ cup finely grated dark sweet chocolate

1. Put the butter in a mixing bowl and blend well with a spatula or a wire whisk. The butter must not be cool. If it is cold it will not blend.

2. Blend the coffee and water and add it to the butter. Add ¼ cup sugar. Beat to blend.

3. Beat the egg whites until partially stiff, using a wire whisk. Gradually add the remaining ½ cup sugar, beating constantly with the whisk. Beat until very stiff. Add half the whites to the butter. Beat well. Add the remaining whites and fold them in with a rubber spatula. Fold in the grated chocolate.

4. Chill until ready to serve. Serve in stem glasses.

Yield: Four to six servings.

Mousse au Chocolat
(Chocolate mousse)

4 ounces sweet chocolate, broken into pieces	3 egg yolks
	3 egg whites
¼ pound butter, cut into small pieces	¼ cup sugar

1. Select a thin, stainless steel bowl with a volume of about 2 quarts.

2. Select a saucepan large enough so that the bowl can fit snugly into it. Add boiling water to the saucepan and sit the bowl in the saucepan. Bring the water to the simmer. Add the chocolate and stir. When it starts to melt add the butter. Continue stirring until well blended and remove the bowl from the heat. Add the yolks and stir until thoroughly blended. Place the bowl briefly in the refrigerator until the mixture is slightly cooler than lukewarm. If it becomes too chilled it will harden. Take care not to overchill.

3. Beat the whites until they stand in soft peaks. Gradually add the sugar beating briskly. Continue beating until the whites are stiff. Fold the egg whites into the chocolate mixture. Spoon the mousse into four individual serving dishes. Chill briefly until ready to serve.

Yield: Four servings.

Index

Anchovy
  dip, cream cheese and, 24
  sauce, squid in, 19
  vinaigrette, sweet peppers with, 253
Appetizers, 13-25
  artichokes vinaigrette, 22-23
  chicken liver mousse, 15
  clams posillipo, 21
  crab salad with jalapeño chilies, 17
  Italian-style shrimp and squid salad, 18-19
  leeks vinaigrette, 23
  oysters with white butter sauce, 20
  smoked brook trout with horseradish sauce, 15
  smoked salmon mousse, 14
  squid in anchovy sauce, 19
Apples
  baked spiced, 279
  with Calvados and ice cream, 271
  crêpes with, 274-75
Armenian rice, 119
Arroz con pollo, 58-59
Artichauts vinaigrette, 22-23
Artichokes vinaigrette, 22-23
Arugula and red onion salad, 259
Asparagus
  and Ham Mornay, 242-43
  pasta with chicken and, 252-53
  with sieved egg, 53
Asperges
  et jambon Mornay, 242-43
  aux oeufs durs, 53
Assorted vegetable vinaigrette, 255
Aubergine
  Niçoise, 260-61
  riz à l', 63
Avocado
  and crabmeat salad, 16-17
  and tomato with lime sauce, 237

Bar rayé Mediterranée, 120-21
Beurre
  blanc, 20, 117
  rouge, 208
Beef, 205-21
  braised, with tomatoes and herbs, 216-17
  chateaubriand, broiled, 214-15
  chili à la Franey, 236-37
  fillet of, with sour cream, 212
  grilled, 208
  meat and potato pie, 220-21
  steak
    marinated, 206-207
    salad, 210-11
  Swedish meatballs, 218-19
Bitoks de porc au chou, 234-35
Blanc de volaille aux crevettes roses, 42-43
Blueberries with Grand Marnier sauce, 278
Boston lettuce salad, endive and, 57
Bread
  crumbs, 31
  Parmesan cheese, 163
  parsley, 139
Broccoli
  purée, 227
  sauté, 185
Brook trout with horseradish sauce, 15
Brown rice, 213, 219
Brussels sprouts with caraway, 169
Bulgur pilaf, 109
Butter sauce
  red, 208
  white, 20, 117
Butterscotch-pecan sauce, 270

Cabbage
  coleslaw, 65
  sautéed, 235
    pork burgers with, 234-35
Calf's liver
  mixed grill, 180-81
  with onions, Venetian-style, 198-99
  with white grapes, 196-97
Calmars farcis, 118-19
Canard grillé, 76-77
Capers
  trout with lemon and, 124-25
  and vinegar, sweetbreads with, 202-203
Caraway
  brussels sprouts with, 169
  rye, pork chops stuffed with, 228-29
Carrelet
  au plat, 106-107
  Provençale, filets de, 108-109
Carrot(s)
  and celery salad, 153
  rice with, 115
  and turnips, 123
  zucchini sautéed with, 229

Carrotte(s)
  et celeri salade, 153
  julienne de légumes, 77
  et navettes, 123
  riz au, 115
  sautés, zucchini et, 229
Casseroles(s)
  eggplant, 260-61
  lamb and eggplant, 261
Cauliflower
  curried, 225
  with egg and parsley, 251
Celeri
  salade, carrottes et, 153
Champignons
  Bercy, huîtres et, 140-41
  épinards sautés aux, 171
  et foies de poussin, riz au, 71
  grillés, 39
  nouilles aux, 143
  pommes juliennes aux, 29
  sauce aux, 61, 221
Chateaubriand
  broiled, 214-15
  grillé, 214-15
Cheese
  and ham, chicken breasts with, 30-31
  mashed potatoes baked with, 199
  noodles with parsley and, 211
  Parmesan bread, 163
  sauce, 173
  soufflé without flour, 91
  Swiss-style dumplings with, 241
  and asparagus, pasta with, 252-53
Chicken
  breasts
    breaded, 37
    with cheese and ham, 30
    in curried cream sauce, 44-45
    with curry sauce, 32-33
    deviled, 38-39
    with mushrooms and ham, 34-35
    with peppers, 28-29
    poached, 33, 83
    with shrimp, sautéed, 42-43
    in tomato sauce, shrimp and, 40-41
  creamed, eggs in ramekins with, 82-83
  with ginger, grilled, 46
  liver(s)
    deep-fried spiced, 64-65
    with garlic, sautéed, 62-63
    mousse, 15, 66-67
    rice with mushrooms and, 71
  Missouri-style barbecued, 72-73
  mousse, 60
  and noodles baked in cream sauce, 54-55
  poached, 55
  rice with, 58-59
  au Riesling, 52

  scarpariello alla Nanni, 50
  stuffed with herbs and mushrooms, 48-49
  and vegetable stew, 56-57
Chiffonade de homard, 134-35
Chile verde, 238-39
Chili
  á la Franey, 236-37
  raita, cucumber and, 45
Chinese seasoning salt, broiled squab with, 74-75
Chocolate
  mousse, 286
  sauce, 269
  soufflé without flour, 285
Chou
  bitoks de porc au, 234-35
  sauté au beurre, 235
Chou de Bruxelles au karvi, 169
Chou-fleur
  au cari, 225
  mimosa, 251
Clam(s)
  dip, cream cheese and, 25
  posillipo, 21
  soup, 130-31
    Italian, 131
  and vegetables, spaghetti with, 254-55
Coconut, rice with raisins and, 33
Cod
  batter-fried fresh, 100-101
  in cream sauce, 102-103, 105
Coffee mousse, 286
Coleslaw, 65
Concombre(s)
  Doria, pommes et, 121
  salade de, 111
Coquilles St. Jacques
  au gingembre, 146-47
  gratin de, 145
  aux huîtres, 142-43
  meunière, 144
  paneés à l'Anglaise, 152-53
  sauce crème et moutarde, 150-51
Cornichon sauce, mustard and, 233
Côtes d'agneau
  champvallon, 168-69
  grillés, 170
  Maintenon, 172-73
Côtes de porc
  bonne maman, 224-25
  charcutière, 226-27
  farcis au karvi, 228-29
Côtes de veau
  belle des bois, 188-89
  Orloff, 190-91
Courgettes, salade tomates et, 85
Court bouillon (for four lobsters), 135
Crab
  Impérial, shrimp and, 164-65

mayonnaise Mexicaine, 17
salad
   avocado and, 16-17
   with jalapeño chilies, 17
Cracked wheat pilaf, 109
Cream cheese
   and anchovy dip, 24
   and clam dip, 25
   and roasted pepper dip, 25
Cream sauce
   cod in, 102-103, 105
   frogs' legs in, 133
   scallops in mustard-, 150-51
   sliced eggs in, 80-81
   veal chops with morels in, 188-89
Crème patissière, 280-81
   aux fraises, 281
   au gingembre, 281
   Nesselrode, 281
Crêpes
   Alaska
      with brandied chestnuts, 274
      with chocolate sauce, 274
      with peach sauce, 273
      with apples, 274-75
      basic recipe for, 272-73
   Normande, 274
Cresson
   à la crème, épinards en branche et, 75
   salade de, et oeufs durs, 263
Crevettes
   chaudes, salade de, 162-63
   et filet de volaille Américaine, 40-41
   Imam Bayeldi, 158-59
   jardinière, 156-57
   roses, blanc de volaille aux, 42-43
   en salsa verde
Croutons, 131
Cucumber(s)
   and chili raita, 45
   and dill salad, 151
   with parsley, potatoes and, 121
   salad, 111
Cuisses de grenouilles
   poulette, 133
   Provençale, 132-33
Cumin rice, 239
Curry(ied)
   cauliflower, 225
   cream sauce, chicken breasts in, 44-45
   lamb, cubed, 176-77
   sauce, breast of chicken with, 32-33

Darne de saumon grillé au beurre blanc, 116
Daube de boeuf Provençale, 216-17
Desserts, 267-87
   apples
      baked spiced, 279
      with Calvados and ice cream, 271
   blueberries with Grand Marnier sauce, 278
   chocolate
      mousse, 286
      soufflé without flour, 285
   coffee mousse, 286
   crêpes
      Alaska
         with brandied chestnuts, 274
         with chocolate sauce, 274
         with peach sauce, 273
      with apples, 274-75
      basic recipe for, 272-73
   fraises Romanoff, 277
   ice cream
      with coconut and rum, 271
      with nutmeg and bourbon, 270-71
   orange
      soufflés, 282-83
      sauce, 283
   pastry cream, 280-81
      with ginger, 281
      Nesselrode, 281
      with strawberries, 281
   pears
      with ginger sauce, 278-79
      with ice cream and chocolate sauce, 268
      in spiced red wine, 278
      pêche Melba, 269
      poached, with Grand Marnier sauce, 227
   strawberry soufflé, 284
   zabaglione with pecans, 287
Dill
   rice with, 141
   salad, cucumber and, 151
Dip(s)
   cream cheese
      and anchovy, 24
      and fresh clam, 25
      and roasted peppers, 25
   gorgonzola with walnuts, 24-25
Duck, broiled, 76-77
Dumplings with cheese, Swiss-style, 241
Duxelles, 173

Egg(s), 79-91
   in cream sauce, sliced, 80-81
   frittata, 87
   hard-cooked, and watercress salad, 263
   omelet with herbs and crabmeat, 84-85
   and parsley, cauliflower with, 251
   in ramekins with creamed chicken, 82
   ratatouille with, 262-63
   sieved, asparagus with, 53
   soufflés. *See* Soufflé(s)

Eggplant
   casserole, 260-61
   and lamb casserole, 261
   ratatouille with eggs, 262-63
   rice with, 63
   shrimp with tomatoes and, 158-59
Emincé d'agneau au cari, 176-77
Endive and Boston lettuce salad, 57
Epinards en branche
   et cresson à la crème, 75
   sautés aux champignons, 171
   soufflé, 90
Escalopes de veau Italienne, 184-85
Escarole Italian-style, 193

Feta cheese, baked red snapper with, 112-13
Fettuccini
   with peas, 246
   con piselli, 246
Filet de volaille Américaine, crevettes et, 40-41
Filets de poisson en papillote, 98-99
Fish, 93-127
   broiled, 96-97
   broth, 121
   cod
      batter-fried, 100-101
      in cream sauce, 102-103, 105
   fillets baked in paper or foil, 98-99
   fluke
      baked with vegetables, 106-107
      fillets with tomatoes and green pepper sauce, 108-109
   monkfish with tomatoes and tarragon, 110-11
   red snapper à la Grecque, 112-13
   salmon steak, broiled, 116
   sole stuffed with shrimp and ginger, 114-15
   soup, 126-27
   steamed whole, 94-95
   striped bass with tomato sauce, 120-21
   stuffed squid, 118-19
   swordfish broiled with mustard, 122-23
   trout
      with lemon and capers, 124-25
      smoked brook trout with horseradish sauce, 15
Fluke
   baked with vegetables, 106-107
   fillets with tomato and green pepper sauce, 108-109
Foies de poussin, riz aux champignons et, 71
Foie de veau aux raisins blancs, 196-97
Foies de volailles
   aux aromates, 64-65
   Provençale, 62-63

Fraises
   Romanoff, 277
   sauce aux, 284
   soufflé aux, 284
Frittata, 87
Frogs' legs
   in cream sauce, 133
   with tomato sauce, 132-33
Fumet de poisson, 121

Garlic
   chicken livers sautéed with, 62-63
   croutons, romaine lettuce with, 149
   mayonnaise, potato and, 127
   potatoes sautéed with, 181
   and tomato sauce, pasta with, 248
Ginger
   grilled chicken with, 46
   scallops with, 146-47
   sole stuffed with shrimp and, 114-15
Glacé
   egg nog, 270-71
   Hawaiien, 271
Gorgonzola
   dip with walnuts, 24-25
   and walnuts, veal scaloppine with, 186-87
Grand Marnier sauce, 276-77
   blueberries with, 278
   poached pears with, 277
Grapes
   ham steaks with, 240-41
   white, calf's liver with, 196-97
Gratin de coquilles St. Jacques, 145
Gratin de volaille Pavillon, 54-55
Greek salad, 179
Green beans
   in cream, 201
   purée of, 187
Green chile con carne, 238-39
Green pepper sauce, fluke fillets with, 108-109

Hachis Parmentier, 220-21
Ham, 223-43
   and chicken breasts
      with cheese, 30-31
      with mushrooms, 34-35
   Mornay, asparagus and, 242-43
   soufflé, Roquefort and, 88-89
   steaks with grapes, 240-41
Haricots verts
   à la crème, 201
   purée de, 187
Herbs and mushrooms, chicken stuffed with, 48-49
Horseradish
   sauce, smoked brook trout with, 15
   tomato sauce with, 101

Huîtres
  au beurre blanc, 20
  et champignons Bercy, 140-41
  coquilles St. Jacques aux, 142-43

Ice cream
  with coconut and rum, 271
  with nutmeg and bourbon, 270-71
  with pears and chocolate sauce, 268
  pêche Melba, 269
Italian clam soup, 131
Italian-style
  escarole, 193
  shrimp and squid salad, 18-19

Jalapeño chilies, crab salad with, 17
Jambon
  aux raisins, 240-41
  soufflé au Roquefort et, 88-89
Julienne de légumes, 77

Lamb, 167-81
  boneless loin of, with tarragon, 174-75
  chops
    broiled, 170
    with mushroom purée, 172-73
    with potatoes and onions, 168-69
  curried cubed, 176-77
  and eggplant casserole, 261
  mixed grill, 180-81
  moussaka à la Grecque, 178-79
Leeks
  in cream, 197
  vinaigrette, 23
Légumes
  grillés, 155
  julienne de, 77
Lemon and capers, trout with, 124-25
Lettuce
  Boston, and endive salad, 57
  salad, 189
Limandes farcis orientale, 114-15
Lime sauce, avocado and tomato and, 237
Linguine
  with oyster sauce, 250-51
  con peperoni freschi, 249
  with roast peppers, 249
Liver(s). See Calf's liver; Chicken livers
Lobster(s)
  court bouillon for four, 135
  mayonnaise with shredded lettuce, 134-35
Lotte Provençale, 110-11

Macaroni
  sauce tomate, 37
  with tomato sauce, 37
Marinated steak, 206-207
Mayonnaise, 17
  potato and garlic, 127

Meat loaf with mushrooms, 194-95
Meat sauce, 265
Meatballs, Swedish, 218-19
Médaillons de boeuf à la Scandinave, 212
Médaillons de porc
  charcutière, 232-33
  grillé aux herbes, 230-31
Menthe, petits pois à la, 191
Mint, green peas with, 191
Missouri-style barbecued chicken, 72-73
Mixed green salad, 91, 125
Mixed grill, 180-81
Monkfish with tomatoes and tarragon, 110-11
Morels in cream sauce, veal chops with, 188-89
Morue
  bonne ma man, 102-103
  frites, filets de, 100-101
  fraîche à la crème, 105
Mouclade, La, 138-39
Moules bonne femme, pilaf de, 136-37
Moussaka à la Grecque, 178-79
Mousse
  au chocolat, 286
  de foie de volaille, 15, 66-67
  au mocha, 286
  de saumon fumé, 14
  de volaille, 60-61
Mushroom(s)
  Bercy, oysters and, 140-41
  buttered green peas with, 243
  and chicken livers, rice with, 71
  chicken stuffed with herbs and, 48-49
  cooked chopped, 173
  grilled, 39
  and ham, chicken breasts with, 34-35
  meat loaf with, 194-95
  noodles with, 143, 151
  potatoes sautéed with, 29
  purée, lamb chops with, 172-73
  sauce, 61, 221
  spinach sautéed with, 171
Mussels
  Charentaise, steamed, 138
  with rice, 136-37
Mustard
  broiled swordfish with, 122-23
  and cornichon sauce, 233
  sauce
    grilled pork with, 232-33
    pork chops with, 226-27
    scallops in a cream and, 150-51

Navettes, carrottes et, 123
Noisettes d'agneau à l'estragon, 174-75
Noodles
  baked in cream sauce, chicken and, 54
  butter fine, 51, 189

[291]

Noodles (cont.)
   green, with Parmesan cheese, 35
   with mushrooms, 143, 151
   with parsley and cheese, 211
   rice with, browned, 113
   spinach with scallops Provençale, 148-49
   with vegetables, 97
   zucchini with, 67
Nouilles
   aux champignons, 143
   fines au beurre, 51, 189
   au Parmesan, 35
   persillées au fromage, 211
   au printemps, 97
   riz au, 113

Oeuf(s), 79-81
   en cocotte à la reine, 82-83
   durs, les asperges aux, 53
   frittata, 87
   omelette fines herbs aux crabes, 84-85
   soufflés. *See* Soufflé(s)
   à la tripe, 80-81
Olives, veal scaloppine with tomatoes and, 184-85
Omelet(s)
   frittata, 87
   with herbs and crabmeat, 84-85
Omelette(s)
   fines herbes aux crabes, 84-85
   frittata, 87
Onion(s)
   lamb chops with potatoes and, 168-69
   pork chops with potatoes and, 224-25
   potatoes with, 175
   red, and arugula salad, 259
   Venetian-style liver with, 198-99
Orange(s)
   sauce, 283
   soufflés à l', 282-83
Oregano, salad with, 59
Oyster(s)
   and mushrooms Bercy, 140-41
   sauce, linguine with, 250-51
   scallops with, 142-43
   with white butter sauce, 20

Pain
   persillé, 139
   de viande champignons, 194-95
Parmesan cheese
   bread, 163
   green noodles with, 35
Parsley(ed)
   boiled potatoes with, 107
   bread, 139
   cauliflower with egg and, 251
   and cheese, noodles with, 211
   potatoes and cucumbers with, 121
   rice, 41, 157, 165

Pasta, 245-55
   with chicken and asparagus, 252-53
   fettuccini with peas, 246
   linguine
      with oyster sauce, 250-51
      con peperoni freschi, 249
   rigatoni with broccoli, 247
   con salsa marinara, 248
   spaghetti with clams and fresh vegetables, 254-55
   with tomato and garlic sauce, 248
   tubular, with broccoli, 247
Pastry cream, 280-81
   with ginger, 281
   Nesselrode, 281
   with strawberries, 281
Peach Melba, 269
Pears
   with ginger sauce, 278-79
   with ice cream and chocolate sauce, 268
   poached, with Grand Marnier sauce, 277
   in spiced red wine, 278
Peas
   in cream, potatoes with, 203
   fettuccini with, 246
   with mint, 191
   with mushrooms, buttered, 243
Pecan(s)
   sauce, butterscotch-, 270
   zabaglione with, 275
Pêche Melba, 269
Pepper(s)
   chicken breasts with, 28-29
   how to roast, 165
   roast, linguine with, 249
   rice with, 49
   sweet, with anchovy vinaigrette, 253
Peppercorn sauce, shallot and, 215
Petits pois
   forestière, 243
   à la menthe, 191
Pilaf, bulgur, 109
Pine nuts
   rice with, 161
   rice with raisins and, 45
Poireaux
   à la creme, 197
   vinaigrette, 23
Poire(s)
   belle Hélène, 268
   au gingembre, 278-79
   au vin rouge, 278
Poisson, 93-127
   grillé à l'Anglaise, 96-97
Poitrine(s) de volaille
   diablées, 38-39
   pochée, 83
Poivrons
   aux anchois, 253
   riz aux, 49

suprême de volaille aux, 28-29
Pommes (apples)
   à la crème, 207
   au four, 279
   Normande à la glacé, 271
Pommes (potatoes)
   bouillies, 105
   boulangères, 175
   et concombres Doria, 121
   de terre
      et pois à la crème, 203
      purée de, 31
      sautées, 209
   juliennes aux champignons, 29
   Parmentier, 181
   purées au gratin, 199
   sautées au beurre, 69
   vapeur, 99, 117, 125, 217
Pork, 223-43
   burgers with sautéed cabbage, 234-35
   chili à la Franey, 236-37
   chops
      with mustard sauce, 226-27
      with potatoes and onions, 224-25
      stuffed with caraway rye, 228-29
   green chile con carne, 238-39
   meat loaf with mushrooms, 194-95
   médaillons
      grilled with herb marinade, 230
      grilled with mustard sauce, 232-33
Potato(es)
   boiled, 105
      with parsley, 107
   in cream, 207
   and cucumbers with parsley, 121
   and garlic mayonnaise, 127
   mashed, 31
      baked with cheese, 199
   with mushrooms, sautéed, 29
   and onions, 175
      lamb chops with, 168-69
      pork chops with, 224-25
   with peas in cream, 203
   pie, meat and, 220-21
   salad, French, 73
   sautéed with garlic, 181
   skillet, 209
   steamed, 99, 117, 125, 217
Poulet
   grillé, au gingembre, 46
   au kari à la crème, 44-45
   poché, 55
   poêlée aux aromates, 48-49
   ragoût de, 56-57
   au Riesling, 52
Poultry, 27-77
   See also Chicken; Duck; Rock Cornish game hens; Squab
Poussins a l'estragon, 70-71

Raifort, sauce tomate au, 101
Raisins
   and coconut, rice with, 33
   and pine nuts, rice with, 45
Raisins (grapes)
   blancs, foie de veau aux, 196-97
   jambon aux, 240-41
Ramekins with creamed chicken, eggs in, 82-83
Raspberry sauce, cold, 270
Ratatouille
   with eggs, 262
   aux oeufs, 262
Red butter sauce, 208
Red snapper
   with feta cheese, baked, 112-13
   à la Grecque, 112-13
Rice
   Armenian, 119
   baked, 159, 177, 231
   boiled, 147
   brown, 213, 219
   with browned noodles, 113
   with carrots, 115
   with chicken, 58-59
   cumin, 239
   with dill, 141
   with eggplant, 63
   with mushrooms and chicken livers, 71
   mussels with, 136-37
   parsleyed, 41, 157, 165
   with peppers, 49
   pilaf, 137
   with pine nuts, 161
   with raisins
      and coconut, 33
      and pine nuts, 45
Rigatoni con broccoli, 247
Riz
   à l'aneth, 141
   Arménien, 119
   à l'aubergine, 63
   au carrottes, 115
   aux champignons et foies de poussin, 71
   au cumin, 239
   au four, 159, 177, 231
   à l'Indienne, 33
   au nouilles, 113
   persillé, 41, 157
   pilaf, 137
   au poivrons, 49
   au sultan, 45
Riz de veau
   Grenobloise, 202-203
   panées à l'Anglaise, 200-201
Roasted pepper dip, cream cheese and, 25
Rock Cornish game hens
   with Chinese seasoning salt, 74-75
   deviled breaded, 68-69
   à la diable, 68-69

Rock Cornish game hens (cont.)
  Missouri-style barbecued chickens, 72-73
  with tarragon cream sauce, 70-71
Romaine lettuce with garlic croutons, 149
Roquefort and ham soufflé, 88-89

Salad(s)
  arugula and red onion, 259
  assorted vegetable vinaigrette, 255
  avocado and crabmeat, 16-17
  carrots and celery, 153
  cucumber, 111
    and dill, 151
  dressing, 97
  endive and Boston lettuce, 57
  French potato, 73
  Greek, 179
  lettuce, 189
  mixed green, 91, 125
  with oregano, 59
  romaine lettuce with garlic croutons, 149
  steak, 210-11
  tomato and zucchini, 85
  tossed green, with herbs, 103
  vegetable, 89
  with warm shrimp, 162-63
  watercress and hard-cooked egg, 263
  zucchini and tomato, 81
Salade(s)
  carrottes et celeri, 153
  de concombres, 111
  de cresson et oeufs durs, 263
  de crevettes chaudes, 162-63
  avec croutons à l'ail, 149
  de crudités, 89
  d'endive et laitue, 57
  grillées, 157
  de laitue, 189
  de légumes vinaigrette, 255
  panachée, 91, 125
  de pomme de terre a la Française, 73
  tomates et courgettes, 85
  vinaigrette aux herbes, 103
  de zucchini et tomates, 81
Salmon
  mousse, smoked, 14
  steak, broiled, 116
Salsa di pomodoro fresca, 248
Salsa verde, crevettes en, 160
Saltimbocca, 192-93
Sauce(s)
  avocado and tomato with lime, 237
  Béarnaise, 171, 215
  breval, 95
  butterscotch-pecan, 270
  aux champignons
  charcutière, 233
  cheese, 173
  chocolate, 269
  diable, 69
  Grand Marnier, 276-77
  meat, 265
  Mornay, 173
  mushroom, 61, 221
  mustard and cornichon, 233
  orange, 283
  raspberry, cold, 270
  red butter, 209
  rouille, 127
  salade, 97
  shallot and peppercorn butter, 215
  strawberry, 284
    hot, 269
  tartare, 153
  tomate, 39, 43, 195, 248
    au raifort, 101
  tomato, 39, 43, 195, 248
    with horseradish, 101
  white butter, 20, 117
Saumon, darne de, grillé au beurre blanc, 116
Scallops
  in a cream and mustard sauce, 150-51
  deep-fried breaded, 152-53
  with fresh ginger, 146-47
  with oysters, 142-43
  Provençale, spinach noodles with, 148-49
  quick-fried in butter, 144-45
  in shells, breaded, 145
Scampi grillées, 154-55
Shallot and peppercorn butter sauce, 215
Shellfish, 129-65
  clam soup, 130-31
    Italian, 131
  crab Impérial, shrimp and, 164-65
  lobster mayonnaise with shredded lettuce, 134-35
  mussels
    Charentaise, steamed, 138
    with rice, 136-37
  oysters and mushrooms Bercy, 140-41
  scallops
    in a cream and mustard sauce, 150-51
    deep-fried breaded, 152-53
    with ginger, 146
    with oysters, 142-43
    quick-fried in butter, 144-45
    Provençale, spinach noodles with, 148-49
    in shells, breaded, 145
  shrimp
    charcoal-broiled, 154-55
    and crab Impérial, 164-65
    in green sauce, 160-61
    with tomatoes and eggplant, 158-59
    and vegetables cognac, 156-57
    warm, salad with, 162-63
Shrimp
  and crab Impérial, 164-65
  charcoal-broiled, 154-55

[294]

chicken breast
   in tomato sauce and, 40-41
   sautéed with, 42-43
and ginger, sole stuffed with, 114-15
in green sauce, 160-61
and squid salad, Italian-style, 18-19
stuffed squid, 118-19
with tomatoes and eggplant, 158-59
and vegetables cognac, 156-57
warm, with salad, 162-63
Skillet potatoes, 209
Smoked brook trout with horseradish sauce, 15
Smoked salmon mousse, 14
Sole stuffed with shrimp and ginger, 114-15
Soufflé(s)
   cheese, without flour, 91
   au chocolate sans farine, 285
   chocolate, without flour, 285
   aux épinards, 90
   aux fraises, 284
   au fromage sans farine, 91
   à l'orange, 282-83
   orange, 282-83
   Roquefort and ham, 88-89
   au Roquefort et jambon, 88-89
   spinach, 90
   strawberry, 284
Soup(s)
   clam, 130-31
      Italian-style, 131
   fish, 126-27
   fish broth, 121
Soupe(s)
   de palourde marinière, 130-31
   de poissons, 126-27
Sour cream, fillet of beef with, 212
Spaghetti
   with clams and fresh vegetables, 254-55
   et palourdes printanière, 254-55
Spaghetti squash, 264-65
Spätzle au fromage, 241
Spinach
   with mushrooms, sautéed, 171
   noodles, with scallops Provençale, 148-49
   soufflé, 90
   and watercress in cream, 75
Squab
   with Chinese seasoning salt, 74-75
   Missouri-style barbecued chickens, 72-73
Squash, spaghetti, 264-65
Squid
   in anchovy sauce, 19
   salad, Italian-style shrimp and, 18-19
   stuffed, 118-19
Steak
   en chevreuil, 206-207
   grillé au beurre rouge, 208
   salad, 210-11
Strawberry(ies)

Romanoff, 277
sauce, 284
   hot, 269
   soufflé, 284
Striped bass with tomato sauce, 120-21
Suprême de volaille
   Eugénie, 34-35
   au kari, 32-33
   Milanaise, 37
   Modenese, 30-31
   poché, 33
   aux poivrons, 28-29
Swedish meatballs, 218-19
Sweet peppers, how to roast, 165
Sweetbreads
   breaded, 200-201
   with capers and vinegar, 202-203
Swiss-style dumplings with cheese, 241
Swordfish, broiled with mustard, 122-23

Tarragon
   boneless loin of lamb with, 174-75
   cream sauce, Rock Cornish game hens, with, 70-71
   monkfish with tomatoes and, 110-11
Tomate(s)
   et courgettes, salade, 85
   grillées, 47
   au raifort, sauce, 101
   salade de zucchini et, 81
   surprise, 258-59
Tomato(es)
   avocado and, with lime sauce, 237
   broiled, 157
   and eggplant, shrimp with, 158-59
   and garlic sauce, pasta with, 248
   and green pepper sauce, fluke fillets with, 108-109
   grilled, 47
   and herbs, braised beef with, 216-17
   and olives, veal scaloppine with, 184-85
   salad, zucchini and, 81
   sauce, 39, 43, 195, 248
      frogs' legs with, 132-33
      with horseradish, 101
      macaroni with, 37
      shrimp and chicken breasts in, 40-41
      striped bass with, 120-21
   summer stuffed, 258-59
   and tarragon, monkfish with, 110-11
   and zucchini salad, 85
Trout
   with lemon and capers, 124-25
   smoked brook trout with horseradish sauce, 15
Truite Grenobloise, 124-25
Tubular pasta with broccoli, 247
Tuna fish
   summer stuffed tomatoes, 258

[295]

Turnips
　carrots and, 123
　julienne de légumes, 77

Veal, 183-203
　calf's liver
　　with onions, Venetian-style, 198-99
　　with white grapes, 196-97
　chops
　　with morels in cream sauce, 188-89
　　Orloff, 190-91
　meat loaf with mushrooms, 194-95
　saltimbocca, 192-93
　scaloppine
　　with gorgonzola and walnuts, 186-87
　　with tomatoes and olives, 184-85
　sweetbreads, breaded, 200-201
Vegetable(s), 257-65
　cognac, shrimp and, 156-57
　grilled, 155
　in julienne, 77
　noodles with, 97
　salad, 89
　vinaigrette, 255
Venetian-style liver with onions, 198-99

Walnuts
　gorgonzola dip with, 24-25
　veal scaloppine with gorgonzola and, 186-87
Watercress
　in cream, spinach and, 75
　and hard-cooked egg salad, 263
White butter sauce, 20, 117
　oysters with, 20
　salmon steak with, broiled, 117
White grapes, calf's liver with, 196-97

Zabaglione with pecans, 275
Zucchini
　et carrottes sautés, 229
　with carrots, sautéed, 229
　julienne de légumes, 77
　with noodles, 67
　aux nouilles, 67
　ratatouille with eggs, 262-63
　et tomates, salade de, 81
　and tomato salad, 81
Zuppa di vongole, 131

About the Author

PIERRE FRANEY is one of the master chefs in this country. His tenure at Le Pavillon caused the critics to unanimously deem it then the best French restaurant in America. His "60-Minute Gourmet" column in *The New York Times* (and 200 other papers across the country) has earned increasing plaudits since its debut several years ago, culminating in the publication of Mr. Franey's best-selling *The New York Times 60-Minute Gourmet.* And his long association with Craig Claiborne has resulted in a number of other books including *Craig Claiborne's The New York Times Cookbook* and *Craig Claiborne's Gourmet Diet,* a best seller for over forty weeks.